MARQUETTE SLAVIC STUDIES

IV

Ukraine and Russia

Ukraine and Russia

A History of the Economic Relations
Between Ukraine and Russia (1654-1917)

By KONSTANTYN KONONENKO

THE MARQUETTE UNIVERSITY PRESS

MILWAUKEE   1958   WISCONSIN

MARQUETTE SLAVIC STUDIES are published under the direction of the Slavic Institute of Marquette University.

Edited by   ROMAN SMAL-STOCKI

Advisory Board   CYRIL E. SMITH
                   ALFRED SOKOLNICKI
                   CHRISTOPHER SPALATIN

The views expressed in the MARQUETTE SLAVIC STUDIES are those of their authors, and are not to be construed as representing the point of view of the Slavic Institute.

Contents

Preface

Most commentators, political analysts, and even scholarly economic students of developments in the Soviet Union — and in Eastern Europe generally — have as yet no keen, appreciative understanding of the strategic position and world-wide significance of the non-Russian nations held captive within the Soviet Union itself. Largely as a result of the educational efforts these past few years of several institutions in the United States, many of these observers have, of course, come to know that there are fundamental differences between the people and history of Georgia, Armenia, Turkestan, White Ruthenia, Azerbaijan, or Ukraine and those of Russia. This knowledge is in itself a measure of real progress. However, it falls far short of a dynamic understanding that with sound perspective can meaningfully relate, for example, Moscow's economic and political concessions to these non-Russian nations with its appeasement policy toward Tito, or patriotic riots in Kiev to the Hungarian revolution, or Moscow's persistent propaganda in Asia about the "independence" of Ukraine and its imperialist drive among the former colonial nations. In short, mere descriptive knowledge is no working foundation for that problem-solving capacity which the subtle maneuvers of the imperialist oligarchy in Moscow challenge daily in its implacable war against Western civilization.

The natural focal point for a problem-solving understanding of the machinations and tactics of the Russian Communist oligarchy is Ukraine. The reasons for this are many, as the Russian oligarchs themselves — beginning with Khrushchev — well know. One rests on the elemental fact that Ukraine is the largest non-Russian nation not only in the substrate empire known as the Soviet Union but also behind the European Iron Curtain. Second, in natural resources—agriculture, coal, oil, iron, etc.— Ukraine is one of the richest and most diversified regions of Europe. Third, for a number of objectives, by geographical position it is strategically located in close relation to Central Europe, the Middle East, the Caucasus, and the open steppes of Russia. Fourth, the heroic record of Ukrainian national resistance to Russian domination, whether Czarist or Communist, is a permanent and very much open chapter in world annals of the struggle for personal and national freedom. And fifth, as a manifest derivative of the above, without its imperialist possession of Ukraine, Communist Russia couldn't possibly maintain for long the substrate empire of the Soviet Union, no less the recently acquired satellite strata of the Russian Communist Empire. Briefly, in terms of history and logic, Ukraine is the jewel in the sickled crown of the Russian Communist Empire, and nowhere, unfortunately, is this appreciated more than in the Kremlin.

The foundation of Russian Communist colonialism, as seen at work in the so-called satellite area, is set in the broad, non-Russian periphery of the Soviet Union. This colonialism far exceeds in exploitation and tyranny anything that might be associated with past Western colonialism. Plainly, the Soviet Union is in reality a totalitarian empire structure. One cannot meaningfully cast and interpret economic phenomena within that structure other than in a monistic framework of totalitarian technique and management in which the production, distribution, and consumption of resources are predicated on totalistic political ends as determined by a ruling minority within a minority nation of this basic empire. Regardless of the superficial de-Stalinization program or the economic decentralization measures designed to enhance productivity as well as integrate the energies of the non-Russian nations in the plan of the empire, the substance of Ambassador Lodge's rebuttal to Vishinsky on August 27, 1953 in the United Nations will remain in force: "Read the reports about the small minority of so-called 'Great Russians' who are crowding the native peoples in the Soviet Union out of choice jobs and are trying to take over everything for themselves. Those are real master-race tactics on the Hitler pattern."

Aside from the magnified effects of modern technology, the institutional facets of this Moscow-centered structure constitute a totalitarian offshoot of the autocratic structure of the Czarist Russian Empire which scarcely existed for the material and cultural betterment of the unvested Russian populace, not to speak of the numerous non-Russian nations it held in bondage. This is an indispensable and valuable perspective for a real understanding of Russian Communist colonialism since the inception of the Soviet Union. The Russian Revolution produced no institutional hiatus as concerns the continuity of Russian imperialism and colonialism. It is this vital perspective that Professor Kost Kononenko supplies in this first volume of an historico-economic analysis of the Russian Empire. Concentrating on the period from 1861 to 1917, this incisive work is well documented, factually descriptive, and analytic throughout. With adequate statistical support, it covers all the major spheres in the economic relationship between Russia and Ukraine, and demonstrates with telling effect the consistent Russian economic exploitation of Ukrainian surpluses. In essence, the solid achievement of Professor Kononenko is seen in his realistic and objective presentation of the essential force of Russian colonialism under the White Czars in a period preceding the intensified continuation of the same force under the Red Czars.

There can be no doubt that this work is a much needed addition to the economic research now being pursued in this country with regard to the past and present Russian Empire. Much of this research, as, for example, *Soviet Economic Growth* (Joint Economic Committee Report, 1957), consists of abstract, aggregative analyses of the economy of USSR that reveal little or nothing of the economic differentials and inequities which exist between Russia and the non-Russian nations in this empire complex. As the quoted report, the research being done usually rests on politically unrealistic assumptions of a "national economy," with a gross national product rather than a gross empire product, and consistently employs Moscow-made monolithic terms, such as "Soviet people" and the like. Obviously such research is of little value when it comes to treating real problems of colonialism and economic disparities within the Soviet Union. This work represents a healthy balance to the usual studies: the promised second volume by Professor Kononenko should deepen American economic scholarship on the Soviet Union immeasurably.

Lev E. Dobriansky
Georgetown University

Introduction

A CLOSE ANALYSIS of Ukraine's history brings into relief an odd phenomenon. It is difficult to understand, how so richly endowed Ukraine could fall behind other lands of Europe; how it could show signs during its historical development, contradicting all the possibilities of its natural resources. Even a superficial survey of the various aspects of the economic position and life of Ukraine gives this astounding impression. For example: this land seemingly destined to take a leading place in world agriculture, has not done so. Yet, it possesses the best soil in all Europe. From Southern Volhynia to North of Mykolaiv, clay-laden black soil often reaches a depth of over three feet, and contains up to 10% humus material. It is also rich in the easily soluble flint-acid combinations needed by plant life. The Ukrainian Black Sea littoral also has very fertile light-brown and chestnut loams. In addition, the soils of Ukraine contain everything that adds to their fertility: the Izyum and Podilla regions have rich deposits of apatites yielding good phosphorous fertilizer, and ammonia manufactured in the Donbas provide azotes.

The climate of Ukraine is quite favorable to the development of agriculture. The land is situated between the 43rd and 53rd degrees latitude North. True, its isotherms are lower than corresponding latitudes of Western Europe. Due to more severe winters, the average annual temperature fluctuates between 43 and 49 degrees Fahrenheit, reaching 56 degrees in the Crimea. But it has a far greater number of days of sunshine in a year than analogous regions of Western Europe, and a much warmer summer. This amount of warmth and the length of the period favorable to vegetation, makes possible the cultivation of a great assortment of farm cultures; rye, barley and cotton among them.

The average annual amount of precipitation in Ukraine is small, varying between 400 millimeters on the shores of the Black Sea and 700 millimeters in Volhynia. This is in large measure compensated, however, by two facts. The rains fall during the optimal periods necessary for agriculture and the soil has high moisture-retaining qualities. Added to this, the Ukrainians are an industrious people who love farming. The

Ukrainians' ability and knowledge is by no means lower than that of many nationals of Western Europe.

Yet Ukraine is behind many lands of the European West in agricultural production. Why?

For the ten-year period before 1917 the comparison of average harvests of basic grain crops and potatoes is shown in the following table:

TABLE I

Yields from 1 hectare in metric hundredweights (of 100 kilograms)[1]

Land	Rye	Wheat	Barley	Oats	Potatoes
Ukraine	10.0	12.0	10.0	11.8	85.0
Russia	8.7	7.8	9.7	9.0	80.7
Belgium	24.7	27.7	30.6	26.4	192.0
Germany	20.2	23.9	24.0	21.2	151.0
France	11.8	14.7	15.5	14.5	97.0

Other extraordinary facts make the picture clearer. Ukraine occupies at present an area of 576.6 thousand square kilometres, with a population of 41,250 thousand. This gives a density of population of 71.3 per square kilometre, much lower than Western Europe. At the same time, in the past fifty years, Ukraine showed all the signs of agrarian over-population. The most significant result of this was the mass migration of the rural population from Eastern Ukraine to lands beyond the Urals and to Central Asia, and from Western Ukraine to Canada and the United States. According to Professor Vobly, in the eighteen years before World War I, from Eastern Ukraine alone 1,600,000 people migrated beyond the Urals. They came mainly from the Poltava region, 23% of all migrants, while Podilla accounted for only 4.5%, although the density of population of Podilla was greater (over 90 per square kilometre) than in Poltava region (74 per square kilometre). Between 1906 and 1910, the number migrating from Poltava region was 174,000, 60% of the natural increase of the population.

Consider the following fact: prior to the revolution the agricultural production of Ukraine of the five basic grain products (rye, wheat, oats, barley, and corn) was 560 kilograms per capita, per annum, while that of Romania was 880 kilograms; of Denmark, 688 kilograms; and of France and Germany, 416 kilo-

---

[1] I. Feshchenko-Chopivsky, *Ekonomichna heohrafiya Ukrainy (Economic Geography of Ukraine)*, Kiev, 1923, p. 36.

grams. But during this same time, Denmark purchased 272 kilograms in addition to a production of 688 kilograms and consumed 960 kilograms; Germany and France purchased 80 kilograms and consumed 496 kilograms each, while Ukraine, from its production of 560 kilograms exported 176 kilograms, and consumed only 384 kilograms, like Russia which produced only 440 kilograms per person.

An analysis of industry produces no less curious a picture. Most striking is the weak development of industry until recent times, when compared with Ukraine's immense possibilities, and then its peculiar trend. The natural resources of Ukraine place it among the most richly endowed in the world. According to data of 1938, geological deposits of coal in the Donets basin are estimated at 70.3 billion tons. They are of a high quality, largely suitable for coking. Coal of the Donbas includes rich deposits of anthracite, up to 97%. Outside of the Donbas there are many other coal-producing areas in Ukraine, from Chernihiv in the Northwest to the Southeastern border, and from Voronizh district in the North to Kuban in the South. Huge deposits of soft coal have been discovered in the regions of Kryvyi Rih, Kiev, Kirovohrad, Ternopil, Rivne, and Stanyslaviv. Large and rich deposits of peat are located in the regions of Kiev, Chernihiv, Zhytomir, and Sumy.

Oil, discovered in the regions of Romny and Lubni in 1936 must be added to the fuel resources of Ukraine. In the Carpathian foothills of Western Ukraine, oil has been extracted for a long time. There are also considerable oil deposits in the regions of Drohobych, Boryslav, and Stanyslaviv. Ukraine is no less endowed with ores, primarily iron and manganese. In the region of Kryvyi Rih the deposits of iron ore are estimated at 1.5 billion tons, exceptionally high in quality, and containing 55% to 62% iron. Much of the ore lies close to the surface, and up to recent times most of it was extracted by strip mining. The Kerch deposits of iron ore are of a lower quality (35% to 45% pure iron), but are three times as large as those of Kryvyi Rih.

These two regions do not contain all the iron ore wealth of Ukraine. Deposits of iron quartzites in Kryvyi Rih and other regions exceed 21 billion tons. So-called "muddy ore" is found in Western Ukraine, containing from 27 to 42% iron. And there is reason to believe that not all deposits of iron have been discovered as yet. Many localities have been found to be magnetically anomalous, indicating the presence of iron ore. Such anomalies have been found in regions of Kremenchuk, Zaporizha, and in the vicinity of Donbas and Kryvyi Rih. In the region of Nikopil are located deposits of manganese ore constituting the largest in Europe and some of the largest in the world. They contain 35% to 48% pure manganese, essential in metallurgy. Deposits are estimated at 522 million tons in the Nikopil region alone, and there are also deposits in the Kryvyi Rih and Odessa regions.

It must be emphasized that the three basic geological regions of coal, iron, and manganese which are involved in metallurgy, are all situated within a triangle whose largest side does not measure more than 300 miles.[2]

Moreover, in Ukraine there are considerable deposits of mercury in the Donbas; of lead and zinc in Haholny Kryah; of copper at the confluence of the rivers Torets and Kalmius, in Volhynia, and South of Kiev. Deposits of rocksalt in the Artemovo-Slavyansk region are estimated in many billion tons, to which must be added salt lakes in Slavyansk and salt deposits by natural evaporation on the bars of the Dnipro estuary. High quality clays are also found in Ukraine, including porcelain and fire-resistant kinds. There is also cement, quartz sand for glassmaking, etc.

With such natural resources, Ukraine should have developed into a highly industrialized land long ago. On the contrary, just prior to World War I, the occupation of the population of Ukraine is characterized by the following data: agriculture, 74.5%; industry, 9%; commerce, 5.3%; transportation, 6.4%; common labor, 4.8%, and all other, 5%. These percentages so contrary to industrial possibilities of Ukraine, appear even more astounding when considered not in proportion to the entire population living in Ukraine at that time, as here cited, but in proportion to the aboriginal Ukrainian population. Then the occupational apportionment is as follows: agriculture, 87.5%; industry 5.1%; commerce, .8%; transportation, .7%; common labor, 3.5%, all other, 2.4%[3]. Thus despite the potential, only

[2] All figures quoted are from: *Ekonomichna heohrafiya Ukrainy* by Feshchenko-Chopivsky, the works of Professor Vobly; "Ekonomichna kharakterystyka Ukrainy" ("Economic Characteristics of Ukraine") by P. Fomin in *Nauchnaya Mysl (Educational Ideas)*, Kharkiv, 1923, and *Bolshaya Sovietskaya Entsiklopediya (Great Soviet Encyclopedia)*, Vol. 55, 1947.

[3] Feshchenko-Chopivsky, *op. cit.* p. 47.

5.1% of the Ukrainian population was in industry and .3% in commerce.

Ukraine is situated on the shores of the Black and Oziv Seas, which are ice-free all winter. These Seas are within the basin of the Mediterranean which has for centuries, been the center of European and world commerce. This location and wealth should make Ukraine a seafaring nation, with a developed sea trade, good ports, a large commercial fleet, etc. But a cursory glance at a map reveals almost no rail connections between ports and interior. In general, the direction of rail lines of Ukraine are: lines connecting the Donbas with the metallurgical region of Kryvyi Rih, with Leningrad (through Moscow), and with the Volga valley; lines connecting the Southwest of Ukraine (basic regions of sugar production) with Central Russia and Leningrad; and finally lines connecting Central Russia with the Black Sea and the Caucasus, which by their direction do not link the basic industrial regions of Ukraine with the sea. The already built Donbas-Moscow line by the Soviets, once more intensifies the connection with the center of Russia, not with the sea. In fact the Donbas is connected with the Oziv Sea only through Mariupil, and Kryvyi Rih has no direct rail connection with the sea at all.

When, toward the end of the 19th century the Donets railroad was opened, Keypen wrote: "Reaching neither the Dnipro, nor the Volga, enclosed by the Oziv and Kozlovo-Voronizh lines, the Donets railroad is placed in a position of complete dependence on the other lines, and for this reason, coal mines situated in its area are unable to develop their productivity in full."[4]

The problem of water transportation is even worse. In 1912 the commercial fleet of ten Ukrainian ports consisted of only 310 steamships, averaging 675 tons, and of 657 sailing vessels, averaging 54 tons.[5] As will be seen from these figures, the commercial fleet did not in any way correspond to the position of Ukraine and the possibilities of participation in world commerce. This fleet was even inadequate to take care of small-scale coastal trade. It is not surprising therefore, that during 1912, the participation of this entire fleet in commercial operations of all Black and Oziv seaports, including Caucasian ports, amounted

[4] N. Keypen, *Krizis 80-tikh godov*, (*The Crisis of the '80's*), Moscow, 1903, p. 29.
[5] We quote pre-revolutionary figures deliberately, because later, during the Soviet regime, the very nature of foreign ties underwent a change. The subject will be discussed in detail later.

to only 11.9% of the number of vessels, and 5.9% of the tonnage handled. The bulk of ocean freight was handled by foreign ships, primarily British, under whose flag sailed 28% of all vessels carrying 47.5% of all tonnage.

Equally striking examples are encountered at every step, no matter what branch of the economic life of Ukraine is considered. The few examples quoted above make it clear that any analysis of social and economic processes of Ukraine cannot be conducted merely by applying data pertaining to these processes themselves. The life of Ukraine was not only determined and directed by such laws of development as would flow from the natural social-economic conditions, but by other forces and factors as well. The economic processes were determined not only by the interests of Ukraine, but by extraneous interests, indeed, the latter were often of decisive importance.

In its historical development, the social-economic life of Ukraine can be understood only by understanding the role imposed upon Ukraine by the interests of the Russian Empire as a whole, be it Tsarist or Soviet. Only then will the anomalies of this development become understandable and the several phenomena will appear in a proper light.

It is in this light that we wish to present the characteristics of basic social-economic processes in Ukraine during the last century. These characteristics should facilitate the understanding of the social-economic background of the Ukrainian national idea.

CHAPTER 1

TOWARD INDUSTRIAL CAPITALISM

The Social Structure of Ukraine after the 1648 Revolution

OUR ANALYSIS of social-economic processes in Ukraine is confined to the period of the last 100 years or, to be exact from the abolition of serfdom. The reason for choosing this date, is that the Manifesto of the Emperor Alexander II, of February 19th (old style) 1861, provided the legal basis for a new social order. From that date the Russian Empire began its period of modern history, a period of capitalist conditions. It is understood however, that a capitalist economy began to develop long before the agrarian reform; that it conditioned the reform, and that it had its reflection in it. Therefore, in order to understand some components of the reform itself, and preceding processes, we have to survey them in the light of prior developments. It will be necessary to turn our attention from time to time to events which took place before the reform. This applies primarily to the agricultural economy, not only because the reform created a change in the agrarian and social conditions in the rural countryside, but also because the agricultural economy was then, and in large measure remains to this day, the basic branch of the Ukrainian national economy. It must also be added that the reform, in its specific application to Ukraine, and against the background of the preceding agrarian structure, in large measure conditioned the sum total of phenomena which characterize the following period.

When referring to the abolition of serfdom in 1861, one must first of all keep in mind that not only was the execution of the reform in many respects different in Ukraine than in Russia, but that serfdom itself was quite different in Ukraine. It did not develop in Ukraine as a result of social conditions, as it did in Russia, but was, to a great extent imposed upon Ukraine, in contrast to the existing order.

Serfdom, which existed in Eastern and Western Europe in feudal times met with mass resistance on the part of the peasants in its different stages, assuming various forms, up to and including peasant wars (Germany). Similar social processes developed in Eastern Europe, in Russia and Ukraine, but were by their nature, entirely different. Although they took place in a single historical period, mid-17th century, political and social conditions in the two lands were different. Therefore the peasants' fight for freedom assumed an entirely different nature. In Russia, by its political content, it was purely a social struggle of the peasants for a change in the structure then prevailing. It was a struggle of those social strata which were subject to the laws of serfdom. It was an exclusively internal process. It assumed the nature of an armed rebellion known as "Razin's rebellion," named for its chieftain, Stenka Razin. The process taking place in 17th century Ukraine was intrinsically different, being primarily a revolution of national liberation and a fight for the restoration of the rights of independent statehood. Social moments played an important part, but in contrast to Russia, this was not an internal struggle of social forces. It was a struggle against a social order which had been forcibly imposed by an alien power, Poland, and for this reason it went hand in hand with national state liberation. It is significant in this connection that the oppressors were mainly Polish nobles, emissaries of the subjugating government. The government of Poland was the source of their social privileges, therefore that part of the Ukrainian nobility which favored Poland was also subject to destruction, because it, too, had become a factor of national oppression. On the other hand, that part of the Ukrainian nobility and clergy which joined the common national front in the struggle for national liberation, was not only not proceeded against by the insurgents, but kept its privileges even after the victorious conclusion of the struggle, notwithstanding the fact that it had been exercising the rights of the serfdom law. Thus, the institution of serfdom as such was not denied, but it was eradicated to the core in those instances where it came into being from the fiat of a conquering nation.

This seemingly contradictory attitude towards serfdom will become understandable when we consider the dissimilar attitude toward this institution in Ukraine and in Poland. In Ukraine, personal freedom was not taken away from the individual, but social obligations were imposed. A person was free to choose the manner of discharging them, either armed service in defense of the community or allocation of part of one's labor to the needs of the community. It did not matter how the latter was made available, either by performance of direct labor for governmental institutions, by delivery of the fruits of one's private enterprise to the state or by work done in the employment of another. The dependence of one person upon another, which came into being at that time, took place as an expression of the person's own will. He would choose this dependence out of economic considerations and even if the choice were made under economic compulsion, it was still never imposed by law. Serfdom, thus, was an institution of mutual agreement, in which both parties carried a legal obligation.

In contrast to this, Polish serfdom was based upon a legal incapacitation of the peasants to dispose freely of their economic activities, and upon a personal allegiance to a master. Ukraine's victory over Poland and the restoration of Ukraine's state independence freed the peasants from servitude and restored their individual freedoms. This applied to all peasants, those who had been subjects of the expelled Polish nobles as well as those who remained dependent on monasteries and Ukrainian nobles who had taken part in the fight for liberation. Unfortunately, legal principles of the new social order cannot be determined with any degree of certainty. The reason is that such legal forms could not be formulated within a short period of regained independence, because of the peculiar state structure of Ukraine where fundamental state power was held by Zaporozhian Cossack military. Subsequently, Moscow deliberately thwarted, to serve her own interest, the all-round development of Ukrainian statehood. The social conditions of Ukraine are all the more significant as they developed from practices beyond the scope of legal control. Thus they provide the main characteristic of the social ideal of the whole nation at that time. Professor Myakotin, analyzing the social structure of the period, came to the following conclusion: "Old legal norms according to which the community was socially stratified had been preserved, but in reality 'society' and 'the common people' into which the population was now divided constituted a single social group with free transfer from one to the other.[6]

[6] V. Myakotin, *Ocherki sotsialnoy istoriyi Ukrainy v 17-18 v. v. (Outline of the Social History of Ukraine in the 17-18 Centuries)*, Prague, 1924, I, 132.

This classification of the time was not, however, of a permanent
nature. As has been noted, it was a social division chosen according to the different obligations to society, the decisive
factor being the kind of burden the individual would be able
and willing to carry for society. A clear and exhaustive description can be found in the 1729 records of oral reports of old
people of the village of Horchaky, Starodub colonelcy: "When
the people settled, the more important (wealthier) registered
as Cossacks, and the inferior (poorer) remained peasants."[7]

"Not mentioning the townspeople," says Myakotin, "even the
peasants were then granted full citizens' rights, including the
complete ownership of their land holdings. The acquisition of
real property rights by the peasants was complete and general
to such extent that it also included those peasants who remained
dependent upon the landed gentry and upon monasteries, those
that is, whose holdings had been left intact."[8]

Both the Ukrainian state and the Ukrainian soil had been
liberated by the effort of the entire people. Hence, the people
recognized in themselves the existence of the right to rule themselves and their land, although the property provisions of the
"Lithuanian Statute" had not been formally repealed, nor new
laws substituted for them. The common law was, in effect, supplemented by creative decisions of the communities which felt
authorized to pass new rules by virtue of being responsible for
the regained freedom. Although this caused some discrepancies
in the manner of local solution of similar problems, yet always
and everywhere one right remained immutable: the people's
right of disposition of the privileges they had gained in their
struggle, primarily of liberty and property. Lazarevsky cites a
vivid example of what the people understood their rights to be
after the liberation from Polish rule. The Cossacks of the village
of Pokoshych stated in 1773: "When with the help of God the
Ukrainians under Hetman Bohdan Zinovy Khmelnytsky liberated with their blood Ukraine from the Polish yoke and from
the rule of Polish kings . . ., at that time . . . on both banks of
the Dnipro all the land belonged to the Ukrainians in full and
in common, until it was first divided among the colonelcies,

The term "society" (*tovarystvo*) denoted the military caste of Cossacks,
and the term "common people" *(pospilstvo)* peasant-farmers, or in a
broader connotation, the taxpaying public.
[7] A Lazarevsky, *Opisaniye Staroy Malorossiyi*, (*Description of Old Little-
Russia [Ukraine]*), Kiev, 1888, I, 381.
[8] V. Myakotin, *op. cit.*, I, 128.

then the captaincies, then the townships, villages, and hamlets, and from the latter among the residences, manors, homes, and homesteads, and therefore all the estates became the property of Ukrainians by entry into possession. The Ukrainians then marked the boundaries of their possessions in various ways; some fenced them, others erected markers and dug canals, and then built whatever they pleased within these bounds."[9]

Therefore, although the wave of rebellion, having destroyed the upper layer of manorial landownership did not touch direct-ly upon other types and forms of land holding in Ukraine, yet it did change the relationship between them, placing them into new forms of development. Among such changes the most note-worthy was that even the common peasants, "serfs" of monaster-ies and nobles, perceived in the regained freedom their right to possess land, and to be able to choose their future social posi-tion. Many such common peasants chose to change their status into Cossacks. According to Myakotin, "Finally the monasteries had to get reconciled with the fact that during the uprisings, and in the first years following, no small part of their 'subjects' went out from under their dominion." They would register as Cossacks, or start farming on their own, or assume a neighbor's obligations, i.e., farm the land of another, taking on all the duties of the former owner. Even later, in 1712, the Archimandrite of the Nizhyn Monastery of the Annunciation complained to Hetman Ivan Skoropadsky that the monastery's "subjects" were selling land, and that "the village of Talalaevka is called a mon-astery village, but many others are in possession of it." It is noteworthy that the Archimandrite did not request that the transactions be made void, but only for permission to buy the land back.

It is obvious that both the monasteries, and since the latter part of the 17th century also private landowners who had had tenant "subjects," asserting their rights upon the unrepealed privileges of exercising dominion over their "subjects," hindered the free transfer of peasants. The Hetman Government consid-ered these claims just, and Hetman Demyan Mnohohrishny for-bade the common subjects of monasteries to change their status into Cossacks. Likewise the Hetmans Ivan Samoylovych and

[9] A. Lazarevsky, "Malorossiyskiye pospolitiye krestyane" ("Little-Russian [Ukrainian] Common Peasants"), *Zapiski Chernigovskogo statisticheskogo komiteta (Proceedings of the Chernihiv Statistical Commission)*, Cher-nihiv, 1866, I, 26.

Ivan Mazepa frequently attempted to return "newly registered" Cossacks to "their former common duties and obedience to monasteries." But such decisions were, first of all, not in the nature of a general order, and in the second place, they could not always be carried into effect.

An opportunity for Moscow to interfere in the area of land ownership came right after the conclusion of the Treaty of Pereyaslav in 1654. Hetman Bohdan Khmelnytsky's envoys to Moscow, the Judge-General S. Bohdanovych-Zarudny and the Colonel of Pereyaslav Teterya requested the Tsar of Muscovy to grant them estates and "subjects," and received them. True, these acquisitions were, for quite a long time kept secret because at that time nobody would dare take away the newly gained freedom from the peasants. This same Teterya requested of the Tsar that "that with which anyone has been endowed by his majesty, should not be ordered made public, . . . because if the Army would find out that he and his comrades had been granted by his majesty such great estates, they would immediately suffer . . . because the members of the Zaporozhian Army may not have any possessions."[10]

Soon thereafter the Ukrainian government was compelled to start endowing the Cossack officer class with "subjects," i.e., with the right to demand of the common peasants certain obligations. Giving land and "subjects" became a means of compensating those who served the government. A significant characteristic of such endowments was the fact that they did not pass into the absolute ownership of the person receiving them. They were so-called "estates of rank" benefiting officers or state employees according to their rank, and only for the duration of their office. In this manner the common peasants did not become serfs of any individual, but rather under duty to the state, which ceded such rights to persons performing certain state functions. Along with "estates of rank," there existed other forms of land tenure, i. e.: 1) peaceful and unimpeded enjoyment, or forever; 2) "at the pleasure of the military," that is until such time when the government would effect a change in possessions, and 3) "in support of the home," as temporary relief given for any good reason. But even in the first instance, when land was granted "forever," it was still not the same thing as the Russian *votchina* (father to son inheritance). First of all, although a

---

[10] V. Myakotin, *op. cit.*, I, 63, 136.

father could give the land he had received to his heirs, the heirs as a rule had to request from the Hetman Government a confirmation of their right (of tenure), and in the second place, the government itself never alienated its right to dispose of such lands otherwise.

Reinstatement of Serfdom

The contractual nature of all forms of land tenure made them similar to "estates of rank." Moscow wanted all the endowments with land and "subjects," which were being carried out on its orders, to assume characteristics peculiar to Muscovite *votchina*, absolute ownership without the right of the Ukrainian government to interfere. In the "Kolomatsky articles"[11] of 1687, on the occasion of the election of Ivan Mazepa to the Hetmanate, it was stated: "Whosoever receives from the Tsar a writ of endowment, he shall have the right of dominion over the mills and the peasants, and the Hetman may not take such writs away, nor violate the Tsar's gracious ukase in any manner."[12]

Such violations of the rights of the Ukrainian people were met with decided opposition on the part of the masses. When Hetman Samoylovych was deposed in 1687, there was a whole series of uprisings. In 1692 a military scribe, Petro Ivanenko Petryk, who first escaped to Zaporozha, and then to the Crimean Khan, proclaimed himself Hetman and called upon the people to rise against Moscow and against Hetman Mazepa. The Zaporozhian Otaman of Kosh (Corps) Husak, wrote: " . . . the common council had carried a resolution that there should be no injustices in Ukraine, and today we see that the poor people in the colonelcies are suffering great oppression . . . Then we had thought that for all time the Christian people would never be in servitude, and now we see that the poor people are worse off than under the Lakhs (Poles), because even those who have no right to have serfs, have them, to haul wood and hay for them, and to stoke their ovens . . ." Dominion by rank did not evoke opposition, as in the minds of the people this was justified: "such men may hold subjects, it does not grieve anyone." But as to others, "just as their fathers ate their bread from labor, so should they eat."[13] It must be stated that until the Poltava

---

11 "Articles" were a Ukrainian-Muscovite treaty concluded at every election of a new Hetman.
12 V. Myakotin, *op. cit.*, II, 79.
13 A. Lazarevsky, "Maloroissiyskiye pospolitiye krestyane," p. 29.

catastrophe of 1709, Moscow's aims could not be widely realized in Ukraine, because Moscow had to deal through the intermediary of the Ukrainian authorities, who were decidedly opposed to letting Moscow lay its heavy hand on Ukraine. The
situation underwent a radical change after the Poltava defeat.
Tsar Peter I issued an order as early as June 18, 1709: "All estates of such traitors like Mazepa, and of others who do not belong to the office of Hetman, are to be listed and reported,
and are not to be given to anyone without a ukase of the great
ruler, and also in the future the Hetman may not give anyone's
wealth nor estates without an explanation as to who receives
what, and for what merit, neither is anything to be taken away
for fault without explanation; and whenever he, the Hetman,
shall see somebody's service which he, even with the consent
of the general officers would reward, he must write of it to
the great ruler, and whosoever shall be at fault for which he
should be deprived of wealth and estates, when the guilty must
be prohibited from exercising power and it must be taken away,
then also it must be written of to the great ruler."[14] In this manner, from then on the Tsar of Muscovy considered himself the
sole owner of the land of Ukraine, empowered to dispose of the
Ukrainian people, and the Hetman Government became merely
a delegate of the Tsar. Although the orders were not always
strictly adhered to, especially in matters concerning holdings of
land and "subjects" of Russian magnates, nevertheless from that
time, the Muscovite system of land tenure and the abolition of
liberties acquired by the peasants came quickly.

Until the time of Hetman Ivan Skoropadsky the Russians
did not have the right to receive estates in Ukraine. An exception
was made in the case of the Tsar's residents attached to the
Hetman, who received land on the rights of "estates of rank."
Now Russian magnates and lesser officials hurried to get rich
with Ukrainian lands, Ukraine being no longer considered a
separate state, but a conquered land. Skoropadsky was powerless
to resist the greed of pretenders to Ukrainian land, and "was
forced to embark upon the road towards which he was being
prodded by the requests of the Tsarist ministers, the road of
granting estates in Ukraine to private individuals who were in
no way connected with Ukraine, who had no previous relations
with Ukraine."[15]

[14] V. Myakotin, *loc. cit.*
[15] V. Myakotin, *op. cit.*, p. 81.

A letter of Count Sheremetiev to Hetman Skoropadsky is significant in this respect: "Not long ago, thanks to the high grace of the Tsar's majesty, in reward for their merits, and thanks to your favorable goodness, his Highness Prince Menshikov, the eminent gentlemen Count Golovkin, Prince Dolgorukov, and Squire Shafirov received estates for themselves in Ukraine; this example has prodded me to make this request" . . . "Receiving estates formally from the Hetman, these magnates were in reality outside of his power, and the Hetman could not only not have any chance of taking away a given estate, but he did not have any influence in this respect."[16] Thus such estates, and peasants inhabiting them, became extra-territorial, not under the jurisdiction of the Ukrainian authorities. A typical colonial situation arose: citizens of the metropolis, not subject to any laws of the colony, established their plantations cultivated by the local population, transformed into serfs. The Russians' appetite for lands and "subjects" in Ukraine was insatiable. Prince Menshikov provides a notable example. No matter how much land he received or grabbed, it was still not enough. The extent of his acquisitions can be attested to by the fact that he forced the entire Pochepsky region to be granted to him, with 6,250 settlements. Later, after the death of Peter I, he received, with others, the city of Baturyn with all the surrounding villages and hamlets. Others were not far behind Menshikov. Similar conditions prevailed, particularly in the South of Ukraine after the liquidation of the Zaporozhian Host in 1775.

Along with the distribution of land those peasants who lived upon it came into servitude. The natural consequence of this was that the number of free peasants diminished at a catastrophic pace. Following the amendments of Hetman Danylo Apostol the number of estates, according to categories, in seven colonelcies out of ten, was: free military, 20,031; city hall, 439; of rank, 6,173; monastery, 9,644; private 19,776; total, 56,063. In all ten colonelcies, the number of common free estates was only 29,321. Thus, 75 years after liberation, the free common peasants in seven colonelcies constituted only one-third of all holdings, city halls less than 1%, estates of rank about 10%, whereas the monasteries and private persons held over 50% of the estates. During the period from 1730 to 1752 the number

---

[16] *Ibid.*, II, 179.

of free common holdings in nine colonelcies (excluding Hadi-
ach) decreased at the rate shown in *Table II.* [17]

TABLE II

After amendments of 1729-30	After amendments of 1743	After amendments of 1751	Status as of 1752
27,559 estates	11,774	6,952 and 5,469 without a landlord	2,859 and 2,682 without a landlord

The problem, however, was not confined to the servitude of
the common peasants. In 1710 Menshikov demanded of Hetman Skoropadsky that the Cossacks residing in the Pochepsky
district which he received also be given him as serfs. Nor was
this an isolated case. During the Hetmancy of Skoropadsky,
some of the Ukrainian Cossacks became the serfs of Russian
magnates. Only much later did some of them succeed in regain-
ing their freedom. Many of those also suffered who had previously registered as Cossacks: a number were deprived of their
Cossack privileges and returned to the status of common peasants. The Cossacks were subject to oppression on the part of
new landowners, Russians who had received Ukrainian lands
from the Imperial Government, and who, leaning on Muscovite
authorities, flouted Ukrainian laws and customs. Receiving
lands settled by common peasants and Cossacks, they would
often assume property rights over inalienable Cossack lands.
Moscow would leave most complaints unanswered, and the
Hetman Government was powerless to right such wrongs. For
example, the Cossacks of the Chernihiv regiment wrote that:
"Before, they could easily bear arms for the state, because they
had sufficient land and other goods, and now they are under
all manner of oppression from the landowners."[18]

The Empress Anna issued a ukase on August 8, 1734, providing that if a Cossack sells his land and continues to live on
it, he must henceforth carry the obligations of a common peasant. This produced the practical result of making land ownership a social category. The final consequence of this was that

[17] Figures cited are from V. Myakotin, *op. cit.,* II, 185-189.
[18] M. Filimonov, *Materiali po voprosu ob evolutsiyi zemlevladiniya*
(*Materials on the Problem of Evolution of Land Ownership*), Perm,
1895 (2d ed.), p. 14.

in 1783 all Cossack regiments were transformed into regular army units, and although the Cossacks did not lose their personal liberty and right of land ownership, they were deprived of their old privilege of self-rule. Matters were also complicated with the new Ukrainian nobility which came into being under conditions of breaking up of old political and social forms. The pre-revolutionary nobility ceased to exist as a separate social class in the middle 17th century. Some individuals of the former nobility survived as landowners, but without any special class privileges. Ultimately the introduction of the Russian order, and the servitude of Ukrainian peasants promulgated by Moscow, brought to the forefront the problem of rights of Ukrainian landowners, because according to Russian laws, only nobles had the right to exercise rule over serfs. Therefore, the Ukrainian landowners who possessed "subjects" wishing to make their class position certain had to take some definite steps. They had already requested on many occasions, that the Imperial Government make them equal in social privileges with the Russian nobility. In a plea of the Hlukhiv nobility to the Imperial Commission charged with the project of a new statute, it was requested: "Permit us, on the same principles as the Russian nobility, to serve where we choose, and to enjoy all our donated and acquired possessions, and such powers of the Russian nobility to be confirmed by high imperial privilege to us and our heirs."[19] The privileges of Russian nobility were extended to Ukrainian nobles in 1785. Many controversies arose from this, the Russian Government frequently refusing to recognize as nobles not only those who had acquired estates in civil service of the Ukrainian state apparatus, but also military elders. These matters dragged on into the 19th century. The Senate created a special commission in 1828 for the ratification of privileges of nobility in Ukraine. As to the Left Bank of Ukraine, the ukase of March 20, 1835 made a final determination, admitting to privileges of nobility descendants of high Cossack officers (inclusive of the rank of "comrades-in-arms"). The problem was more acute on the Right Bank where, following the revision of 1838, only 587 persons of the former nobility were recognized as nobles, 22,000 were classified as doubtful cases, and 87,121 were deprived of privileges. In Podilla, 83 were recognized, and

[19] V. Myakotin, *op. cit.*, II, 183.

48,545 refused, and the corresponding number for Volhynia was 73 and 31,411.[20]

As is well known, the Russian Government abolished the autonomous Hetman Government of Ukraine in 1764, and in 1781-1782 *"gubernial* ordinance" was extended to Ukraine, with the enforcement of Russian laws, and by Empress' Catherine II ukase of May 3, 1783 even those common peasants who had not theretofore been "subjects" of landowners were declared serfs. They became "state peasants" (*gosudarstvenniye krestyane*), serfs on state lands, such lands being the acquisition of the Russian Government of both free lands, and of those belonging to free peasants. Only those Cossacks who remained professional soldiers retained personal freedom and the rights of land ownership.

Freedom gained in hard struggle was taken away, and serfdom imposed on the peasants whose system of land ownership was wrecked. The land itself became in large measure the property of Russian magnates and nobles, the Ukrainian peasants becoming serfs on their plantations. In place of the Ukrainian State, which concededly had as yet been unable to perfect its governmental structure, came an artificial division into administrative-police units, the *gubernias,* under an autocratic order. Ukraine ceased to exist as a state-political body.

Conditions of Serfdom

It cannot be stated that conditions of serfdom were more oppressive in Ukraine than in Russia. The treatment of serfs was perhaps even more gentle and more humane than in Russia. The reason was that alongside the serfs there existed the free class of Cossack-peasants, who held on tenaciously to the tradition of defenders of the people's rights. It was also of decisive importance that the entire people had preserved the spirit of freedom, of struggle for it, and that memories of a free life were quite fresh. Serfdom itself was considered as a trampling of people's rights by an alien power. It is not surprising therefore, that the peasants frequently rose in rebellion against the oppression of the landlords. According to computations of M. Drahomanov, between 1836 and 1848 there were sixty-eight peasants' uprisings in Slobidska Ukraine, with twenty

---

[20] M. Slabchenko, *Materialy do ekonomichno-sotsialnoyi istoriyi Ukrainy 19-oho Stor.* (*Materials on the Economic-Social History of Nineteenth Century Ukraine*), Kharkiv, 1925, I, 59.

landowners killed. In the Right Bank Ukraine there were twenty-six uprisings between 1845 and 1849. Escape was another form of reaction against the landlords' oppression, the flights frequently assuming mass proportions. Most of the escaping peasants went to Southern Ukraine, to the Don and Kuban regions where the descendants of Cossacks, whose Zaporozhian Host was ruined by the Russian Government in 1775 had found refuge. There were so many of these serfs-escapees that the Tsarist Government was powerless to restore them to their masters, and in 1832 permission was granted "for the successful settlement of the Northeastern coast of the Black Sea, to let 'tramps' settle there who had come without proper documents (passports)."[21] This thirst for freedom and for throwing off the yoke of serfdom imposed by Russia never died among the peasants, and it kept all life at a point of high tension, decidedly influencing relations between masters and serfs. On the eve of the abolition of serfdom, Ukrainian peasants embarked upon a mass migration to the Crimea, just following the Crimean War. From two counties only, Verkhnedniprovsk and Katerynoslav, 9,000 peasants escaped, and 3,000 from Kherson. Great masses also came from the *gubernias* of Poltava, Kharkiv, and Chernihiv. The government was compelled to set up a military guard across the Perekop Peninsula; the escaping peasants staging pitched battles against the regular army. Some part, albeit a very insignificant one, was played in this cautious treatment of the serfs by the fact that not all the old rules of law had been abrogated. The Emperor Alexander I decided to effect a codification of laws, intending initially to conduct the work in two directions: for the whole empire, and for those preserving a different language and laws. Ukraine was supposed to constitute such a separate part. The project dragged on, and a code of local laws was not compiled until 1829, but "on the part of local administrators (Russian officials), the compiled code was met with an unfavorable attitude. The Governor-General of Kiev, Bibikov, was particularly hostile, because he gave precedence to Russian law and would not agree to the continuance of separate courts on the Right Bank, adhering to a strictly 'Russifying policy.' "[22] County marshals (administrative officials) meeting in Poltava in 1840 expressed themselves in a similar vein, demanding the abolition of Magdeburg Laws and of the Lithuanian Statute, alleging

[21] M. Slabchenko, *op. cit.*, I, 138.   [22] *Ibid.*, I, 111.

that "differentiating features have been erased, and one can observe an identity of laws" with those of Russia. As a result of this, the Lithuanian Statute was repealed in 1842,[23] and general laws of the Empire substituted for it. The Magdeburg autonomous laws of the cities of Ukraine were abrogated even earlier, between 1831 and 1835.

In the light of what has been said above, it is clear why the state administration of Ukraine frequently interfered in the relations between landlords and peasants with the object of regulating them, and of curtailing the nobles' license which contributed to the already existing tensions. Serfdom in Russia was based on the principle of almost complete denial of any rights to the serf. The serf was deprived of human honor and dignity, and therefore had no right to appeal to a court for slander. He could not testify under oath, although an oath of allegiance was required of him in military service. He was a *res* of the owner, an *instrumentum vocale* in the full meaning of the term. M. Slabchenko quotes the words of Tsvetayev which vividly characterize the Russian understanding of serfdom: " . . . servitude is one of the most important political rights, according to which one belongs as a thing, as far as his property is concerned, therefore the right to possess serfs should be the privilege of the first estate in the nation, which consists of persons prominent, either by their own merits or by ancestry."[24]

In relation to his serfs the landlord was not only the master of their land and labor, but also their administrative and judicial authority. According to Russian law, the landlord could, for transgressions against others and against himself, impose penalties upon serfs up to 40 lashes, imprisonment up to two months, prescribe forced labor up to three months or transport to arrest detachments up to six months. By act of 1846 the landlords were permitted to maintain their own jails and to put prisoners in chains. The only prohibition was inflicting bodily injury upon serfs. Serfs could be exiled to Siberia after 1822. According to an act of 1857, corporal punishment was a mandatory addition to every penalty imposed upon a serf.

The landlord also had a right to sell his serfs. The law of 1808 prohibited the sale of serfs without land, and the law

[23] Only some provisions of the Lithuanian Statute remained in force (particularly in domestic relations and laws of inheritance), and were the law of the Left Bank of Ukraine until 1917.
[24] M. Slabchenko, *op. cit.*, p. 116.

of 1833 without the serf's family, but it became permissible after 1841 to purchase serfs for resettlement on other land. The cus-
tom was for a serf to work for three days in a week for his
master, and the rest of the time for himself, but the ukase of
April 5, 1797 provided that such a division was only advisory,
and not mandatory. In fact, the landlord himself would determine the number of days of weekly servitude, sometimes the
entire week.

Complete enforcement of all these rules of servitude throughout Ukraine was impossible due to historical circumstances. This
is not to say there was no cruel conduct against serfs in Ukraine.
There was, not infrequently. But despite everything, the Ukrainian peasants never lost their feeling of human dignity, and never
acquiesced to the condition of servitude. Hence the need for
controlled relations between landlords and serfs, to prevent or
weaken eruptions of opposition. Indicative of this were the so-
called "Inventory Rules" introduced by the Governor-General of
Kiev, Bibikov in the 1840's. According to these rules, every estate had to be described in detail, with an estimate of the labor
of serfs in all categories. The serf's duty to render labor was
based on the amount of the landlord's land he was using; his
labor therefore was like payment of rent for using land. According to the amount of labor to be rendered, the serfs were divided
into: 1) draught-serfs (a draught meant 3 to 4 teams of oxen or
horses), 2) semi-draught, 3) gardeners, and 4) *bobyly* (landless
workers). The serfs in the first category had to work for the
master three days a week, in the second two days. In addition
they had to fulfill 12 "gathering" days per year (during the
period of greatest activity when all the able-bodied were "gathered" for work), and 24 days of guard duty. If a landlord was in
need of more labor, he was to pay for it according to schedule.
The gardeners had to give 12 more days of labor per year in
addition to the 12 gathering days and 24 guard days, and to
pay for the land they were using for themselves according to
schedule. Work in the manor, i. e. everyday labor on the estate
of the landlord could only be performed by *bobyly* (landless
peasants) and orphans, and for wages. An accounting of labor
performed had to be entered into a book of every serf. Serfs
obligated to perform labor were men from 17 to 55, and women
from 16 to 50. Labor for the landlord had to be done during
the first days of the week, holidays excluded, also days of sick-
ness if no substitute was available. Working off debts for any

goods received from the landlord was not permitted during periods of field work, and no more than one day in a week could be given for this purpose.

After taking a detailed inventory of the estate, with an exact description of the duties of each serf, one copy of it was kept by the landlord, another was announced by the minister in church and kept by him. It is obvious that the landlords made a determined stand against this control of obligations, and wherever possible circumvented the rules and avoided making inventories. Landlords would often substitute so-called *uroky* (annual days) for obligatory labor days, which was permitted by law. But tasks to be performed on *uroky* were often of such magnitude that it took an entire family a week to complete them.

The milder and more restrained forms of servitude in Ukraine, as compared to Russia, cannot be presumed to furnish proof that there was no oppression in Ukraine. Such a false conclusion could be reached by assuming that Ukraine was an ordinary colony, in all respects behind its metropolis, something on the order of Asian or African colonial lands. Russia, however, came to Ukraine possessing a much more backward system of social order, a system of deep social cleavages and dark slavery. Ukraine, following the revolution of national and social liberation of 1648, stood in the ranks of the leading nations of Europe of the day.[25]

Thus, the lesser degree of trampling of human rights was not the result of any privileged position of Ukraine. It furnishes only one more proof that the conquest of Ukraine by Russia constituted an act of extreme retrogression for the former. Of equal importance is the fact that the serf's position was characterized not only by the curtailment of his human rights. In evaluating his position, the economic status of the serf was of prime importance. In this respect the Ukrainian peasant was always below the comparable Russian. This was due not so much to conditions of agricultural productivity as to the general economic conditions to which Ukraine was subjected.

The Ukrainian peasantry was by no means homogeneous in the social and legal sense. It was more varied than the Russian. Besides the Cossacks who had not lost their personal freedom and right to own land, and the insignificant number of free

---

[25] An analogous situation could be observed in Finland after its conquest by Russia. Finland's social order was without comparison more liberal and democratic than Russia's.

peasants, there were also many alien colonists in Ukraine, who were free and their own masters. We do not mean the Russian peasants-serfs who were imported into Ukraine by tens of thousands to provide labor to the Russian landlords on their Ukrainian plantations, but colonists from various lands of Europe. They flocked to the rich lands of Ukraine. Indeed, the Russian Government took pains to settle and assist such colonists. "The Committee for the settlement of aliens admitted in 1870 that one family of colonists cost the treasury 5,000 rubles, while subject peasants who were migrating from overpopulated *gubernias* to sparsely settled areas, and created the most profitable settlements from a state viewpoint, were hardly ever granted any loans."[26] One of the motives behind attracting alien colonists was a desire to establish military settlements which would provide the government with better support in turbulent Ukraine. This was one of the primary reasons for settling a large number of Serbs in Ukraine, who established the so-called New Serbia, receiving a grant of 1,421,000 *desiatynas* of land. Thus, thanks to conditions created by Russia, there was this curious phenomenon in Ukraine that Russians and emigrants from various lands were colonizing Ukraine, while Ukrainians were leaving en masse for Kuban, the Crimea, etc.

The basic element and largest part of the rural population was the serfs. They were in turn divided into serfs of the state, crown and landowners. State serfs were those who occupied state lands and tilled them. Crown serfs were those on land belonging to the reigning dynasty. These classes of serfs were created by the Imperial Government's confiscation of lands which were either the property of the Ukrainian nation or the private property of the peasants. We have previously stated what conditions prevailed in Ukraine after the liberation from Polish rule. The Russian Government, in distributing the land, along with its peasants, among Russian landowners, and keeping the remainder, thus assumed property rights to the land. The peasants, by acquiring rights to till the land became obligated to the landlords or the government. Thus the duties imposed upon the serfs for the right to till the land flowed from the usurpation of the rights of these very same peasants by the Russian Government. We are emphasizing the nature of agrarian conditions of this period because we shall encounter analogous con-

[26] M. Slabchenko, *op. cit.*, I, 22.

ditions again, in discussing agrarian policy of the Bolshevik regime.

Troynitsky's work *"O chisle krepostnikh v Rossiyi"* (*On the number of serfs in Russia*), quotes the figures, in *Table III*, on the number of landowners' peasants (in thousands).[27]

TABLE III

Region:	1803	1837-38	1857-58
Volhynia	345,3	451,5	440,5
Katerynoslav	117,9	155,8	158,8
Kiev	488,4	504,6	521,2
Podilla	454,4	462,7	485,9
Poltava	616,1	337,0	325,3
Kharkiv	191,6	226,1	223,5
Kherson	96,5	151,4	151,1
Chernihiv	(included in Poltava)	290,4	277,1
TOTALS:	2,310,2	2,579,5	2,583,4

The above figures deserve some study. As we can see, the total number of serfs is almost stationary. For the 35-year period between the first and second census the increase is only 10.5%; for the 20-year period between the second and third census, the number is almost stabilized. Such odd census results require some explanation. By natural increase alone, the number of serfs should have doubled in 55 years, and in addition there were other factors contributing to the increase of the number of landlords' serfs. First of all, at the beginning of the 19th century the process of distributing land among Russian magnates still continued. Secondly, during the first half of that century mass settlement of Russian serfs continued on Ukrainian estates of Russian landlords.

The cause of these census results is in a small degree the liberation of some serfs by purchase, but the real and main cause is their mass flight to the Don and Kuban regions. During those times, Kuban became almost exclusively settled by Ukrainians, and thus by its national composition became a Ukrainian land.

Not the lack of land, nor its poor quality were then the cause of a mass flight of Ukrainians from their homeland, but conditions created by Russia in Ukraine.

[27] N. Troynitsky, *O chisle krepostnikh v Rossiyi* (*On the Number of Serfs in Russia*), Poltava, 1907, p. 26.

Table IV shows the number of state serfs (in thousands).

TABLE IV

Region:	1851	1858
Volhynia	24	197
Katerynoslav	425	426
Kiev	206	205
Podilla	146	167
Poltava	866	949
Kharkiv	638	687
Kherson	97	97
Chernihiv	628	666 [28]
TOTALS:	3,030	3,394

For clarity the number of landlords who owned serfs, with a division into groups according to the number of serfs owned, should be shown (in *Table V*): this will be necessary to shed some light on conditions at the time of the reform of 1861.

TABLE V
Classification of Landlords as of 1857

Region:	to 20 serfs	to 100 serfs	to 500 serfs	to 1,000 serfs	over 1,000 serfs
Volhynia	511	709	851	112	63
Katerynoslav	881	1,063	410	33	15
Kiev	188	353	563	138	78
Podilla	310	376	570	148	105
Poltava	5,195	1,504	578	53	39
Kharkiv	2,236	1,109	472	44	43
Kherson	1,175	1,059	333	28	5
Chernihiv	3,342	932	350	67	46 [29]
TOTALS:	13,838	7,105	4,127	623	394

Significantly, over 80% of all serfs belonged to estates which held 50 and more serfs, and over 37% to estates which held 1,000 and more serfs each. This shows that the dominating feature of landlord possession was the huge estate, typical of an agricultural economy of slave labor in a colony.

According to the ukase of December 12, 1801, a serf desiring to purchase his liberty had not only to pay for his personal liberty, but also purchase his land, which had previously been taken

[28] *Ibid.*, p. 30.   [29] *Ibid.*, p. 36.

away from him. After 1826, personal liberty could be purchased without land.

The obligations of a serf to the landlord consisted of two
main forms: *panshchyna,* labor for the master, and *obrik,* rent,
or the product of his labor in the form of produce or money.
The master's demand of labor can be considered the more oppressive form, inasmuch as the master could demand the highest
degree of efficiency during the period the serf was working
for him. The obligation of paying rent could be accomplished
with a more leisurely pace of work. It would be complied with
by simply surrendering to the master a certain percentage of
the crop. But there were also instances where the rent would be
computed in an absolute figure of produce or money without
regard to the serf's income. In such cases the tenant could apply
more intensive methods and all the surplusage would accrue to
him. He could also engage in a trade or in commerce.

In Ukraine, labor for the master was the dominant form of
serfdom, tenancy with payment of rent being infrequent. As
we shall see later, this circumstance was of prime importance in
determining the development of the nation's economy and its
agrarian conditions.

According to compilations of Maslov, the number of tenants
paying rent reached 16.7% in the Left Bank and Slobidska
Ukraine, 6.5% in the steppe region, while it was only 1% in the
Right Bank region.[30] The number of serfs who gave labor was
(regions): Poltava, 98.86%, Chernihiv, 97.44%, Katerynoslav,
99.8%. There were 524 villages of rent-paying State serfs in 1851,
whose population was 182 thousand, about 6% of all serfs in
this category.[31]

The amount of rent in produce averaged in the Kharkiv region one-third of the gross crop, and in Volhynia from two-
thirds to three-fourths of the crop. In addition there was a cash
rent of 3 to 4 rubles per household, and in the region of Poltava,
5 rubles. On a cash computation the average annual rent per 1
desiatyna of ploughing soil was (regions): Katerynoslav, 27
rubles, 98 kopecks; Kherson, 30 rubles, and Kiev, 2 rubles, 92
kopecks.

Before making conclusions as to all peasant obligations, exclusive of taxes, the so-called military settlements must be con-

---

[30] P. Maslov, *Agrarniy vopros v. Rossiyi (The Agrarian Problem in Russia),*
St. Petersburg, 1908, II, 141.
[31] M. Slabchenko, *op. cit.,* p. 123.

sidered. The idea of military settlements occured in Russia in 1685, at first for the organization of Cossack military service, but after the Poltava catastrophe the Russian Government sought a foundation for its rule in Ukraine in the establishment of a landed militia system. The Napoleonic War of 1812 accelerated the plan for military settlements in Ukraine.[32] The composition of military settlements was quite varied. Cossacks and State serfs, it also included Russian peasants purchased from their masters by the government at the following rates: a child to 11 years, 390 rubles; a youth, 750 rubles; an adult, 1,000 rubles. These settlers lived in separate settlements, including all who belonged to that category. In Ukraine military settlements were located in the *gubernias* of Kharkiv, Katerynoslav, Kherson, Kiev, and Podilla, totaling 36 battalions of infantry and 249 squadrons of cavalry. The basic form of obligation of these settlers was military service, and also so-called "bivouacs," i. e. maintenance of armed detachments in temporary quarters. Military settlers were divided into a first and second rank. The first included men who had no less than four oxen or horses and received 15 *desiatynas* of ploughing soil, the second with 2 oxen or horses would get half as much land. There were also such settlers who tilled only truck gardens, and received one-fifth as much land as the first rank. They were free to do their work whenever necessary, but for the purpose of safeguarding some of their time for military duty, there was a certain amount of regulation.

Pre-capitalist Trade and Commerce

In order to recognize the economic conditions of the Ukrainian peasants, and the degree to which they differed from Russia, we must go beyond an analysis of the agricultural economy. It would be futile to merely mention considerable differences in the conditions of production. Quality of soil, climate, availability of space in the Southern steppes all made the position of the Ukrainian peasants superior to that of many Russian regions. The difficult situation of the Ukrainian peasants, and of all other workers, was conditioned by those social and economic circumstances which encompassed the entire economy and life of the population. The natural environment did not have the decisive influence in this case.

[32] *Ibid.*, p. 76.

As early as the 18th century the Ukrainian agricultural economy began to enter a money economy. It showed signs of developing industries, and in general far out-distanced Russia, then
still remaining in the stage of an agriculture strictly for consumption. In methods of agriculture Ukraine was not inferior to the
leading lands of Western Europe. Even in antiquity tools were
used in Ukraine which Russia adopted only several centuries
later. Aristov wrote in 1866: "Tools used for tilling the soil in
Ukraine, were the same which we now see in our agriculture."
The iron plough was used more in that antiquity than *sokha*.
(The wooden *sokha* was the most widely used tool in Russia as
late as the 17th century). *Ruska Pravda* of the 11 to 13th centuries contains references to iron harrows and scythes. In the 1267
chronicle of the Tartar Khan Temir there is mention of water
mills. The chronicle of 997 describes spring and winter sowing,
and such cultures as wheat, rye, oats, barley, peas, lentils, hemp
and flax.

During those ancient times, Ukraine-Rus also engaged in
commercial activity on the markets of Europe, trading mainly
with lands of the Danube and with Greeks. According to the
chronicle, the Great Prince Svyatoslav said: "I do not like to
stay in Kiev. I would rather be in Pereyaslavets on the Danube
as that is the center of my land, all goods are gathered there:
from the Greeks, gold, textiles, wines, all kinds of fruit; from the
Czechs and Magyars, silver and horses; from Rus, furs, wax, hon-
ey and servants."[33] It is therefore not surprising that, coming
under the sovereignty of Russia, Ukraine was already at a high
stage of commercial development. Among the many articles of
commerce, grain occupied a place of prime importance because
of natural circumstances and transportation facilities. Developing grain exports gradually, by the middle 19th century
Ukraine assumed a leading position on the grain markets of
Europe. It exceeded Russian foreign grain trade sixty-fold.
During the period 1846 to 1852, Ukraine exported the following
quantities of grain in units of *chetvert*:[34] to France, 4,413,616; to
Italy, 4,149,597; to Austria, 2,076,997; to Turkey, 4,117,163; to
England, 4,071,330; to Greece, 172,308, etc.[35]

[33] N. Aristov, *Promishlennost drevnoy Rusi (Industry of Ancient Rus')*, St.
Petersburg, 1866, p. 17.
[34] *Chetvert* is a measure of volume equaling about 210 pounds for oats,
to 350 pounds for wheat.
[35] M. Slabchenko, *op. cit.*, p. 243.

Ukrainian industry also developed rapidly. Various trades and home industries had already existed during the Hetmanate period, and factory industries had made a start. In the 1830's when factories began to crowd out individual tradesmen, the region of Poltava had 4,216 artisans; Kharkiv, 3,083; and Kiev 10,080, of whom about 4,000 were in the City.[36] Some home industries, in the nature of peasant handicrafts, produced goods having a wide market: rugs of Kharkiv county; earthenware of Vodolahy and Valky; silk shawls of Okhtyrka; lace and linen of Izyum; Reshetyliv ribbons in the Poltava region; tablecloths and towels from Krolevets near Chernihiv; fishing nets for the Oziv Sea of Ostri; sails of Novozybkiv; furs of Ostri; fur garments in the tens of thousands from Berezniany region, and many others. Industrial production also reached wide proportions. Weaving of woolens was an old and highly developed industry of Ukraine. Looms (for weaving cloth) were standard equipment in most households.[37] The flowering of the woolen industry reaches the early 18th century, when Ukraine already had huge sheep ranches of a high technical standard, with a rich and varied assortment of production. The regions of Chernihiv and Volhynia produced most of the heavy cloth. Kiev, Podilla and Poltava produced fine cloth.

Similarly, the manufacture of linens developed at a fast pace after the 18th century. The main centers were in the regions of Chernihiv (Pochep, Sheptaky, Topal), Volhynia (Rivne) and Kiev (Shpola). Other developing branches of industry were glass, porcelain, metalware (mainly tools for agriculture) and others.

We are not now attempting to give a detailed description of the level and condition of Ukrainian industry of the 18th century. The data briefly furnished merely emphasizes that as early as the period referred to, Ukraine was already well on the way towards a broad developing industry based on natural and economic conditions, and had achieved a position of prominence in international commerce. The retreat from this path of historical development occurred under pressure of alien forces, in consequence of Russia's colonial policy in Ukraine.

---

[36] *Ibid.*, p. 201.
[37] O. Ohloblyn, *Ocherki istoriyi Ukrainskoy fabryki. Manufaktura v. Hetmanshchyni (Outline of History of Ukrainian Factories. Manufacturing in the Hetman Period)*, Kiev, 1925, p. 87.

Ohloblyn gives an accurate estimate of the situation which
came about as a result of an advanced and stronger economic
system being conquered by a weaker and under-developed system: "The foundation of the Ukrainian and Russian economy
of the 18th century was the same: rural agriculture. But at a
time when the products of the Ukrainian economy were already, for a few centuries, known abroad, having travelled a
beaten path there, the Russian agricultural economy had only
just started on that path. Russian commercial capital, taking a
freer look at Europe through a window just opened, should
have taken pains to close some doors, primarily to independent
Ukrainian trade, in order to keep out drafts detrimental to itself. Russian industry, young and weak, could not alone compete with the old and strong Western European industry for
the Ukrainian market. The interests of Russian business unequivocally dictated the liquidation of Ukrainian commerce. The
problem was to divert Ukrainian commerce to new and unknown paths.[38]

"In the struggle against the economic independence of
Ukraine, Moscow attempted not only to take this foreign trade
into its own hands (apparent in the first stages from the desire
to curtail Black Sea trade), but also to crowd Ukrainian goods
out of the Russian market and to transform Ukraine into a market for Russian products. These attempts became evident even
in Khmelnytsky's time, when duties were imposed on Ukrainian
goods . . ." Russia made wide application of its customs duties
policy in the struggle against Ukrainian industry and commerce.
"The Russian bourgeoisie of the 17th and 18th centuries did not
feel comfortable when Ukrainian factories grew and would send
their goods to Western lands and to Russia, where Ukrainian
products competed with the Russian easily. The reasons cited
brought barriers to industry and commerce, with whose aid the
Imperial Government could regulate Ukrainian exports and imports. The fiscal interests of the Empire were being simultaneously safeguarded:[39]

Customs duties was not the only weapon of Russian policy
against Ukrainian industry and commerce. Many other means,
including outright wrecking of industrial plants were employed.
At the election of Hetmans, it became almost a rule to introduce

[38] *Ibid.*, p. 38.
[39] M. Slabchenko, *Orhanizatsiya khozyaystva Ukrainy* (*Organization of
the Economy of Ukraine*), Kharkiv, 1925, II, 92.

"a series of articles providing for the curtailment of Ukrainian trade within the borders of the Russian State."[40] In 1718, the erection of new potassium plants was prohibited. Then came the prohibition of free exports of potassium, tars, and saltpeter, which ultimately resulted in complete decline of these previously highly developed industries.

A similar fate befell the Ukrainian glass industry, which had reached a high stage of development and was Russia's chief supplier of glass and glass products. Legal restrictions put this industry into a difficult position. "Ukraine could not only no longer sell her glass on the Russian market, but her own market began to feel insufficient production of this article."[41]

A stage was reached where some branches of Ukrainian industry encountered artificial barriers erected by Russian competitors. Thus, for example, in place of ready made products of the porcelain works of the village of Poloshky, Hlukhiv county, clay was exported to Moscow and Petersburg, to plants of Russian manufacturers. Russia did not hesitate to wreck Ukrainian enterprises outright. The fate of the large linen factory of Pochep was sealed by an ordinance stating: "this summer the factory is to be transported to Great Russian cities," and it was dismantled and re-erected in Russia. In general, the woolen and linen industries were the object of the most acute oppression on the part of Russia. This can be readily understood, since their widely used products offered the most tempting opportunities in Ukraine for Russian manufacturers. The Ukrainian textile industry was brought to a decline by a series of ordinances, especially of a customs fiscal nature. Thus, for example the woolen industry of Kiev region declined 44.1% between 1842 and 1847, from 668.5 thousand rubles to 373.3 thousand. Other localities had a similar decline.

All this had repercussions on sheep ranching. The demand of wool on the part of the Ukrainian mills, as well as Russian manufacturing and the markets of Western Europe, caused the development in Ukraine of fine-fleece sheep. From the very beginning, the ranching was of a colonial nature. Merino sheep made their first appearance in Ukraine in the late 18th century. In 1804, the Russian Government, through a German named Miller, brought a large flock of merino sheep to the Odessa region. This kind of sheep ranching took great strides with the

[40] *Ibid.*, III, 146.   [41] M. Slabchenko, *op. cit.*, p. 150.

establishment of huge ranches, mainly in Southern Ukraine,
and thus Ukraine became a wool center both for Russia and
Europe. In 1848 there were 3,700,000 merino sheep in the south
of Ukraine, with some ranches raising tens of thousands. Exports
of wool through Black Sea ports reached the following figures:
1831, 3,140,000 pounds; 1840, 6,418,000 pounds; 1860, 20,577,-
000 pounds; and in 1838, the Russian mills purchased 3,200,000
pounds on the Troitsky market in Kharkiv.[42]

After closing the borders of Ukraine to Western European
textiles and wrecking the Ukrainian woolen and linen industries, Russia, in order to procure for herself a monopoly of the
Ukrainian market and its colonial exploitation, undertook measures to prevent even Polish textiles from reaching Ukraine. "An
increase of imports of Polish manufactures, mainly cloth, and
primarily into Ukraine, was the cause of initiating special tariff
measures in 1832 to curtail Polish imports into the borders of
Russia and Ukraine."[43]

In this connection Slabchenko wrote: "Russian merchants
were particularly interested in Ukrainian markets, because there
they not only got raw material, but also disposed of goods of
inferior quality . . . goods delivered from Russia were of much
lower quality then those distributed in Russia itself, and prices
obtained in Ukraine were 15% to 20% higher. The tariff of 1822
secured particular privileges to Moscow merchants, and in this
connection a lot of so-called 'fancy goods' (textiles) were pushed
into Ukraine. The Kreshchensky and Illinsky fairs alone handled
almost 22 million rubles worth of Russian manufactures, which
was about one-third of the total production. Russian textile
goods crowded out the Ukrainian altogether."[44]

Ohloblyn gives this exact analysis of the Ukrainian market
of the period: "In the middle 1850's the process of capturing
the Ukrainian market by Russian capital was almost complete.
Russian industry sold on the markets of the Left Bank and
Southern Ukraine 20 million rubles worth of textiles alone. (Almost one-third of the general textile production of the Empire).
In 1854 this was 86.9% of the total sales of textiles, and nearly
a quarter (28.8%) of the gross sales at Ukrainian fairs. The participation of foreign capital in the textile trade of the Ukrainian

[42] M. Slabchenko, *Materialy . . .*, p. 31.
[43] M. Volobuyev, "Do Problemy Ukrainskoyi Ekonomiky" ("On the Problem
   of the Ukrainian Economy"), *Bolshevyk Ukrainy*, Kharkiv, 1928, ("From
   Manuscript").
[44] M. Slabchenko, *op. cit.*, p. 228.

market in the middle of the century amounted to only 1 million rubles, constituting 4.3% of the total sale of textiles."[45]

The grain trade was more complicated. Russia could not do the same thing as in industrial products, squeeze the Ukrainian agricultural economy and put Russian production in its place. But the large grain trade volume opened wide possibilities of increasing national commercial capital. Exports of Ukrainian grain in great quantities facilitated, because of the influx of foreign exchange, exports to Ukraine of Western European industrial products, with which Russia could not hope to compete. Moreover, the inclusion of foreign importers in the activities of the Ukrainian market in connection with grain trade was fraught with dangers, particularly in the grain price policy. Thus, the grain trade of Ukraine became the main problem to be solved before Russia could conquer the Ukrainian economy completely.[46]

What made the situation even more complex was the fact that Ukraine, situated on the seaboard, was naturally drifting into participation in world ocean trade and was thus becoming an organic part of the European economy. Under such circumstances the development of Ukrainian grain trade based on Black Sea routes was self-evident. As early as 1802 Napoleon wrote to Tsar Alexander I: "Your Highness' State and France would benefit much if direct trade were opened between our ports through the Black Sea. We could bring from Marseille to Black Sea ports products of our colonies and of our manufacture, and in exchange would take grain, lumber, and other goods which are easy to carry down the great rivers flowing to the Black Sea."[47]

The attractive power of the Black Sea was being felt to such a degree that not only Ukraine, but also Russian *gubernias* bordering on Ukraine directed their goods to this arterial highway of commerce. During the 1820's, 90% of all goods from the *gubernias* of Orlov, Smolensk and Kaluga went down the Desna and Dnipro rivers to the Black Sea.

These natural factors of the Ukrainian economy were so strong that in spite of all obstacles, Black Sea trade kept increasing considerably. Shipbuilding increased, both of seagoing

[45] O. Ohloblyn, *Peredkapitalistychna fabryka* (*Pre-Capitalist Factories*), Kiev, 1925, pp. 44-45.
[46] M. Slabchenko, *op. cit.*, p. 41.
[47] K. Skalkovsky, *Russky torgoviy flot* (*Russian Merchant Marine*), St. Petersburg, 1909, p. 17.

and river vessels, and seaport improvement was begun. Following a plan of Count Vorontzoff, a guild of so-called "free sailors' unions" was established to guarantee crews for ships.

An important stage in the development of seagoing trade, subsequently playing an important part in its further growth, was the granting to Odessa, in 1817 of free customs zone privileges, finally effectuated in 1819. This made Odessa a warehousing point for foreign goods and guaranteed duty-free exchange of goods within the prescribed zone. The extent of the Black Sea foreign trade is shown by the fact that between 1851 and 1853 the number of vessels entering Black Sea ports was 3,916 and sailing for foreign ports, 11,074.

This situation created for the Russian industrialists and merchants a dual problem. First, they had to remove from the Ukrainian markets the foreign exporters dangerous to them and replace them with their own capital, and then they had to impair the significance of the Black Sea and turn Ukrainian grain northward to their ports on the Baltic. The Crimean War of 1854 to 1856 helped realize the first task, "removing the foreigner and putting in his place the Russian exporter aided by tariffs." The war also helped in lessening the importance of the Black Sea not only by halting all traffic for the duration, but also by destroying the merchant fleet. The restoration of this fleet proceeded under the new form, completely in the hands of Russian capital of the "Russian Company for Steam Navigation and Commerce."

The channeling of Ukrainian grain northward required more complicated steps. One of them was the price policy of grain. In Ukraine, local prices were kept at a much lower level than in regions which gravitated to Baltic ports. Freight rates and duties were much lower in the Baltic than in the Black Sea ports in spite of a greater distance of grain producing areas from the former.

Table VI gives comparative prices of grain in Baltic and Black Sea ports (per unit of 1 *chetvert* (approximately 360 pounds in rubles). On the other hand freight and duty per *chetvert* were 1.67 rubles in the Baltic ports and 2.99 rubles in Black Sea ports. "The growth of the Ukrainian grain trade could not be looked upon with comfort by Russian black-soil landlords, therefore they made demands that duties be imposed on Ukrainian grain in the interests of Russian black-soil agriculture."[48]

48 M. Slabchenko, *op. cit.*, p. 41.

TABLE VI

Years		Baltic	Black Sea
1822-26	....	5.70	4.20
1827-31	....	5.80	4.25
1832-36	....	5.80	5.10
1837-41	....	8.15	5.40
1842-46	....	7.80	5.10

This difference in freights and tariffs was felt even more acutely when Russia started building railroads, and halted them in Ukraine. In the correspondence of a Ukrainian landlord, Andry Storozhenko, with his son, we read: "But they did not hurry with Ukraine, although Ukrainian merchants and landowners were already vociferous about this matter (construction of railroads). Conversations started in connection with the fact that American grain began to take the place of Ukrainian on foreign markets. Our wheat was locally cheaper: in Odessa in 1840, 6.10 against American 7.92; in 1841, 5.60 against 7.85; in 1842, 5.55 against 7.39, in 1843, 4.85 against 7.00. But both freight and insurance were higher in Ukraine (insurance from Odessa to London was 2.5% and from New York to London 1.5%. It took almost twice as long to ship grain from Ukraine as it did from America."[49]

Ukrainian landowners were very busy in the matter of building railroads, but "the Government made such severe demands on corporations that they could not be complied with."[50]

The results of this policy soon became apparent. "In the 1850's England was lost as a purchaser, now being able to buy the same Ukrainian grain in Baltic ports, the Scandinavian nations also, although the Black Sea still offered stiff resistance to encroachments of Baltic ports and Russian exporters, even during periods of lowest depression."[51]

The Black Sea grain trade itself finally came under Russian control, being unable to avoid the general process of colonial exploitation. *Table VII* shows ethnic division of industrialists and merchants of Ukraine for 1832.

"Russian merchants and owners of factories often lived in Russia, and administered their Ukrainian enterprises from there."[52]

---

[49] *Ibid.*, p. 249.
[50] P. Fomin, "Ekonomichna kharakterystyka Ukrainy" ("Economic Characteristics of Ukraine"), p. 51.
[51] M. Slabchenko, *op. cit.*, p. 146.   [52] O. Ohloblyn, *op. cit.*, p. 47.

TABLE VII

	Proprietors of Industrial Enterprises	Merchants
Russians	44.6%	5.26%
Ukrainians	28.7%	22.2%
Jews	17.4%	20.9%
Foreigners	3.6%	1.9%
Others	5.7%	2.4%

Even the sugar refining industry, where Ukraine was clearly outside of any competition by reason of having the greatest yield per area and the lowest production costs, was subject to attempts to have its development thwarted by a system of tariffs. There were 45 sugar refining plants in Ukraine in 1840, and 229 in 1852, but notwithstanding the prime position of Ukraine, considerable quantities of unrefined sugar were shipped to Russia for refining (e.g. the Koenig plant in Petersburg).

The position of Ukraine as a result of this policy was aptly characterized in 1813 by V. Karazyn, the founder of the first Ukrainian university in Kharkiv: "We are forced to sell our products in that form in which nature has given them to us, and being rich in all material for manufacturing, almost all our needs have to be satisfied by imports from afar, paying for freight to inside Russia and back, and paying with our poor money the net gains of middlemen through whose hands pass first of all raw materials extracted with our hands, and then when they come back to us in the shape of manufactured goods."[53]

We refer again to the basis of the Ukrainian population, the peasants. In the light of what was said above, it is clear why their position was much worse than that of the Russian peasants. The productive nature of Ukrainian agriculture induced the landowners to increase its extent, imposing serf labor upon the peasants. Hence the practical absence of a rent system in Ukraine, the complete dependence of the peasants on the manors and the servitude. Added to this are the extremely limited opportunities of wage labor, because of an artificial stifling of Ukrainian industry. The Ukrainian peasant simply had no place to earn wages even if he only had to pay land rent. The policy of low grain prices in comparison with Russia, diminished even further the income from that part of the peasants' production

[53] Quoted in M. Slabchenko, *op. cit.*, p. 10.

that went to market. At the same time, the fiscal policy of the Imperial Government based on the principle of privileges for the landowners and favoring young Russian industry, transferred the greater part of the tax load onto the shoulders of the peasants. The landowners' peasants paid a head tax of 95 kopecks, 49.5 kopecks of land dues, and a whole series of local assessments, such as quartering soldiers, furnishing labor for road construction, and traction power for hauling. D. Zhuravsky in his *Statisticheskoye Opisaniye Kievskoy Guberniyi*, computed the cash expenditures of a peasant family in the 1830's in Kiev region at 29 rubles, 25 kopecks, of which 15 rubles went for taxes, 3 rubles for communal dues, and 1 ruble for religious dues. The balance went primarily for tools, scythes, wheels, axlegrease, etc. Only tiny amounts were available for consumption and clothing, the main item being the cost of salt.[54]

Thus, the purchasing power of the main part of the population, a decisive factor in any nation's economy, was extremely low. But even these modest financial needs could not be met by farming. Comparing the cash income and cash outlay of a medium sized household, we find an average annual cash deficit per family of 7 rubles, 25 kopecks. This caused a continual accruing of huge tax deficiencies owed by the peasants, which the government was frequently compelled to write off as not collectible, only to have them pile up again, in even larger amounts. In 1817 the landowners' peasants owed 879,000 rubles in deficiencies, which were written off. By 1839 there was a new deficiency of 5.5 million rubles. A manifesto of 1826 wrote off similar deficiencies of state serfs, but in 1858 the latter again owed 797,000 rubles in rents and 787,000 rubles in taxes. An extremely tight money situation was then characteristic of the Ukrainian farm economy; caused on the one hand by agrarian conditions existing in Ukraine, and on the other by the colonial position of the Ukrainian economy, particularly of industry and commerce. This crisis, as we shall see, played a decisive role in the subsequent history of Ukrainian agriculture, and of the economy as a whole. Ukraine entered the period called the "era of industrial capitalism" under these handicaps. The beginning of the period is the abolition of serfdom, in February, 1861.

[54] M. Slabchenko, *op. cit.*, p. 148.

Earlier, Empress Catherine II wrote to Prince Vyazemsky: "We must eradicate the indecent idea [of the Ukrainians], according to which they consider themselves to be an entirely different nation from this [Russian]. Little Russia, Livonia, and Finland are provinces governed by privileges confirmed to them; it would not do to violate them all at once, but nevertheless calling them foreign (nations) and treating them on such a basis is more than a mistake, it can be called sheer stupidity. These provinces, also the Smolensk, must be brought by easy stages to such condition that they become Russianized, and stop looking to the woods like wolves."[55]

The policy of Russianization was, as is well known, the backbone of Russia's attitude toward Ukraine over the centuries. It would, however, be a grave mistake to believe that the aim of this policy was complete unification of Ukraine with Russia, i. e. the transformation of Ukraine into an equal Russian territory. On the contrary, Russian economic policy always aimed at differentiating Ukraine from Russia, and of keeping Ukraine in the status of a colony.

[55] Serhiy Yefremov, *Istoria Ukrainskoho pysmenstva (History of Ukrainian Literature),* Kiev, 1924, I, 272.

CHAPTER 2

POST-REFORM AGRARIAN CONDITIONS IN UKRAINE

Pre-conditions to the Reform of 1861

THE MANIFESTO of February 19, 1861, abolishing serfdom and introducing a change in agrarian conditions, instead of solving the difficulties of the Ukranian peasants resulting from the economic subjection made them even more complicated. The causes of this were both the nature of the reform itself, as well as the peculiar situation in which the Ukrainian peasants were placed in relation to Russia, again in the interests of the latter.

The abolition of serfdom had at that time become an historical necessity, moral motives never being decisive in the policy of the Russian Government. The main compelling reason was the course of Russia's economic development. A further growth of industry, already occupying in Russia an important position was meeting with two insurmountable obstacles. First of all, industry needed a mass consumption market for its production, because at that time, light industry was the dominant mass production manufacturer. Serfdom excluded the possibility of creating such a market. The labor of the peasant on the landlord's estate was in the nature of work dues (a certain number of days in the week), having no reflection in the peasant's cash budget. His own enterprise was also of a natural-consumption character, and his connection with the cash-commodity market went no farther than the purchase of salt, axle-grease, scythes, etc. Most satisfied their needs with their own farm and handicrafts products, or by bartering food products for products of other artisans. This characterized not only the level of the needs of the peasants, but also the style of their living, reflected in the commercial relations of the period. The produce of the peasants' farms (bread, vegetables, milk, meat) had no local market, and the masses of the local population

had to be their sole consumers. If a person needed such products, he would buy them not for cash, but for repayment in
kind. Consumer goods produced by the peasants then could
only get a market value upon reaching a city market. But the
distances from such markets with almost no established roads,
and the small amount of production, were an obstacle to the
participation of the peasants in market activities. Cash was badly needed for the payment of taxes, and this determined the
extent to which the serf farmers took part in market activities.
According to budgetary research, in 1858 in the Kiev region the
payment of taxes and local assessments reached two-thirds of all
cash expenditures of the average household. It is quite clear
then, that under such internal market conditions, any large-scale
development of capital industry was out of the question. Life
demanded a breaking down of the natural forms of the economy. It demanded the inclusion on a much larger scale than
before of the peasants as the basis of the population (constituting over 75% of Empire's entire population) in the system of
monetary circulation. For this purpose it was necessary, on the
one hand, to endow the labor of the peasants on landlords' estates with the forms of hired labor, paid in wages, and on the
other, to increase the peasants' needs for cash, mainly by increasing their taxes and other obligations.

The Imperial Treasury had a direct interest here. The economic condition of the Russian Empire, backward in relation
to Western Europe, was becoming hard pressed and threatening.
The aureole of glory and the leading role in Europe secured
by Russia as a result of the war against Napoleon vanished
quickly, and Russia faced the danger of a decline of her importance in European politics. The Crimean War of 1854-56 gave
the situation a vivid emphasis. It was becoming clear that it was
no longer possible to base the power of the state exclusively
upon the human masses. With the gigantic industrial development of Western Europe during the 19th century, if Russia were
to remain industrially stagnant, she would invariably lose all
her positions gained in almost uninterrupted wars of aggression.
(According to the Russian General Kuropatkin, during the 200-
year period of the 17th and 18th centuries Russia had 72 years
of peace and 128 years of war, out of which 101 years, 22 wars,
were for the conquest of alien territories.)[1]

---

[1] "Natsionalne pytannya na skhodi Evropy" ("The Nationality Problem in

The necessary tempo of development could not be provided by Russian industry's own resources, because up to this time it had been existing under favorable conditions of the natural economy of serfdom and did not possess sufficient capital. Therefore, in order to achieve its goal, the government had to embark upon the development of a state industry, and furnish aid to industry in the form of grants, credits, and a favorable customs policy. This required a considerable increase in the state budget, impossible to realize under conditions of serfdom. In a natural economy, the peasants could not become the basic tax-bearing category. On the other hand, the class nature of the Tsarist Empire, the privileged position of the nobility, and the political weight of the latter, stood in the way of increasing the tax load of the landowners. Thus, this facet also demonstrated the need for abolishing serfdom, so as to change the peasants into a basic source of the state's income. The main emphasis was that only by liberating the peasants, would Russia, as the metropolis, get rich at the expense of her colonies. This was, in fact, realized in full measure, as we shall see later. Colonial exploitation had, in the case of Russia, the same decisive meaning in the development of industry, as it did in the case of Western European empires.

The interests of industry also demanded the abolition of serfdom, because the problem of availability of labor hinged upon this. Binding the peasants to the soil caused a lack of labor for industry, and supplementing the cadres of labor from the ranks of rent-paying peasants (released for wage-earning by the landowners) created on the other hand a condition of fluidity which precluded establishing a permanent class of qualified labor, a prerequisite for the ever-increasing technical level of the industrial process.

The government had earlier sought a solution to the problem of industrial labor by submitting state-serfs to serfdom in industrial plants. The metallurgical industry of the Urals was based upon such serf labor, and the Luhansky State Metallurgical Plant in Ukraine was also based on this plan. But this proved to be so unproductive that it was impossible to even think of organizing any normal production schedules with it. Industry needed a free market of hired labor; it needed the abolition of serfdom.

Eastern Europe"), *Materyaly i Dokumenty* (*Materials and Documents*), Prague, 1925, p. 31.

Finally, the landowners themeselves were, in a large majority, interested in such reform, not because serf ownership was
onerous to them, but because it would provide a means of rem-
edying their hopeless financial position. The crux of the matter
is that the monetary system of the economy was unable to include in its orbit even the landlords, whose economy, as has
been mentioned above, was based upon a natural system. The
new style of life created an acute need for money which the system of the time was unable to satisfy. Hence the great indebtedness of the landowners, the mortgaging of properties, etc. Redemption payments, due the landowners according to the 1861
reform, the land becoming the property of the peasants who had
been tilling it just as before the reform, thus became a considerable financial aid to the landowners. In reality endowing the
peasants with land along with their liberation was nothing but
compulsory purchase, and at prices much in excess of the real
market value of the land. This was the reason behind the interest
of the landowners in the reform. It is true that they became ap-
prehensive, lest after the liberation a lack of labor for their estates might ensue, and that cash payments for labor may become
a great load upon their economy, and for that reason they demanded certain guarantees to be given along with the reform
which would safeguard them against such dangers, and this, as
we shall see later, they were successful in getting.

Abolition of Serfdom and Endowment with Land

The abolition of serfdom was then an historical necessity
of the period. It was not only in the interests of the commercial and industrial classes, but also of the whole state, and
even of a large part of the gentry. Serfdom was abolished
on February 19, 1861, after lengthy preparations by the government. The Tsar's Manifesto granted the peasants personal
freedom and abolished their subjection to the landowners,
but the peasants were still a class of limited rights. They
had no right of absolute freedom of movement, they were subject to the jurisdiction of special courts, corporal punishment
could be inflicted upon them at the hands of so-called *Zemsky
nachalnyky* (Landchiefs) an office created in 1889 of a purely
administrative nature, though also endowed with certain judicial functions. These conditions were, however, uniform for the

whole Empire, and in this respect Ukraine did not differ from Russia. But in application of rules the Russian bureaucrats in Ukraine displayed much more of a "fighting spirit," mentioned by the Russian journalist Danilov in his work *Obshchaya politika pravitelstva i gosudarstvenniy Stroy.* He wrote: " . . . this (policy) was dictated by a desire to bolster among the organs of the authorities that 'fighting spirit' which is created by a military command in borderlands; it was dictated by the tide of a multiplied bureacracy which was directly augmented from the milieu of the land-poor gentry, clergy and officialdom, running after jobs and rewards . . . Finally, this 'fighting' policy was, in relation to borderlands, people of other race and other faith, the means suited best for directing their feeling of anger and dissatisfaction on a false path, a feeling that was embracing more and more of the aboriginal Russian population which was being forced to take it out against other nationalities by oppressing them, for their own miserable and poor existence."[2]

In Ukraine, this "fighting spirit" became more acute by special efforts of the government, directed at eradicating everything that had any relation to national separateness. In 1863 the Ukrainian language was prohibited in religious, popular and scientific printing and textbooks. Later, in 1876, a circular letter extended the prohibition to all forms of works in the Ukrainian language. Anything that contained traces of nationalism in any form was placed outside the law.

But the Russian Government did not stop at national oppression or cruel administrative policy. In Ukraine, the reform itself was surrounded by a whole series of legal norms, differing from those for Russia, such that they not only preserved the colonial position of the Ukrainian agricultural economy, but conditioned its increase.

The endowment of the peasants with land, by way of purchase from the landowners, was itself very unjust, as far as Ukraine was concerned. We have already mentioned in the previous chapter how serfdom originated in Ukraine. It was nothing but an usurpation of the peasants' property rights to land. Unlike Russia, the introduction of serfdom in Ukraine consisted not only in depriving the peasants of their personal freedom,

---

[2] F. Danilov, "Obshchaya polityka pravitelstva i gosudarstvenniy stroy" ("General Policy of the Government and State Structure"), *Obshchestvennoye dvizheniye v Rossiyi (The Social Movement in Russia),* St. Petersburg, 1910, I, 211.

and imposing labor obligations on them in relation to landowners, but also in robbing them of their own land properties.

The Ukrainian peasantry has always remembered this violation of its property rights to land. It long continued, contrary to alien legal rules, to exercise property rights in land by alienation, lease, etc. And these acts of the peasants were recognized even by the landowners as part of the common law augmented by tradition. Thus, the very decision concerning purchase of land from the landowners hit hard on the consciousness of the Ukrainian peasants. To them it was nothing, but this: the purchase of their own property from those who had stolen it from them.

The average price of one *desiatyna* of land at the time of the abolition of serfdom was 123 rubles in Ukraine, and 187 rubles in European Russia. This differential was caused by the low price of land in the steppes where, at that time, little was under cultivation. The differential of the price of land is given varying analyses by different authors. Some stress the privileged position of the Russian landowners as compared to that of the landowners of Ukraine; others, contrariwise, mention the better position of the Ukraine peasants than those of Russia. We believe that a correct estimate of the situation would be to look at it from the aspect of its future influence upon the Ukrainian peasants. First of all, the figures cannot be taken in their absolute dimensions. We have mentioned before that the cash budget of the Ukrainian peasants was because of the suppression and deliberate wrecking of Ukrainian industry, relatively lower than of the Russian peasants, who had opportunities for extra wage income in industry. We shall see later what a large number of Russian peasants had winter home-wage opportunities in, for example, textile industry, preparing thread for weaving. Hence the payment of 123 rubles was no less onerous to the Ukrainian peasant than 187 rubles to the Russian. Neither can we overlook the fact that 123 rubles was an excessive price for the period, in comparison with the real value of the land. Professor Slabchenko cites computations of Professor Khodsky, according to which the purchase price exceeded average bank valuations (and these, as we shall see were higher than average market prices) in the Chernihiv region by 3.9%; in Kherson, 11.2%; in Katerynoslav, 18%; in Kharkiv, 23.2%; in Poltava, 35%; in Volhynia, 81%; in Kiev, 96.5%; and in Podilla 100.9%. In localities of the greatest density of population, and the least land availability, they were double of the current real values.[3]

Even this excessively high price of land in Ukraine did not add to the landlords' desire to transfer larger areas of land to the peasants than was done in Russia. The natural and economic conditions in Ukraine at the time determined a capitalistic nature of large agricultural enterprises. This was the cause of the landowners desire to hold on to as much land as possible, because land played the role of capital. This process of capitalization of the agricultural economy did not reach the same degree in Russia, and moreover, the higher price of 187 rubles favored a larger distribution of land among the peasants.

A decrease in the amount of peasant holdings in Ukraine was also in the interests of the Imperial Government. In it was perceived the best guarantee against the danger of a lack of human labor on the large estates, in whose conservation it was interested, because they provided the main source of exports of goods, the profits of which, as we shall indicate later, benefited the Imperial Treasury. The nine-year obligation of former serfs to work on lands of their former masters authorized by the *Polozheniye* and the so-called "obedience" provided a temporary solution of the problem. The "peasant intermediaries," authorized to conduct the land reform put into effect in that spirit the matter of endowing the peasants with land.

The results were these: the peasants of the centrally located and more industrialized regions of the Empire lost only 9.9% of their former land uses, while in Ukraine, where the land was the sole source of income for the mass of the population, the area of land used by the peasants decreased by 30.8%.[4] The reform cost the peasants almost one-third of that land, off which they lived before 1861. But of itself this large average loss of peasant lands does not provide a complete picture of the decrease of peasant land uses, nor of its economic consequences, because that average was in large measure determined by the land-rich steppe, where the amount of such losses was much smaller, and where the peasants' purchases were much larger. The real and catastrophic significance of these land losses were felt in regions where "land was tight," and where the population was dense, on the Right Bank and in Slobozhanska region, where

[3] M. Slabchenko, *Materialy . . .*, II, 36.
[4] N. Olezhko, *Agrarna polityka Bolshevykiv (Agrarian Policy of the Bolsheviks)*, Munich, 1947, p. 8.

the losses were greater, and the area of land coming to the
peasants did not warrant the normal development of the economy. To compute the "head-tax," a periodic census of the population was taken following the revision. Between the two revisions
the real number of the population exceeded by far the number
of "taxable souls." Thus, per "taxable soul" there were 3.5 desiatynas of land before 1861, and only 2.5 after. Less than 3
desiatynas per "taxable soul" were given to peasants in the Kiev
gubernia to 72%; in Podilla to 77.5%; in Volhynia to 33.7%; in
Kharkiv to 33.5%; in Poltava to 70.5%, and in Chernihiv to
40%.[5] On the occasion of the reform the peasants of the Poltava
gubernia lost 449,765 desiatynas; of Katerynoslav, 198,838 desiatynas; of Kharkiv, 187,128 desiatynas; of Chernihiv, 59,015
desiatynas, etc.[6] It must be added that the extent of the losses
varied, depending on the area of the estates. As a rule, the larger
the estate, the larger the losses to the peasants of land which they
had been using. These losses amounted to 50% and more. P. Maslov, in the work quoted gives collected data on the gubernia of
Volhynia. According to him, the peasants suffered the losses
shown in Table VIII on the occasion of their liberation in 1861.

TABLE VIII

	% of their former land use
On estates of less than 100 desiatynas	8.2%
On estates from 100 to 500 desiatynas	28.8%
On estates from 500 to 1,000 desiatynas	30.4%
On estates from 1,000 to 5,000 desiatynas	43.4%
On estates from 5,000 to 10,000 desiatynas	56.5%
On estates over 10,000 desiatynas	74.6%

[7]

There were then serfs who received only one-fourth of the
amount of land which they had been using before the reform.
We must bear in mind that land-rich owners holding 1,000
desiatynas and more, who had taken the most land from the
peasants, held on the Left Bank 71.1% of the total area of land
owned by the landlords, on the Right Bank 86.9% and in Southern Ukraine also 86.9%.[8]

[5] P. Maslov, Razvitiye zemledeleniya v Rossiyi (Development of Land
Distribution in Russia), Moscow, 1912, p. 123.
[6] M. Slabchenko, loc. cit.
[7] P. Maslov, op. cit., p. 129.
[8] M. Ogonovsky, Individualnoye zemlevladeniye (Individual Land Ownership), Moscow, 1912, p. 79.

Monetary Restrictions

Thus the Ukrainian peasants had been robbed twice: when serfdom began their land property was taken away; when serfdom ended they were robbed by means of payments and decrease of the land area used by them. Land-tight conditions thus created, became as we shall see later, a decisive factor in the entire development of the Ukrainian economy, and in the structure of economic conditions. It determined a standstill, and in some fields even a retrogression of agricultural production. It caused an awful breaking up and differentiation of farm units. It created an exceptional increase in differential rent and land value, as capital. It finally created that crisis of the means of production and costs in the agrarian economy which characterized the entire system of agrarian conditions, and in large measure predetermined the position of the peasantry in the social processes of following periods, including the Bolshevik period. All this, in turn, brought about the fiscal forms of colonial exploitation of Ukraine; a decline of large-scale agricultural production; difficulties in the accumulation of national capital which is a basis of the development of a national economy; a *sui generis* capitalization, and its capture of foreign capital. It is difficult to find any branch of the Ukrainian economy during the last century, wherein in greater or lesser degree, conditions of the agrarian economy did not have repercussions. It is quite understandable when we consider how important the agricultural economy was to the basic mass of the population of Ukraine. We noted in the introductory remarks to this work that as late as the eve of World War I, 87.5% of all the Ukrainian population, or 74.5% of all the population of Ukraine were engaged in agriculture. These are the reasons which compelled us to consider all the foregoing, for without it one could not understand the nature of many social and economic processes in Ukraine. And one could not uncover, in full measure, the colonial position of Ukraine.

The obligation to pay off the "purchase price" of land under conditions of a natural-consumption character of the agricultural economy, and in absence of opportunities for gainful employment outside the home farm, coupled with a decreased land area used by them, descended as a great weight upon the backs of the peasants, it immediately created a deep internal economic and financial crisis, which influenced the economy for a long

period of time. It was not within the peasant's own powers to
cope with the obligation. He was therefore compelled to apply
for a state loan, authorized by the reform of 1861. This transformed the "purchase price" into a form of obligation to the
state, turning the government into a collection agency. In the
minds of the peasants the borderline between the current payments of these obligations and ordinary taxes was thus often ob-
literated.

Nobody was able to pay the purchase price of land in the
gubernias of Podilla and Volhynia, in Kiev *gubernias* only 0.1%;
Poltava, 2.6%; Chernihiv, 3.6%, Kharkiv, 5.4%, and only in the
land-rich regions of the steppe the percentage was higher,
reaching 13.9% in Kherson, 32.3% in Katerynoslav, and 35% in
Tavria. Almost all peasants signed up to buy land. (See *Table
IX*).

TABLE IX

In the region of	Total number taxable souls	Number signing up
Kharkiv	179,248	164,211 - 97.8%
Kherson	117,093	94,580 - 94%
Katerynoslav	130,596	82,467 - 63.8%
Chernihiv	235,116	199,385 - 88.9%
Poltava	284,078	210,356 - 76.8%

In other regions almost all peasants signed up. But still, by
1874, when the aforementioned nine-year term of "obedience"
finally expired there remained, in different regions, a certain
number of peasants obligated to the landowners, and unable to
perform them partially. The number of peasants so obligated
reached 26.7% of all peasants in the Poltava region. And in all
regions without exception, from the very first year of accounting for endowed land there were deficiencies, peasant indebtedness for current payments which often, increasing from deficiencies of prior years, reached the dimensions of the peasants'
total cash expenditures during an entire year. The picture becomes more clear when we consider the extent of these obligations. In the Kherson region, for each "soul endowment" the
following payments had to be made annually: 7 rubles, 20 kopecks for the purchase price amount, 1 ruble, 80 kopecks to the
landlord for the same account, 2 rubles head tax under the
"taxable soul" revision assessment, and 80 kopecks for local
needs. All this excluded assessments in kind. The total amounted

to 2 rubles, 12 kopecks per *desiatyna*. Assessments were even higher in other regions. According to data of the Kharkiv County Administration for the year 1869, the assessments for every *desiatyna* of land were: Kharkiv, 3 rubles, 79.5 kopecks; Poltava, 3 rubles, 70 kopecks; Kiev, 4 rubles, 27 kopecks; Podilla, 3 rubles, 87 kopecks; Volhynia, 4 rubles, 27 kopecks, etc.[9]

Professor Slabchenko says that "conditions became such that in some localities payments exceeded land income." This may sound incredible, but we must consider that the tax amount of 4 rubles from one *desiatyna*, under the then prevailing agricultural system of rotation which left one-third of the land fallow, really meant 6 rubles in relation to the crop-yielding area, equal to 25% of the gross crop (less seed). An endless number of other taxes increased the burden. Beside the purchase price, they had to pay state and local property taxes, city taxes, the head-tax, military levy, assessments in kind and many others. A large part of the taxes (especially those imposed locally) changed frequently, usually increasing, making accounting of the peasants out of previous payments more difficult. In some *zemstvos*[10] these taxes equalled, and sometimes exceeded, the totals of all other assessments. Thus, e. g. in the Vovchansky county of Kharkiv *gubernia*, the taxes reached almost 5 rubles per *desiatyna*.

In addition to cash taxes the peasants had to bear a whole series of assessments in kind; "road duty," labor on road construction and maintenance; hauling duty, transporting goods and people; *desiatske*, police aid work with local authorities, etc. Such taxation of the peasants was without comparison higher than that of the landlords. Prof. Bogolepov compiled the following table of land taxes (exclusive of redemption price payments, military levy, assessments in kind, etc. of which the landlords were entirely free). He compared, see *Table X*, the taxes paid by peasants and landlords during the periods of 1891 and 1899 (in rubles and kopecks per *desiatyna, per annum.*)

In some counties, local assessments narrowed the gap, but the difference was still great. In the Poltava region, the peasants

[9] M. Slabchenko, *op. cit.*, pp. 267-269.
[10] *Zemstvo* was an organ of local self-government in which representatives of the nobility were in a dominant majority. Delegates of the peasants numbered no more than one-third of the voting land deputies. Participation of the peasants in the executive organ of the zemstvo, *Uprava*, was insignificant. Among the competences of zemstvos were: rural primary education, health, maintenance of roads, vital statistics, agronomic and veterinarian aid, and other similar measures in aid of the peasants. Financially the zemstvos relied on the power of taxing the peasants.

TABLE X

Region	1891		1899	
	Peasants	Landowners	Peasants	Landowners
Left Bank	1.68	0.40	1.80	0.70
Right Bank	1.93	0.35	2.06	0.18
Steppe	1.17	0.26	1.70	0.29

[11]

paid from 10% to 150% more than the landowners and in Cherni-hiv, 8% to 71%. This difference became greater when, following requests by the landowners, their land taxes were twice reduced.

True, some taxes of the peasants were also reduced. Thus, the head or soul tax was abolished in 1883, and the passport fee in 1892. But in general the taxes increased by means of new forms, mainly local collections. For the three-year period, 1875-1877, *zemstvo* averaged 6.2 to 6.5 kopecks per *desiatyna* per an-num for landowners lands. Those of the peasants were 13.9 to 14.8 kopecks. Along with a decrease in direct taxes, there was, as a rule an increase in indirect taxes. Between 1881 and 1892, direct taxes in the whole Empire came down from 139.9 million rubles to 91.3 million rubles (not including local taxes, whose sum total did not decrease, but increased). But during the same period indirect taxation increased from 327.7 million rubles to 466.9 million rubles. Per capita indirect taxes amounted to about 3 rubles in 1871, and to 5 rubles, 20 kopecks in 1901.[12]

Moreover, there was an unequal distribution of taxes within the peasant class itself. Former state serfs were better positioned than former serfs of private owners, and they also, as we shall show, received more land. In the Poltava region, as has been noted, former landowner serfs paid an average of 3 rubles, 70 kopecks per *desiatyna*, while former state serfs paid only 1 ruble, 63 kopecks. Corresponding figures for the Kherson region were: 2 rubles, 12 kopecks and 1 ruble, 19 kopecks. It may seem unnecessary to devote so much attention to the matter of taxes, since neither the sole fact of taxation nor its amount, if figures are taken in the abstract, reveal an unusual situation. However, when one considers the total position of the peasants these pay-ments and all other money burdens which descended upon the peasantry of Ukraine as a result of specific measures applied to them on the occasion of the reform, the picture differs.

[11] P. Bogolepov, *Gosudarstvenniye i miestniye nalogi* (*State and Local Taxes*), Kharkiv, 1902, p. 39.   [12] *Ibid.*, p. 53.

Moreover, tax itself is not of basic importance, but the expenditure of tax money. In this respect Ukraine was again in a different position than Russia: the bulk of taxes was not applied to the servicing and development of the Ukrainian population's economy. All taxes went into the Imperial Treasury and came back to Ukraine only in insignificant amounts, mostly for the upkeep of the Imperial governmental apparatus which was by its composition, mainly Russian. Thus on the Right Bank, for example, out of the entire Ukrainian population there were employed, on government jobs in the army, administration, courts and police, as well as in the free professions, only 5.5%. The number of Russians was 47%; Jews, 17.5%; Germans, 8.8%; and Poles 29%.[13]

Most of the taxes paid by Ukrainian peasants went toward the economic development of Russia and toward increased armed forces, necessary for the realization of her policy of aggression, particularly in Central Asia and in the Far East.

We have already indicated that the Russian Government organized state industrial enterprises, and developed a network of state railroads in Russia proper, excluding non-Russian territories, Ukraine among them. In 1876, when Russia already possessed 17,652 *versts*[14] of constructed railroads, Ukraine had only 587. Later, when railroad construction assumed a much faster pace in Ukraine, its financing was carried out not by the state, but by private capital, mostly foreign.

All these expenditures were labelled in the budget as "extraordinary." Ukraine's position in the Imperial budget will be analyzed in detail later, we now mention these "extraordinary" expenditures only to stress the fact that taxes both exploited the rural economy, and failed to invigorate the national economy.

The best indication of burdensome tax loads are tax deficiencies. From year to year these deficiencies invariably characterized the ability of the peasantry to pay. Tax indebtness grew constantly, notwithstanding the fact that taxes were collected very ruthlessly, and their collection was facilitated by the existence of the so-called *Kruhova poruka* (liability), which will be described later. There were many instances of the auctioning of the peasants' household effects and livestock for these tax de-

---

[13] M. Porsh, "Iz statystyky Ukrainy" ("From Ukrainian Statistics"), *Ukraina*, Kiev, 1907, III, 34.
[14] 1 *verst* = 1.066 km., or roughly two-thirds of a mile.

ficiencies. But these measures were incapable of solving the
problem, and the government was frequently compelled to write
off, or reduce the deficiencies. And nevertheless they grew
anew. For the five-year period, 1891 to 1895, tax deficiencies of
the Ukrainian peasants reached 95.2% of the annual tax assessment.[15]

A vivid illustration of the fact that taxes were an unbearable
load is the remarkably extensive practice of usury which fed
on the peasants' misery. Professor Slabchenko cites the following: "in the villages of the Right Bank, Jews, who paid the taxes
for the peasants charged 3 kopecks per week interest per ruble
(156% a year), or if the peasant borrowed 5 rubles from the landlord for that purpose, he had to work for the landlord for two
months of 30 full days under penalty of 5 rubles."[16]

Of course the government, in spite of its attempts to collect
from the population as much as possible, could not be blind
to the great economic degrading of the peasants not only in
non-Russian territories, but also in Russia. The famine of 1891-
92 in the Volga regions was particularly hard-felt. Struck by
it, the Secretary of the Treasury Witte wrote: "The village is
impoverished under the tax load . . . It would be better to halt
the construction of railroads temporarily, or to build them with
borrowed funds, than to continue this financial policy, ruinous
to the population under which money is collected not from income, but from capital."[17]

In a confidential note *Strain on the Paying Ability of the
Population* (1903) Witte wrote: " . . . we cannot close our eyes
to the indubitable fact that the development of the people's
prosperity is going at an uneven and much too slow pace, and
in places the level of the economy is even declining."[18] Witte
cites in support of his statement the words of the Chief of the
Council of Ministers of 1891 Bunge, that "under existing conditions of life in the villages, the people will not come out of the
hopeless situation. It is imperative to think about removing the
evil. If we do nothing to get the rural population out of the position in which it remains, then famines which occur almost an-

---

[15] F. Danilov, *op. cit.*, I, 187.
[16] M. Slabchenko, *op. cit.*, p. 273.
[17] *Ibid.*
[18] S. I. Witte, *O narpryazheniyi platezhnikh sil naseleniya* (*The Strain on
the Paying Ability of the Population*), Stuttgart, 1903, p. 213.

nually, will become more frequent, and will encompass ever larger territories."[19]

In seconding this idea, Witte was also worried about repercussions on the state treasury: "The total amount of postponements and cancellations of deficiencies equals this year the sum of 41.5 million rubles. In addition, for 1894 there remains 1,074,-000 rubles deferred, and not paid on time, and we can expect a further increase of this debt; in 1898 taxes in kind for 1891-92 were forgiven in the amount of 170 million rubles; a quite sizable reduction of state land taxes was put into effect; the passport tax was repealed, etc."[20] But all these worries apply to "tensions of the paying ability of the population of the central Russian *gubernias.*" This characteristic of the peasant situation did not consider those in borderlands, nor in non-Russian territories. On the contrary, unable to foresee an improvement at the expense of alleviating the tax load of the central regions (because this would be a burden on the state treasury), Witte openly proposed transferring this load onto non-Russian territories. "All states," said Witte, "profit by their colonies as a source of income and a means of increasing their prosperity; we, however, apply quite contrary principles, . . . we place the burden of taxes upon Russia proper."[21] He claimed that in 1896 expenditures in the Caucasus exceeded collections by 6.5 million rubles, and in Central Asia by 6.6 million rubles, although basically these expenditures were related to the maintenance of the imperial apparatus in the colonies, and to the army maintenance. He was indignant that "the above mentioned regions do not participate in general expenditures for the central government, in payment of interest and retirement of state loans," although the loans were taken for the construction of railroads in Russia proper and for financing her wars of aggression, and the retirement of these loans, as we shall see later, fell almost exclusively upon Ukraine, to the detriment of Ukraine's favorable foreign trade balance.

In the opinion of Witte the colonies should reimburse Russia for the military expense of their enslavement. He said: " . . . the great expenses which Russia bore for the annexation of these borderlands and for their cultural development [which in reality consisted of the introduction of a Russian administration and

---

[19] *Ibid.*, p. 218.   [20] Witte, *op. cit.*, pp. 220, 221.
[21] *Ibid.*, p. 218.

a destruction of native culture—(*Author*)] have fallen upon, and continue to bear upon European Russia with all their weight."[22] Witte resorted to unusual calculations in order to prove the allegedly insufficient taxation of the colonies and to justify a transfer to them of a greater measure of obligations. He ignored problems as: rentability of the economy, nature of market relations, extent of production of goods, place of accumulation of differential rent, and the entire system of economic relations, of all that, in other words, which determines the amount of payments a given population is capable of bearing. Instead he took the total of all tax payments per capita of population, including not only land, and other taxes, but also income from realty, income from industry and commerce and redemption payments. It is obvious that such taxes, as those from commerce and industry which were more developed in Russia, increased the total sum of taxes. The same applies to income from realty, naturally much higher in the industrialized regions of Russia. But he did not feel restrained to compare the per capita tax load of Russia in the amount of 1 ruble, 84 kopecks with that of 92 kopecks of Central Asia, nor to deem this an "obvious illustration of the burden carried by central *gubernias* in favor of borderlands." He stated that a correction of this, the transfer of a great part of the tax load to the colonies, will be "the subject of detailed studies and measures of the Ministry of the Treasury."[23]

Even this dubious method of computation showed that the tax burden of black-earth regions, including Ukraine, of 1 ruble, 97 kopecks per capita was in excess of the tax burden of the central industrial region of Petersburg, where the per capita tax load reached 1 ruble, 3 kopecks.[24]

Subsequently, when we shall analyze state budgets of these times, we shall indicate what huge amounts were annually drawn from Ukraine in favor of Russia.

The Granary of Europe

Such an approach to the problem of taxing the population of the borderlands, wherein the amount of taxes was not determined by the total economic conditions of the land, but a colonial obligation to serve the development of the prosperity of the metropolis, and its policy of military aggression, brought about

[22] *Ibid.*, p. 228.   [23] *Ibid.*, p. 221.   [24] *Ibid.*, p. 224.

a situation under which the excessive taxation of the Ukrainian peasants was one of the prime causes of the impoverishment of large masses of them. An acute shortage of tools of production, and to a certain extent a deterioration of the economy resulted. Excessive taxes and curtailment of the area of land use were twin dilemmas for the Ukrainian peasants. Their very life was subject to an attempt to solve the problem: how to feed the family, and where to get the money for taxes. Under existing conditions both problems were, to a majority of the peasantry, incapable of solution. What is more, the natural increase of the population, whose surplus could find no outlet in industry even during the period when industry began to grow quite noticeably, made the problem more and more acute. If we compare the area of land used by the peasants in 1860 with the area in 1890, considering the increase in population, and losses suffered as a result of the reform, we get the figures in *Table XI*.[25]

TABLE XI

Land area per 1,000 population	1860	1890	% of decrease
Right Bank	1,404 desiatynas	695 desiatynas	50.5
Left Bank	1,562 desiatynas	898 desiatynas	42.6
Southern Ukraine	3,017 desiatynas	1,243 desiatynas	58.8

This decrease in land holdings was a continuous process, and by 1900 the average holdings per household, as compared with 1863 (the year of separating the holdings of the peasants) are shown in *Table XII*.[26]

TABLE XII

Region	1863	1900	% of decrease
Kharkiv	4.5 desiatynas	1.9 desiatynas	57.6
Poltava	2.5 desiatynas	1.5 desiatynas	40.0
Chernihiv	3.4 desiatynas	2.0 desiatynas	41.2
Kiev	2.9 desiatynas	1.2 desiatynas	58.5
Volhynia	4.2 desiatynas	1.7 desiatynas	51.5
Podilla	2.6 desiatynas	1.2 desiatynas	53.8
Kherson	6.1 desiatynas	2.2 desiatynas	63.9
Katerynoslav	6.0 desiatynas	2.3 desiatynas	61.6

[25] V. Kosinsky, *K Agrarnomu voprosu (The Agrarian Problem)*, Moscow, 1911, I, 479.
[26] M. Porsh, *loc. cit.*

Under pressure of such curtailment of cultivated land, the peasants utilized every bit of suitable land for ploughing. Even considering this, the decrease of land under cultivation per 1,000 people was: on the Right Bank, 29.9%; on the Left Bank, 42.3%; and in Southern Ukraine, 26.7%. The utilization of land for ploughing reached such an extent in Ukraine, far in excess' of analogous indices for other European countries, including Russia. (See *Table XIII*).

TABLE XIII

County	Ploughed land and gardens	Grass-lands	Forests	Unsuitable	Total area of cultivation
Ukraine	70.3	12.3	10.6	6.8	82.6
England	12.9	65.8	3.9	17.4	78.7
Italy	42.6	25.0	15.7	13.1	67.6
France	59.4	10.5	15.8	14.3	69.9
Germany ...	48.7	16.2	25.8	9.3	64.9
Russia	28.2	16.4	39.2	16.2	44.6

At the beginning of the 20th century there were, per 100 *desiatynas* of arable land, the following rural dwellers: England, 79; France, 84; Germany, 107; and in Ukraine's regions: Kiev, 178; Podilla, 160; Chernihiv, 157; Volhynia, 147; Kharkiv, 137; Poltava, 124, and only in the regions of Katerynoslav and Kherson were the figures equal to those of Germany and France, respectively.[27]

It is evident that such a density of the rural population per arable unit of land, coupled with a lower fertility than that of Western European countries, did not provide sufficient food for the population. This is a seeming contradiction of the general estimate of pre-revolutionary Ukraine as the "Granary of Europe" which exported its grain products in great quantities to foreign countries. Judging by grain export figures, it would be erroneous to explain these exports solely by the existence of grain surpluses. Exports were in large measure the result of economic difficulties of the peasants, and the tax policy illustrated above contributed in no small degree to the existence of these difficulties. *Table XIV* is a comparison of average annual yields of the chief cultures for the ten-year period of the end of the 19th and beginning of the 20th century (in pounds per 1 *desiatyna*).[28]

[27] Feshchenko-Chopivsky, *Ekonomichna heohrafiya Ukrainy*, p. 36.
[28] *Ibid.*, p. 41. The original quotes figures in *poods* which the translator has calculated in pounds at 36.113 pounds per *pood*.

TABLE XIV

Country	Rye	Wheat	Barley	Oats	Corn	Potatoes
Russia	1,878	1,697	2,094	1,950	2,428	17,478
Ukraine	2,136	2,600	2,172	2,464	3,358	18,417
Belgium	5,344	5,994	6,608	5,705	....	41,530
Germany	4,369	5,164	4,983	4,536	....	32,754
France	2,464	3,178	3,358	3,142	2,089	20,940

We have already indicated that the "Granary of Europe" consumed less grain per person than any other Western European country. (See *Table XV*).[29]

TABLE XV

	Grain production per capita	Grain imports	Per capita consumption
Denmark	1,552 lbs.	614	2,166
Germany	939	180	1,119
France	939	144	1,083
Hungary	1,480	216 expt.	1,264
Bulgaria	1,300	325 expt.	975
Ukraine	1,264	397 expt.	867
Russia	1,011	144 expt.	867

One must not lose sight of the fact that the extent of grain consumption stands in reverse ratio to the consumption of other products. Therefore Ukraine, where bread is the basic food, has more need of grain than for example, Denmark or Germany.

Thus, the amount of bread alone per person is, during this period, not nearly enough to satisfy the population's grain needs. Hence, the annual export figure of almost 14.4 billion pounds of grain is no indication of a sated internal market. The surplus is comparable not with the need, only with the purchasing power of the population, especially of the rural population, a majority of whom appeared on the markets as bread consumers when, a short time before, they had been vendors.

The result was that Ukraine, producing 25% per person more than Russia, exported 397 pounds of grain per capita, as against Russia's per capita export figure of 144 pounds. Thus Ukraine brought her consumption down to the same level as Russia's, 867 pounds per capita. These figures become much more convincing if we apply them not to the average data of Ukraine as a whole, but to the peasants' consumption. If we consider 720 pounds

[29] Feshchenko-Chopivsky, *op. cit.*, p. 35.

per capita as the norm of peasant consumption (including fodder), an absolutely inadequate quantity, then we see that even under this norm, the Right Bank has a deficiency of 216 pounds, or 31.5%, the Left Bank a deficiency of 234 pounds, or 32.5% and only the steppe region has a surplus of 644 pounds, or 89%. Kosinsky concludes that "people and cattle were equally undernourished."[30]

As has already been noted, the taxes were assessed on the land area without regard to the fact whether this unit yielded an income, or only minimum livelihood. In addition, the statistics refer to total cultivated land areas, including leased land, the rent for which, as we shall see later, was extremely high. In order to satisfy the need for cash, the weakest economic groups had to be vendors of grain in the fall, only to become purchasers soon after Christmas, or else consumers of substitutes for bread, most often potatoes. This explains why the price of rye, which constituted the basic ingredient of bread in the peasants' consumption, went up much faster than the price of the most valuable grain, wheat. Even during the first decade following the abolition of serfdom, the price of rye went up more than 70%, while wheat rose only 38%. In order to understand the extent of the rural economy production in relation to its population, and in order to be able to realize the real nature of the so-called "relative agrarian overpopulation" in Ukraine, which is always referred to as the most characteristic feature of the Ukrainian rural economy, it is necessary to consider in more detail the matter of peasants' land holdings.

Land Shortage

When the peasants were endowed with land, they lost a considerable part of the land which they had been using before the reform. In 1877, after the land allotments were almost completely finished, the entire agricultural area of 37,460,633 *desiatynas* was divided into the following categories: private property, 17,952,886 *desiatynas,* or 47.9%; endowed property, 16,762,-066 *desiatynas,* or 44.6%; state, church, etc., 2,745,681 or 7.5%.[31] During the next 10 years the general arable land area was increased by 1.4 million *desiatynas* by putting hitherto unused

[30] V. Kosinsky, *op. cit.,* I, 482.
[31] M. Porsh, "Statystyka zemlevolodinnya i mobilizatsiya zemelnoyi vlasnosty v Ukrainy" ("Statistics of Land Ownership and Mobilization of Land Property in Ukraine"), *Ukraina,* 11-12, p. 146.

land under cultivation, increasing the total of 38.8 million *desiatynas*. During the same period, the area of peasant endowments was increased by 1.5 million *desiatynas* so that peasant endowments increased to a total of 18,169,922 *desiatynas*. Since that time, there were no changes of any significance.[32]

The endowed land was divided, on an average per household, as shown in *Table XVI*.

TABLE XVI

Region	Endowed land	Households	Per household
Right Bank	6,159,829	1,134,654	5.4
Left Bank	7,187,809	1,178,345	6.8
Southern Ukraine	4,822,284	565,121	8.5

[33]

Thus that average land endowment per household in Ukraine was 6.3 *desiatynas*. But this figure does not sufficiently characterize the problem of land use. Besides regional variations, we must bear in mind that former state serfs were in a much better position on land endowment and tax assessment (See *Table XVII*).

The matter will become even more clear when we consider in *Table XVIII* the groups of households among which the endowed land was divided.

Thus, from the very beginning there existed a deep discrepancy in peasant land holdings, where 32.3% peasants' farms had only 13.3% of the land with an average holding of less than 4 *desiatynas* per household, or under the minimum required for a bare living. But outside of that there were also landless peasants, constituting 19% of all peasant households, 3,595,500 people. If we take all peasant households who could not be provided with a livelihood from the land, their number rises to 44.7%. In other words almost half of the Ukrainian peasants were land-hungry immediately following the land reform.

A question naturally arises whether such land holding was peculiar only to Ukraine, or whether the same picture is presented by all European Russia in the post-reform period? Unfortunately we have no data pertaining to the last quarter of the 19th century, because not all *zemstvos* kept statistics of land holdings. There are some data pertaining to the first years of the 20th century, but these, to some extent, indicate a better

[32] *Ibid.*   [33] *Ibid.*, p. 164.

TABLE XVII

State serfs received	8,616 thousand desiatynas for	1,137 thousand households,	or average 7.5 each
Landowners serfs received	8,167 thousand desiatynas for	1,617 thousand households,	or average 5.0 each
Freemen received	24 thousand desiatynas for	5 thousand households,	or average 4.6 each
Leaseholding serfs received	110 thousand desiatynas for	41 thousand households,	or average 2.6 each
Colonists received	1,246 thousand desiatynas for	78 thousand households,	or average 15.9 each [34]

TABLE XVIII

Group	Farms (households) number	%	Land area in desiatynas	%
Under 1 desiatyna	84,691	3.0	39,074	0.2
1-2 disiatynas	132,104	4.6	208,387	1.1
2-3 desiatynas	326,087	11.5	841,617	4.7
3-4 desiatynas	376,607	13.2	1,318,852	7.3
4-5 desiatynas	383,667	13.4	1,731,693	9.5
5-10 desiatynas	1,155,667	40.5	8,269,232	45.7
10-50 desiatynas	397,174	13.9	5,592,864	30.9
50-100 desiatynas	1,378	0.0	82,373	0.4
Over 100 desiatynas	195	0.0	30,428	0.2 [35]

[34] *Ibid.*, p. 163. [35] *Ibid.*, p. 168.

position of Ukraine because, as we shall see later, the Ukrainian peasants were buying up the landowners' estates on a large scale. There are grounds to believe that immediately after the reform, conditions were even worse. But under any conditions, the different situation of Ukraine becomes immediately apparent.

If we divide all peasants into three groups, those with insignificant land holdings, medium holdings, and large holdings (including in the latter group all farms of ten *desiatynas,* and over), then *Table XIX* gives proportionate figures for different regions of the Empire (in percentages).[36]

TABLE XIX

Region:	Small holdings	Medium	Large
Central Chornozem	23.7	56.0	20.3
Middle-Volga	17.9	50.0	32.1
Ukraine			
South	35.4	36.6	28.0
Right Bank	57.6	33.0	9.4
Slobozhanska	44.8	43.0	12.2
Industrial region	16.8	58.7	24.5
Byelorussia	7.9	63.6	28.5
Lithuania	4.0	19.0	77.0
Lake region	5.1	43.5	51.4
Baltic region	1.5	0.7	97.8
Ural region	10.0	11.6	78.4
Northern region	19.9	24.7	55.4
Lower Volga	5.4	9.2	85.4

As can be seen, Ukraine differs greatly from the other territories of the Empire by the large preponderance of small peasant holdings and by an insignificant percentage of large holdings. Only northern Ukraine has a number of large holdings equal to that of other regions, but the number of small holdings here is also much greater than elsewhere.

This single comparison suffices to prove that Ukraine, as a result of Russia's colonial policy, was under entirely different conditions. An additional factor must be noted which was of great importance in the matter of land holdings. It is of servitudes, or easements. Ukraine is poor in pastures and forests: only 12.3% of the usable land area is pasture land, and 10.6% forests

[36] P. Maslov, *Agrarniy vopros v Rossiyi,* I.

(compared to the respective figures for Russia of 16.4% and 39.2%). For this reason, the accumulation of hay and fodder for cattle was always an acute problem. During the land reform a large part of such lands (pastures and forests) were excluded from peasant allotments and reserved as servitudes, or lands of common use. For example in Volhynia in 1885 there were 1,926 thousand *desiatynas* of servitude lands; in Kiev, 647 thousand *desiatynas;* in Podilla, 991 thousand *desiatynas,* etc. But in 1886 the senate passed a ukase which gave the landlords the right "to decide the matter in the interests of farming." From that time the landlord had a right to "place his sown field according to his convenience, without considering the servitudes."[37]

In reality this was an abolition of the right of easement which deprived the peasants of the opportunity to use pastures and meadows, and transformed these lands into the private property of landowners. Mass litigation in this matter brought no changes.

This caused a land shortage, the amount of land in possession of the peasants could not absorb all available labor of the peasants. A surplus rural population came into being and continued increasing, thus causing an "agrarian overpopulation" which is justly "relative," because at its basis lay not an absolute lack of land, only its artificial apportionment. This land shortage, in relation to economic conditions, of which it was the main cause, became the chief obstacle on the road toward an intensification of the rural economy, and prevented the increased use of labor per area of surface.

As early as the 1870's the land with which a peasant household had to work, under conditions of the period in the Poltava region, sufficed for only one worker. "The second and following workers in households of no land and small land holdings were superfluous, unless the farmer leased other land."[38]

S. Korolenko estimated the surplus rural population for the 1880's to be 5 million, with only about half able to find work locally, or in the immediate neighborhood; the remainder leaving for work in distant places. Thus, the entire natural increase of the rural population, with the very small exceptions pertaining to larger farm holdings, became "surplus" and had no opportunity to earn a living. Ukraine had neither sufficient industry to

[37] M. Slabchenko, *op. cit.,* p. 169.
[38] S. Vasylenko, *Kustarni promysly (Home Industries),* Kiev, 1913, p. 23.

absorb this surplus nor off-season home-wage earning opportunities which would compensate for the inadequate income derived from agriculture, and would employ people beyond the period of seasonal farm work.

The peasants of industrially developed Russia were, in this respect, in an entirely different position. In addition, they had much better farm land. The peasants of Russia not only found ample employment opportunities in industrial plants, but also had good chances of additional wages by working for the same industries at home during the winter season. "Over and above factory industries, in the *gubernias* adjacent to Moscow, home cotton manufacturing industries were widespread. They employed 350 thousand people." Those peasants, employed at home, turned out semi-finished products for the factories. "In addition, outside of the factories, the linen industry employed 3 million spinners and half a million weavers, and in the preparation of flax another half million peasants found work. This working population belonged to the northern and central *gubernias.*"[39]

The Ukrainian peasants did not have such opportunities nor any real chance of full-time employment in industry. Their home industry of preparing flax and hemp, which also existed, had an entirely different character. For the most part it was merely to satisfy their own family needs.

A situation thereby arose in which the peasants found themselves chained to the soil. Outside of agriculture they did not, in fact, have any chance to work. It is then natural that the increase of the population contributed to the splitting of peasant holdings and to the increase of the number of landless peasants. Professor M. I. Tuhan-Baranovsky cites changes which occurred in the division of peasant land holdings in nine counties of the Poltava *gubernia* during the ten-year period from 1889 to 1900. (See *Table XX.*)[40]

We have here a very characteristic picture. The general increase in the number of farms was 14%, at a time when changes among the groups are far in excess of this increase. We see then, not only a distribution of the increase of the population, but also translocations within the groups. The most stable appear

[39] N. Yasnopolsky, "Ekonomicheskaya buduchnost yuga Rossiyi i sovremennaya yego otstalost" ("The Economic Future of South Russia and Its Present Backwardness"), *Otechestvenniye Zapiski* (*Home Notes*), St. Petersburg, 1871, p. 292.
[40] Quoted from Fomin's "Ekonomichna kharakterystyka . . .," p. 59.

TABLE XX

Household (farms) in thousands									Total
	Land-less	Under 1 des.	1-2 des.	2-3 des.	3-6 des.	6-9 des.	9-15 des.	15-50 des.	ov. 50 des.	
1889	56.7	6.8	19.4	25.5	61.1	33.5	19.0	6.9	6.3	235.2
	24.2	2.9	8.2	10.8	26.0	14.2	8.1	2.9	2.7	100
1900	48.2	15.2	30.6	32.0	71.7	30.6	18.5	8.9	13.6	269.3
	18.3	5.8	11.6	12.1	27.1	11.6	7.2	3.4	2.9	100

Approximate
percentages
plus and minus
changes —15 +124 +60 +20 +8 −9 −3 +29 +117 +14

to be the three middle groups, from 9 to 15 *desiatynas*. The extreme groups underwent significant changes, such changes being more pronounced in those groups which are farthest from the center. This means that there was a process of land splitting; the weaker units of the middle groups joined the lower groups, and the latter went down even further. On the other hand, the more wealthy farms of the middle groups, went higher.

Regarding the decrease in the number of landless households, we have not an acquisition by them of land, but, undoubtedly, a complete abandonment by them of farming. This finds support first of all in the insignificant percentage increase of the total number of farms in relation to the natural increase of population, and in the second place in the fact that by 1900 the Donbas industry had already grown considerably, and was able to accommodate a large number of workers from the neighboring Poltava region. Such a large percentage of landless peasants and a constant increase of the number of small holdings was prevalent not only in the Poltava region which experienced the worst "land shortage," but also in the land-rich regions of Southern Ukraine. Peasants who could not cultivate land (a certain percentage of the landless took land on lease) numbered: in Berdyansky county, 6.7%; of the total number of households, in Melitopil county, 7.5%; Oleksandrivsky, 16.8%, Ananievsky, 13.1%, Bakhmutsky, 15.4%, Slavyanoserbsky, 22%, etc.

The data regarding Mariupil county, shown in *Table XXI* are entirely analogous to those of Poltava, only in a different numerical expression, and in reference to farming not only the peasants' own land, but also leased land.[41]

---

[41] A. Knipovich, *K Voprosu o diferentsiyatsiyi krestyanskogo khozyaystva* (*On the Problem of Differentiation of the Peasants' Economy*), Katerynoslavskoye Gubern. Zemstvo, 1903, p. 78.

A statistical study, conducted in Bakhmutsky county in 1886, gave the results shown in *Table XXII*.[42]

We see then that even farms of medium land holding joined the landless class.

This loss of land in certain counties and within certain categories of peasants reached extraordinary proportions. In 1882, *Table XXIII* shows numbers of landless peasants in Poltava region.

In 1917, in general, the peasants of Ukraine were divided, as *Table XXIV* shows, into categories according to land holding.[43]

TABLE XXI

	1886	1901
Not cultivating	4.6%	6.8%
Under 5 desiatynas	19.3%	15.7%
5-10	28.7%	28.0%
10-20	35.1%	29.8%
20-50	11.6%	17.6%
Over 50	0.7%	2.1%

TABLE XXII

Number Receiving Land in 1861	*Quantity per household*	*Became landless*
4581	up to 4 desiatynas	977 - 21.4%
6193	over 4 desiatynas	444 - 7.2%
6402	up to 8 desiatynas	990 - 15.4%
8075	over 8 desiatynas	846 - 10.8%

TABLE XXIII

	Myrhorod county	*Poltava county*	*Zinkiv county*
Among Cossacks	16.5%	29.8%	18.8%
Among Peasants	36.3%	36.0%	53.8%

TABLE XXIV

Amount owned	*Families in thousands*
Landless, or with only a house and yard	700 - 15%
1 to 3 desiatynas	800 - 20%
3 to 5 desiatynas	1,000 - 22%
5 to 8 desiatynas	950 - 21%
8 to 10 desiatynas	600 - 13%
10 to 20 desiatynas	300 - 7%
Over 20 desiatynas	80 - 2%
Total	4,430 - 100%

[42] M. Slabchenko, *op. cit.*, p. 179.
[43] Feshchenko-Chopivsky, *op. cit.*, p. 53.

It should be noted that this last listing of land holding should be considered in relation to the time, 1917; the process of mobilizing land by the peasants had been going on for several years by means of purchases of land by the peasants. This will be discussed in more detail later.

Lease of Land

The land situation of the Ukrainian peasants here described brought about quite naturally a situation, under which all the peasants' attention was concentrated on the problem of getting more land, because they had no place to earn a living outside of agriculture. The peasants had only two ways open to them: purchase or lease. The third way, one of fighting for their rights, at first assumed the form of mass lawsuits for lands held by prescription, for rights to servitude (easement), and later, of rebellion and open revolutionary warfare for land. This did not, however, bring about any changes in peasant land holdings up to 1917.

Speaking of leasing land, we must first of all note its peculiar nature which has given rise to the apt designation, "lease in kind." For most peasants, the taking of land under lease was not in contemplation of increasing production in order to take in an increased profit, but merely a means of getting additional produce in order to feed the family. A lease was "a continuation of the farmer's work on his own land, the former and the latter constituted a single economic activity." The large number of people who took land on lease can be explained by the fact that the area of land per household was two to three times smaller than necessary.[44]

To determine the essence of the "lease in kind" we must understand first the objective the peasant had in mind when he decided to take land under a lease, and secondly the price he had to pay. The decisive factor was that the grain from his own farm would not suffice the family for a year, and a certain number of pounds must supplement it. He could not buy the grain for money earned elsewhere, because he could not find work during the off season in agriculture. What remained was to lease some land, not for reward, but on the risk that the additional amount of grain, after payment of rent, would suffice

[44] V. V. *Ocherki krestyanskogo khozyaystva (Outline of the Peasant Economy)*, Moscow, 1903, pp. 83-100.

to cover his deficit in kind. The essential attributes of a lease were its compulsory nature and the attempt of the peasants to solve their subsistence budget with its aid, not stopping to consider its economic fallacy in the sense of a much lower reward for labor when compared with the price of labor. Professor Slabchenko wrote in this connection: "The peasant did not stop to consider the obvious inconvenience of a lease, in the Poltava region, e. g. the gross income from 1 *desiatyna* of land was 19 rubles, 26 kopecks, and the cost of tilling 11 rubles, 76 kopecks, while the rent was 9 rubles, 6 kopecks. This meant there was no profit, only a loss of 1 ruble, 51 kopecks."[45]

Thus rent for land was not determined by the interest on land as a capital investment, (not by the level of an absolute land rent). Instead, secondary considerations fixed it, considerations which had no direct relation to the amount of industrial income from the agricultural enterprise, cost of labor, and prices of agricultural products. The rent was created by conditions resulting from post-reform land relations. It became, of itself, a factor which determined the value of land as capital.

In *Table XXV*, Professor Kosinsky, in his *K Agrarnomu voprosu* shows a balance, quoted in full, of economic results of tilling leased land in five counties of the steppe. They clearly show the economic nature of this kind of land area exploitation, when the problem is approached from the criterion of normal industrial enterprise interests:[46]

TABLE XXV

(*In Rubles*)	*Oleks-andriv*	*Elysave-thrad*	*Anan-iev*	*Odessa*	*Kherson*
Net income from 1 desiatyna	3.98	3.94	4.01	6.27	7.48
Rent on long-term lease..	6.28	5.56	5.00	4.84	5.52
Rent on 1 year lease	9.96	9.60	7.58	7.97	8.76
i.e. loss (−) or profit (+)					
Under long-term lease	−2.30	−1.62	−0.99	+1.43	+1.96
Under 1 year lease	−5.98	−5.61	−3.57	−1.70	−1.28

The nature of the phenomenon becomes even more apparent, when we consider gross income as seen in *Table XXVI*.[47]

---

[45] M. Slabchenko, *op. cit.*, p. 268.   [46] V. Kosinsky, *op. cit.*, p. 291.
[47] *Ibid.*, p. 292.

TABLE XXVI

	Oleks-andriv	Elysave-thrad	Anan-iev	Odessa	Kherson
Total gross included					
from 1 desiatyna	12.30	12.30	11.30	13.40	14.80
Long-term lease	+6.98	+6.74	+6.30	+8.56	+9.38
1 year lease	+2.34	+2.70	+4.72	+5.43	+6.60
Hired Labor per					
1 desiatyna	8.32	8.36	7.29	7.13	7.32
Hence, the result of					
long-term lease	−1.34	−1.36	−0.99	+1.43	+1.96
1 year lease............	−5.96	−5.66	−2.57	−1.70	−1.32

As we can see, the economic nature of a peasant's work on leased land was such that it was rewarded at a much lower rate than the hired labor market offered. On a one-year lease, the peasant of Oleksandriv county received only 28% of what he would earn working as hired labor. The remaining 72% of his labor accrued to the landowner, creating a differential land rent. To the peasant there was significance not in the reward for his labor itself, but in additional sum total of natural products. To that end, he increased the leased area (calling on existing manpower in the family) to such a degree that as a result, he would either get the amount of produce needed, or else he would have to curtail his needs either by reducing the number of cattle, or simply by undernourishing the cattle . . . and his own family. Obviously the existence of such high rental rates for land determined by its "yield in kind" nature is, from the economic viewpoint, an anomaly. The explanation has to be sought both in the division of land on occasion of the reform, and in the economic subjection of Ukraine to Russia. The former created an artificial surplus of the rural population with its "relative agrarian overpopulation," the latter tied this population to the soil.

Thus, a constant and ever growing demand for land on terms of lease was created. A continual increase in land rent resulted.

In the Poltava region, rents increased at the following rate (in rubles): 1861, 0.75; 1872, 1.50; 1892, 10.14; 1900, 11.92; 1901, 13.00, and 1902, 13.85.[48]

In 1916 average rents in Ukraine were on the following level for spring sowing (double for winter sowing): Volhynia, 12.00

[48] M. Slabchenko, *op. cit.*, p. 312.

rubles; Kiev, 12.50; Podilla, 16.00; Kherson, 12.00; Poltava, 18.50; Kharkiv, 12.00; Katerynoslav, 12.00; Tauria, 18.00. The average for all of Ukraine was 14.00 rubles. "This gave the landowners no less than 175 million rubles. Before, the entire servitude gave the landlords less than only the land rent now. And at that, as they say, without any trouble."[49]

And so it was. In the 1890's, in the same Poltava region tilling of 1 *desiatyna* by the landlords cost 27 rubles, and the income was 34 rubles. But even at that time, rents were higher than that difference of 7 rubles and the landlord could get a higher income from rent without the trouble of conducting an enterprise.

Although since that time yields became higher, and the prices of grain increased also, neither the former nor the latter went hand in hand with the increase of rent. The increase in rent was in no degree determined by the market for grain or for labor, only by the hopeless position of the peasants, for whom the lease was for the most part the only means of preserving life. This, in turn, caused a demand for land. If the Poltava peasant in 1916 had, from 1 *desiatyna* of leased land 2,275 pounds of barley (or corresponding amounts of other grain, the harvest that year being about average); then, after deducting the seed, he had a marketable product (grain and straw) valued at 29 to 32 rubles, out of which he paid a rent of 18.50 rubles or 58% to 63% of the total. After deducting all other expenses, such as traction, tools, threshing, etc. only a miserly amount was left over for his own labor. But the decisive factor was that otherwise he would have had nothing, and he had this additional amount without leaving his farm.

It must be noted that these average rental sums contain large hidden differences, depending on the term of the lease and the area of the land leased. We had the opportunity to observe, on studying five counties of Southern Ukraine, that a one-year lease was 60% to 65% more expensive than a long-term lease. Differences are even greater when the area is considered. Thus, in Berdyanske county, for example, a lease of up to 5 *desiatynas* of land cost 11 rubles while larger leases of over 50 *desiatynas* called for a rent of only 4.20 rubles. The corresponding figures for Dniprovske county were 15.25 rubles and

[49] S. Ostapenko, "Kapitalizm, na Ukraini" ("Capitalism in Ukraine"), *Chervony Shlakh* (*Red Path*), Kharkiv, 1924, p. 26.

3.55 rubles. It was like this all over. This naturally gave rise to speculation in leases. "In the Poltava region, a speculator would take land at 8 rubles and sublease it at 15 to 35 rubles and even at 50 rubles, depending on the culture for which the land was used." (Truck garden rents were as high as 60 rubles.)[50] Extra high rents were also charged for grazing. On the Left Bank, they were 7 to 10 rubles per *desiatyna*, between one-quarter and one-third of the value of the cow itself.

There are no data available showing the exact amount of land leased by the peasants. Professor Slabchenko cites estimates of Vasylchykov pertaining to the 1870's, according to these estimates the peasants leased. (See *Table XXVII*). Professor Ogon-

TABLE XXVII

(In desiatynas)

Region:	Former landlords' lands	Former state lands
Kharkiv	1,366,235	89,750
Chernihiv	1,612,577	5,129
Poltava	1,942,137	10,603
Kiev	1,808,424	144,776
Podilla	1,601,590	42,456
Volhynia	2,256,338	135,199

[51]

ovsky reports for approximately the same period that in Southern Ukraine the peasants took on lease 2,761,500 *desiatynas* of land.[52]

In total, this gives a sum which equals 73% of all private land holdings, at that time 17 million *desiatynas*. We are inclined to believe that these figures are excessive. They might include servitude lands which still existed at that time, and comprised several million *desiatynas*. The estimates of P. Maslov may be considered as the more accurate, also those of Posnikov. Both state that at the beginning of the 20th century, the landlords cultivated only 56% of the land they owned. If we take this figure, and if this percentage is not underestimated, it would appear that at that time about 4.5 million *desiatynas* were taken in lease by the peasants annually (the area owned by landowners had by then declined to 10 million *desiatynas*).

[50] M. Slabchenko, *op. cit.*, p. 372.   [51] *Ibid.*
[52] M. Ogonovsky, *op. cit.*, p. 161.

The average rent then as has been stated above was, in Ukraine, 4 rubles per *desiatyna*. This means that every year 63 million rubles were taken from the peasants in the form of payment for temporary use of land. Where this money went, and what the repercussions were upon the entire Ukrainian economy, we shall show later.

Knipovich gives a vivid picture, reproduced in *Table XXVIII*, of the meaning of land leases among the various groups of peasants in his work *K voprosu o differentsyatsiyi krestyanskogo khozyaystva.* [53]

Although the data apply to the relatively land-rich Katerynoslav region where, as we see, the percentage of landless peasants, and of those who only had a cottage, equalled only 8.1% as against 36% in the Poltava region, and although the data are cited for the period when the Katerynoslav region had an already noticeable industry which, to some extent, freed the peasants from the land. Nevertheless, even under such conditions we can see what a decisive role leasing of land played in the lives of the peasants of that region. Only in the last group of those having over 25 *desiatynas* does the lease occupy an auxiliary place in the general land holding, and at that, at the expense of land acquisition. But even in this group the percentage of farms which took land in lease was not lower than in other groups. In general, more than half of all the farms resorted to leasing. It is a striking fact that along with a general land hunger and mass resorting to leasing, all groups include a certain part which gave out land under lease. This is particularly noticeable in the groups holding fom 5 to 10, and from 10 to 15 *desiatynas* per farm, precisely in the middle groups, where the equilibrium between labor available in the family and the amount of land is at an optimum. This phenomenon resulted from many causes. Among them, the more significant, though not decisive, was an insufficient supply of farm tools. But the main cause was that the region of Katerynoslav, unlike many other parts of Ukraine, was a *gubernia* governed by the Russian-imposed system of community land holding, a situation to which we shall return later. This form of land holding caused a great splitting of land into strips, where one farmer would have to use many small pieces of land each in a different location. In the

---

[53] A. Knipovich, *op. cit.*, p. 137.

TABLE XXVIII

Groups of farms	% of farms	% of population	Arable land per farm unit (in desiatynas)	Persons per farm unit	% of farms which bought land	Land bought per farm unit	% of farms taking leased land	% of farms giving land in lease	% of Land in Group			% of farms hiring labor	% of farms with home industries	% of farms without tools
									Endowed	Bought	Leased			
Landless	4.9	4.0	...	5.1	...	...	52.3	...	...	...	100	26.1	35.7	43.0
Under1 des.	3.2	2.6	0.3	5.2	12.3	0.4	43.0	1.6	6.0	1.1	92.9	2.9	27.0	59.4
1-3	11.2	9.3	2.0	5.1	10.9	1.5	54.3	16.0	24.5	2.3	73.2	3.1	39.4	39.6
3-5	19.5	15.7	3.6	5.0	9.5	2.2	44.8	21.2	45.9	2.8	51.3	2.8	29.7	36.2
5-10	35.2	35.0	7.1	6.2	12.9	4.1	37.5	27.1	62.6	5.0	32.4	3.2	28.8	20.7
10-15	15.3	18.8	11.7	7.6	18.8	7.2	44.0	26.0	61.8	8.1	30.1	3.8	29.8	11.1
15-20	5.1	7.2	16.5	8.8	22.6	10.7	48.3	24.5	56.3	9.7	34.0	7.8	23.7	6.3
20-25	1.5	2.4	21.9	9.6	36.3	14.9	64.1	15.5	48.9	16.1	35.0	14.0	23.0	2.4
Over 25	4.1	5.0	59.5	7.6	55.0	57.4	53.7	12.6	39.6	44.9	15.5	59.9	7.3	1.6

steppe area these distances sometimes reached eight and more miles. The cultivation of a small piece of land at a distant location was naturally a losing proposition; hence the owner would let it out in lease, in order to lease for his own use more closely located land. This was the cause of mutual leases in the groups of farmers. In the higher groups, however, leasing of land assumed proportions of normal industry. As far as the group holding 1 to 3 *desiatynas* is concerned, the fact that 16% of them gave land in lease cannot under any circumstances mean that they had a surplus of land. This is a group which abandoned farming, and appears to be artificially tied to the land by norms of the so-called Stolypin law of community property, *obshchina.*

Likewise the large percentage, 26.1%, of labor hired by the landless cannot be considered proof of a lack of labor in comparison with the land area. This is nothing but hiring to till the land of those who possessed the needed tools, by those who did not. In general, we can see that the utilization of hired labor by all groups, with the exception of the last, was so insignificant that even on farms with sufficient land it could not be taken as proof of the lack of an adequate labor supply in relation to the land. We should also not overlook the significant percentage of farms in all groups that engaged in home industries. The nature of the home industries and their differences from those of Russia have already been commented upon. This was not factory work which would bring in extra income. It merely satisfied their own needs, primarily in textiles. This fact proves that the economy was of a consumer nature, and that there was a lack of money which prevented the peasants from joining in the market turnover.

The "lease in kind" nature of leasing land in Ukraine (the most appropriate name for it would probably be "lease in order to live") was, according to the number of leases, the most widespread. Its chief mark was that it was dictated by the hopeless situation of the peasants. Nevertheless, there were forms of leases which peasants undertook not by compulsion, but out of consideration of a more rational and more profitable conduct of their farm enterprise; there were also business leases designed to effectuate a large production of cereal goods. In his *Opys Poltavskoyi huberniyi,* Imshenetsky divides leases into three groups: 1) lease out of necessity, in which he includes all leases under 10 *desiatynas;* 2) economic leases of 10

68   *Ukraine and Russia*

to 30 *desiatynas,* and 3) industrial leases of 30 *desiatynas* and
over. A division into the above groups gives the picture shown
in *Table XXIX*.[54]

TABLE XXIX

	Group I	Group II	Group III
Land given in lease	13.9%	35.7%	50.4%
Leases	51.7%	37.2%	11.1%

Mobilization of Land

It is quite evident that the Ukrainian peasants were seeking
a solution of the artificially created land shortage by means other than taking land in lease. Strenuous efforts were directed by
them toward acquisition of land outright. Here again, as in the
analysis of leases, we shall encounter a series of phenomena,
basically different from their analogies in Russia. They came
into being as a result of specific economic conditions to which
the entire economic life of Ukraine was subject in the interests
of the metropolis.

The process of diminishing landlord land ownership is
characteristic of the entire European part of the former Russian
Empire. Its causes were many. First of all, the huge area of land
acquired by the landowners during the reform, by far exceeded
present adequate production capital in the shape of tools, material, cash, etc. necessary for the exploitation of such great areas.
Prior to the reform, the majority of labor was performed with
agricultural tools of the serfs. In the second place, the diversion
of the economic attention of the peasants towards their own
land created, particularly during the seasonal peak of activity,
a lack of labor available from local reserves. Thirdly, capital
invested in agriculture brought much lower returns than in other
forms of production because of the poverty of the internal market
caused by the agrarian nature of the country, underdevelop-
ment of transportation, etc.

In Ukraine, however, in addition to the general causes, there
existed others, created by peculiar conditions. It is obvious
that the demand for land, prompted by the "land shortage" contributed to a greater increase of prices for land than in Russia.

[54] N. Imshenetsky, *Opys Poltavskoiy huberniyi (Description of Poltava
Governorship),* Poltava, 1907, p. 43.

But in a much greater degree leasing was a contributing factor. Extremely high rental values of land given in lease determined the capitalized value of the land. Similarly, as the market value of stock rises according to higher dividends declared upon it, aiming toward an average yield on invested capital, so also prices of land changed continually, determined by lease rents as land rent.

If we adopt the figure 100 as the price of land and the rent value for the period 1904 to 1908, subsequent changes are in the following relation shown in *Table XXX*.[55]

TABLE XXX

	Rent	Price of land
1904-08	100	100
1909-1913	138	130
1913	165	165

As we can see, there is a complete concurrence, and it is also clear that the decisive role is played by the rent, i.e. the price paid for using land.

This is where we have to look first for an explanation of why there occurred extreme variations in prices of land which, during the reform, were more or less on an even level and during the determination of reform acquisition payments were higher in Russia than in Ukraine. Land in Ukraine in fact became several times more valuable than in Russia.

In *Table XXXI* we give a comparison of and prices in various regions of the former Empire during the period of 1854 to 1858 and 1898 to 1902 from which one can also see to what extent

TABLE XXXI

Price per 1 desiatyna of land in outright purchase (rubles):

Section	1854-1858	1898-1902
Central industrial region	14.82	56.25
Western land	15.63	42.76
Eastern land	5.82	32.05
Ukraine:		
Left Bank	17.78	119.80
Right Bank	12.75	99.12
Southern	11.34	123.97

[56]

---

[55] S. Ostapenko, *op. cit.*, p. 126.   [56] P. Maslov, *op. cit.*, II, 211.

the prices fixed at 187 and 123 rubles at the time of the reform exceeded the real value of land at that time.

Subsequently the price differences became even greater. At five-year intervals the purchase value of land in Ukraine, per 1 *desiatyna* increased at the following rate: 1868 to 1872, 28.1%; 1873 to 1877, 21.9%; 1878 to 1882, 14.9%; 1883 to 1887, 38.2%; 1888 to 1898, 16.8%; 1893 to 1897, 17.3%; 1898 to 1902, 36.1%.[57]

Wherever the rental value reached its highest peak, the pace of price increases of land was also the fastest. Thus, in the Poltava region the price of 1 *desiatyna* in 1897 was 103 rubles; in 1902 it was 207 rubles; in 1905, 236 rubles; in 1908, 281 rubles; 1909 to 1912, 236 rubles, and in 1913, 451 rubles.[58] Within sixteen years the price more than quadrupled. It is understood that neither the profit income from land, nor price profit from land could, or did grow in the same proportion. It was nothing else but robbing the peasants under specifically created conditions.

A similar process went on in all other parts of Ukraine, although not in the same degree as in the Poltava region. In Southern Ukraine, the increase of prices of land for the eight-year period from 1892 to 1900 went on at the pace charted in *Table XXXII.*

TABLE XXXII

| | County of | | |
	Oleksandriv	Ananiev	Kherson
1892	97.5	88.3	94.9
1893	126.7	100.1	110.6
1894	138.3	96.0	117.5
1895	113.2	93.2	122.8
1896	120.5	97.7	130.6
1897	147.1	101.7	132.8
1898	158.3	110.5	146.6
1899	174.2	133.9	174.6
1900	201.5	139.9	188.6

And people still continued to buy land. During the period 1893 to 1896, the peasants bought land for the following amount (in thousands of rubles): Left Bank, 10,188; Right Bank, 10,208, Southern Ukraine, 15,832.[59]

[57] *Ibid.*, p. 213.   [58] *Ibid.*, also S. Ostapenko, *op. cit.*, p. 128.
[59] M. Slabchenko, *op. cit.*, p. 378.

When we emphasize the mass and increasing demand for land on the part of the peasants, we may not lose sight of one factor which proves conclusively that it was not the demand which created such an unbelieveable increase in the price of land, because offers of land always exceeded the demand.

During the first decade following the reform collections of redemption payments by the landlords contributed in large measure to the betterment of the financial position of the landlords who, as has been stated above, felt a lack of capital for conducting their enterprises under new conditions. The capital rent on their own grain production was immeasurably lower than the average capital gains of the period, thanks to general economic conditions and, primarily, to grain prices, tariffs, customs policies, the details of which will be discussed later.

Land purchase (under the reform) payment alleviated the situation to a certain degree. But already in the second decade they collected only 25% of the previous decade's amount, and during the five-year period of 1893 to 1898 only 1% of the initial amount. Against this background there appeared, on the part of the landlords, a continuing demand for credit.

In 1885 the "Gentry's Land Bank" was established, for the purpose of issuing land mortgage loans at 5.25% interest rate, as against the lowest prevailing rate of 6%. In 1889, a lottery premium loan was floated by the bank which increased its capital by 90 million rubles, and reduced the interest rate by .5%. Mortgage loans extending from 60% to 75% of the bank's valuation of the land were given.

Already in the 1890's, 41,788 landlords' estates in Ukraine. or 42.1% of the total number were pledged with banks. They were valued at 1,129 million rubles, and were pledged against loans of 714 million rubles, 63.5% of their valuation.[60]

The extent of indebtedness was reached by reason of the over-evaluation, conducted in 1888. To the old indebtedness was added a new one, in the following amounts per *desiatyna*: in Volhynia, from 26.25 rubles, to 32.61; in the regions of: Katerynoslav, from 21.05 to 27.85; Kiev, from 27.97 to 35.08; Poltava, from 39.96 to 53.20, etc. During the same period the landowners possessed in tools per 1 *desiatyna* in Volhynia, 1.92; Poltava, 6.03; Podilla, 2.70; Kiev, 4.07; Chernihiv, 4.77, etc.[61]

---

[60] M. Porsh, *op. cit.*, p. 46.   [61] M. Slabchenko, *op. cit.*, p. 361.

From the reports of the "Land Banks" of Kiev, Poltava, Tauria, Kherson and Kharkiv one can get an approximate idea of the indebtedness of the gentry's lands in Ukraine. As of January 1, 1913, these banks reported loans issued in the amount of 596,800 thousand rubles, and unpaid loans in the amount of 543,800 thousand rubles, or a total of 1,140,600 thousand of rubles. This was far in excess of the indebtedness in Russia. For examples, for 1 *desiatyna* of land, there were loans in the regions of: Kiev, 62 rubles; Poltava, 69 rubles; Kherson, 70 rubles; Kharkiv, 73 rubles; Tauria, 77 rubles; while at the same time the figures for the Petersburg and Tula *gubernias* were 32 rubles; Moscow, 43 rubles; Nizhegorod, and Samara, 14 rubles.[62]

By government decree of May 18, 1882, the Peasants Land Bank was established for the purpose of facilitating the purchase of land by peasants from landlords, or, to be more precise, to facilitate the landlords' sale of land. A source of capital of this bank was an annual issue of 5.5% government bonds in the amount of 5 million rubles, which were subsequently quoted on foreign exchanges. Already in 1884 this issue proved insufficient. It was increased from year to year. In 1894, the interest rate on bonds was reduced, and in the following year the bank was authorized not only to give loans for the purchase of land, but also to give mortgage loans against previously purchased land. In addition, it could purchase land itself for the purpose of resale.

The bank's favorable attitude towards the landowners was manifest from the very outset, when prices for land sold to peasants were fixed at a higher rate than their existing market value at the time. Thus, the Kharkiv Peasants Bank valuated 1 *desiatyna* in 1893 at 102 rubles, as against the current value of 83 rubles; in 1895 at 102 rubles against 88 rubles. Similarly the Podilla Bank sold estate lands in 1894 for 127 rubles against the current value of 116 rubles.[63]

Banks paid these high prices for the landowners' land in spite of the fact that the demand never equalled the supply. In 1905 to 1906, filled with hopes resulting from the revolution, the peasants sharply curtailed their purchases of land; but this did not prevent the banks from making further purchases. At the same time, as we have had occasion to observe in the Poltava region, the prices went up at an even faster rate. As of May 1,

[62] S. Ostapenko, *op. cit.*, p. 130.   [63] M. Slabchenko, *op. cit.*, p. 361 ff.

1907 the bank owned already 2,095,365 *desiatynas* of land valued at 205,401 thousand rubles, and the bank sold, from November to May, only 170,000 *desiatynas*. The remainder owned by the bank, yielded only .15% interest.[64]

The above quoted facts are quite sufficient to prove that the mobilization of the landlords' land by the peasants and the prices paid for land were in no way the result of a healthy competition between two forms of an agricultural economy: the large and the small. Neither did they indicate healthy market conditions. At the basis of all this lay, on the one hand, the "land shortage," and on the other special measures taken by the Russian Government which was interested in the exploitation of the Ukrainian economy. Russia made good use of the consequences of anomalous land conditions created by it at the time of the reform. The operations of the land banks permitted the government to place the bonds of the banks on foreign exchanges, and thus to draw into Russia the capital necessary for the development of Russian industry. Just as in the matter of leases, the "land shortage" compelled all groups of peasants to participate, similarly in the purchase of land all peasants took part, the poorest included, though of course, in unequal degree.

Land purchased through banks, amounted to the quantities per person of a peasant household shown in *Table XXXIII*. Out

TABLE XXXIII

Landless	1.4 desiatynas
Those owning less than 1.5 desiatynas	0.8 desiatynas
Those owning from 1.5 to 3 desiatynas	0.8 desiatynas
Those owning from 3 to 6 desiatynas	2.6 desiatynas
Those owning over 6 desiatynas	5.6 desiatynas

of the land purchased by the peasants personally between 1875 and 1895, small purchases (under 25 *desiatynas*) accounted for 16% to 20% of all land alienation, and the greater part (80% to 84%) were larger transaction (over 25 *desiatynas*).[65]

During the reform the Ukrainian peasants possessed, as private property, much less land by far than the Russian peasants: only 432 thousand *desiatynas* out of a total of 5,745 thousand

[64] P. Maslov, *op. cit.*, II, 227.   [65] P. Maslov, *loc. cit.*

desiatynas of peasants owned land, i.e. 7.5% in proportion to 23% of the population. By 1877 this private property increased to 776 thousand *desiatynas* and continued to increase very rapidly, leaving a similar Russian land mobilization far behind.[66] As has been noted, in that year there were 17,953 thousand *desiatynas* of privately owned land in Ukraine. This land was distributed among the categories of owners shown in *Table XXXIV*.

TABLE XXXIV

Landowners (gentry)	15,174 thousand desiatynas
Monasteries and churches	96 thousand desiatynas
Merchants	1,172 thousand desiatynas
Townspeople	346 thousand desiatynas
Peasants	776 thousand desiatynas
Aliens	151 thousand desiatynas
Others	76 thousand desiatynas
Unclassified	162 thousand desiatynas
TOTAL	17,953 thousand desiatynas

Subsequently the redistribution of real property among the categories of owners took place almost exclusively at the expense of the landowners (gentry). As early as the latter part of the 19th century, the landowners' property declined in some regions to its former half, and at the beginning of the 20th century the process quickened noticeably. If we assume the extent of the gentry's holdings to be represented by the figure 100 as of 1862, the year of the reform, the decline of these holdings is represented by the figures in *Table XXXV*.[68]

TABLE XXXV

	1862	1867	1877	1887	1897
Left Bank	100	98	90	79	68
Right Bank	100	101	97	93	87
Southern Ukraine	100	94	84	66	56

By 1905 the area of landowner holdings decreased (from 15,174 thousand *desiatynas* to 9,985 thousand *desiatynas*) by 5,189 thousand *desiatynas*. Those 5 million *desiatynas* were dis-

[66] *Statistika po dvizheniyu zemlevladeniya v Rossiyi*, 1911 ed., p. 17.
[67] M. Porsh, *op. cit.*, p. 148.   [68] P. Maslov, *loc. cit.*

tributed among all groups, the greatest area being taken over by peasants.[69]

During the same period, *Table XXXVI* shows changes which took place in the peasants' land holdings.[70]

TABLE XXXVI

Years	Endowed	Purchased	Total (*in desiatynas*)
1877	16,672,066	775,908	17,447,974
1905	18,169,922	4,536,525	22,706,447
Increase	1,497,856	3,760,617	5,258,473

We have data for the same period referring not only to peasant households, but all farms, including those of colonists, townspeople settled in villages, and others. We quote them in *Table XXXVII* because they provide a more complete picture of the structure of productive peasant landholding:[71]

Land from the landowning gentry was purchased not only by the peasants, but also by other categories of land holders. Merchants increased their holdings during this period by 160 thousand *desiatynas*, townspeople by 524 thousand *desiatynas* and others by 451 thousand *desiatynas*.[72]

After 1905, when by ukase of November 1905 the operations of the Land Bank were considerably broadened, the mobilization of landowners' land by the peasants, which had subsided during the years of the revolution, increased again very quickly. In 1906 the Land Bank in Ukraine had been offered 1,453 thousand *desiatynas* of land for sale, of which 1,289 thousand *desiatynas* were offers of the gentry landowners.[73]

During the following five years, up to 1910, the peasants of Volhynia, Kiev and Podilla regions acquired an additional 340 thousand *desiatynas;* of Poltava, Kharkiv and Chernihiv regions, 425 thousand *desiatynas;* of Katerynoslav, Tauria and Kherson regions, 711 thousand *desiatynas,* or a total of 1,476 thousand *desiatynas.*[74]

Professor Peshekhonov wrote in 1922: "During the years following, the transfer of absentee owners' lands into the hands

[69] M. Porsh, *op. cit.,* p. 146.   [70] *Ibid.*
[71] "Sils'ke hospodarstvo Ukrainy" (Ukrainian Agriculture"), *Narkomzem Ukrainy,* (*Peoples' Commissar of Agriculture*), Kharkiv, 1923, p. 10.
[72] M. Porsh, *op. cit.,* p. 148.   [73] M. Porsh, *op. cit.,* p. 153.
[74] P. Fomin, "Ekonomichna kharakterystyka Ukrainy," p. 97.

TABLE XXXVII

	Endowed	Purchased	Total	% of purchased in relation to endowed	Per household		
					Endowment	Purchase	Total
1877							
6 gubernias of the Left Bank and the Right Bank	12,161,448	391,006	12,552,454	3.2	8.1	0.2	8.3
3 gubernias of the Steppe	6,561,239	761,973	7,323,212	10.1	15.1	1.8	16.9
Total for Ukraine	18,722,687	1,152,979	19,875,666	6.1	9.7	0.6	10.3
1905							
6 gubernias of Left Bank and Right Bank	13,347,638	2,568,901	15,916,539	19.2	5.8	1.1	6.9
3 gubernias of the Steppe	6,779,816	3,044,708	9,824,524	44.9	9.7	4.4	14.1
Total for Ukraine	20,127,454	5,613,609	25,741,063	27.9	6.7	1.9	8.9

of the peasants went on at an even faster pace, and holdings of the peasants increased annually by 200 to 220 thousand *desiatynas*. By 1917 the peasants of these nine *gubernias* possessed as we can assume, over 28 million *desiatynas*, or 64% of the total area."[75]

It appears, therefore, that the Ukrainian peasants acquired, between the time of the reform and the 1917 revolution, over 8 million desiatynas of land.

Average prices of land increased from 72 rubles in 1888 to 1896 to 196 rubles in 1906 to 1914.[76] Inasmuch as the bulk of the land was purchased by the peasants at the end of the 19th century and the beginning of the 20th, it would not be too risky to assume that the average price for the entire period was between 160 and 170 rubles. It follows therefore, that the Ukrainian peasants, besides paying an annual round figure of 60 million rubles for rent, also spent another 1,360 million rubles in purchasing land.

If we take to consideration that during this period the Ukrainian peasants paid over 3 billion rubles in rent, then the sum total is very close to 5 billion rubles. This sum is to be accepted at its value then, when it was much higher than the sum total of all capital invested in the entire Ukrainian industry on the eve of the revolution.

Thus, over a period of more than half a century, the huge aggregate of the labor energy of the multi-million Ukrainian peasantry, instead of being spent on the acquisition of products of human enterprise went merely for the right to use the land, i.e. to use the natural property of the people. What necessitated the shifting of the right of the use of land was at first Moscow's wanton disregard of existing land conditions in Ukraine, and later an even further deterioration of these conditions during the reform of 1861.

Such an accumulation of the national income, effected at the cost of pitiful living conditions of the great masses of peasants and the halting of the development of their economy could be, if not excused, at least understood, if these accumulated values had gone toward the development of the national economy, toward the development of national industry, or at least toward

[75] A. Peshekhonov, "Zemlevladeniye" ("Land Ownership"), *Narodne Khozyaystvo Ukrainy (National Economy of Ukraine)*, Kharkiv, 1922.
[76] "Sils'ke hospodarstvo Ukrainy."

a rational organization of production of the large agricultural enterprises themselves.

Nothing like this ever happened. The overwhelming part of those huge material contributions of the Ukrainian people was completely excluded from the Ukrainian economy. Those huge amounts flowed from Ukraine in a wide river to Petersburg, Moscow and abroad.

This statement is not too difficult to prove. If we divide all the landowners according to the extent of their holdings, we get the figures shown in *Table XXXVIII* for the year 1877.

In the Kiev region, owners of over 10,000 *desiatynas* held 17% of all private land holdings, and in Volhynia, 24.2%.

Discarding the group of landholders under 100 *desiatynas,* the overwhelming majority of whom were peasants, we have the right to come to the conclusion that Ukraine was a land of large estates. Three thousand owners of large estates who constituted only 1.5% of all landowners held more than 50% of all privately owned land. Those billions of purchase price money, rents and other payments went into their pockets.

For the most part the owners of the large estates did not administer them directly. They did not even live on them, visiting them only once in a while. They constituted the close circle of the Tsar's court, the upper echelon of the government hierarchy, the higher aristocracy. In short, they were the *haut-monde* of the two capitals of the Empire who also filled the fashionable places of France, Switzerland and Germany. It was into the pockets of the Koenigs, Kleinmichels, Sheremetevs, Bobrinskis, Sanguszkos, Branickis, Potockis that the Ukrainian peasants, money flowed. Money in payment for the right to till their own Ukrainian land. The peasants' concentration on extending their land holdings absorbed all their economic resources and became the main obstacle to the development of agricultural production commensurate with its natural potential, a potential which would have guaranteed Ukraine a foremost place among the countries of Europe. This is what prevented the intensification of agriculture and increase of the amount of labor per unit of area, and which gave rise to that so-called "relative agrarian overpopulation."

As is well known, the basis of a rational organization of agricultural production is a harmony between its three basic factors: land, labor and tools. The land conditions created in Ukraine

TABLE XXXVIII

Size of holdings	Number of holdings in thousands	Amount of land in thousand desiatynas	Holdings in %	Land in %
Under 10 desiatynas	123.0	412.4	64.3	2.7
11 to 50 desiatynas	41.3	933.2	21.5	6.2
51 to 100 desiatynas	8.7	626.4	4.5	4.1
Total under 100 desiatynas	173.0	1,972.0	90.3	13.0
101 to 500 desiatynas	12.1	2,834.0	6.3	18.6
501 to 1000 desiatynas	3.4	2,421.6	1.8	15.9
Total under 1000 desiatynas	15.5	5,255.6	8.1	34.5
1001 to 5000 desiatynas	2.8	5,253.5	1.5	34.5
5001 to 10,000 desiatynas	0.1	1,183.4	0.0	7.8
Over 10,000 desiatynas	0.0	1,555.1	0.0	10.2
Total over 1,000	2.9	7,992.0	1.5	52.5

77 M. Porsh, *op. cit.*, p. 156.

produced a surplus of labor in relation to the land: financial
burdens came into existence as a result of land conditions, a
deficiency of tools, even in relation to the insufficient amount
of land. What is more, already toward the end of the 1880's,
when rents began to rise much faster, the payment of rent was
in large measure accomplished at the expense of a reduction in
the basic tools of production. This was a direct sign of a decline
of the economy. It was felt most acutely in the supply of working
and production animals. Censuses of horses, *Table XXXIX*, for
military purposes conducted between 1888 and 1901, show the
changes in the supply of horses (the year 1888=100).[78]

TABLE XXXIX

Farms without horses	122	Farms with 4 horses	57
Farms with 1 horse	125	Farms with 5 horses	45
Farms with 2 horses	96	Farms with 6 horses	41
Farms with 3 horses	65		

This indicates that the number of households with one horse
and without any increased at the expense of a sharp decline
in the number of multi-horse farms.

As early as 1882 the number of farms without a horse was,
in relation to the total number of farms: in Chernihiv, 31.4%;
Volhynia, 39.8%; Katerynoslav, 40.9%; Kharkiv, 41.7%; Kherson,
44.7%; Podilla, 51.4%; Kiev, 58.2%, and Poltava, 58.6%. It is not
surprising therefore that even in such a relatively wealthy county
as that of Mariupil "teaming up" by several neighbors for common tilling of land reached 53.5% of all field work: hiring of
horses, 21.4% and only 20.7% of the area was cultivated by the
farmer's own animal power.[79]

A similar process of impoverishment could also be observed in
relation to food animals. The number of animals in the wealthiest food producing Kherson area is shown in *Table XL.*[80]

Maslov noted the relationship between this phenomenon and
anomalous land conditions in these words: "The process of the
impoverishment of the peasants permitted a continuation of lease
of land, as long as there was an opportunity to supplement the
budget of the household by means of curtailing the tools of production."[81]

[78] P. Maslov, *op. cit.*, II, 63.   [79] M. Slabchenko, *op. cit.*, p. 111.
[80] *Ibid.*, p. 112.   [81] P. Maslov, *op. cit.*, II, 69.

TABLE XL

| | Per 100 population | | Per 100 desiatynas of land | |
	Cattle	Sheep	Cattle	Sheep
1882	64.4	206.0	...	...
1887	70.2	131.2	34.8	69.5
1896	46.4	76.5	24.5	40.7
1900	44.2	65.7	22.9	32.0

An even more vivid illustration of the impoverishment of the peasants is provided by *Table LXI*, a closer analysis of the supply of production tools and dwellings.[82]

TABLE XLI

Average per one farm (value in rubles):

	Buildings	Farm tools	Animals	Production tools per one desiatyna	All capital invested per one desiatyna
1 desiatyna and less ..	236	8	14	22	258
1-2 desiatynas	266	90	35	84	260
2-3 desiatynas	207	104	38	57	140
3-4 desiatynas	256	160	74	67	140
4-5 desiatynas	274	167	70	53	114
5-6 desiatynas	380	212	104	58	126
6-9 desiatynas	445	312	134	46	106
9-15 desiatynas	598	402	136	45	95
15-25 desiatynas	361	607	195	40	58
25 to 30 desiatynas ...	2,080	981	490	54	130

Noteworthy is not only the low amount of invested capital, but also the fact that its absolute increase in the higher groups of land holding is so insignificant that it conclusively indicates rather an increase in tools of prime necessity, such as ploughs, harrows, etc., rather than any application of improved machinery. Very significant also is the fact that the value of buildings in all groups except the last is almost unchanging: all peasants live in primitive cottages and have primitive quarters for their animals. Most indicative is the extremely low value amount of animals, which even in the groups of 6 to 9, and 9 to 15 *desiatynas* does not exceed in value 2 to 3 head, horses included.

Even in the 1880's only the percentage of peasant land holdings shown in *Table XLII* were tilled with the aid of machines.

[82] S. Ostapenko, *op. cit.*, p. 119.

⸱

TABLE XLII

	Sowing	Reaping	Threshing	Winnowing
Right Bank	5.7	1.3	29.4	32.1
Steppe	20.7	20.3	36.3	no data

[83]

According to the census of 1917, when the peasants were in fact cultivating nearly 27 million *desiatynas* of area, they had: 2 million metal ploughs: 1.5 million tillers; 4 million harrows; 2.6 million carts; only 7,000 steam threshers; 55,000 seeders; 43,000 reapers; 156,000 winnowers, etc.[84]

From the mere fact that there was one seeder for every 500 *desiatynas* and one winnower for 175 *desiatynas*, we can judge the straightened financial circumstances in which the peasants remained as far as equipment is concerned. This situation was caused primarily by the burden of payments for land.

It must be stated here that in the enterprises of a capitalistic nature, of the landowners and of other owners, the sum total of capital investment in buildings, tools and animals equalled only 1,145 million rubles. It was far smaller then, than these enterprises received for land and in the way of annual income from production. This is convincing proof that a great part of such income was kept from use in the national economy and consumed beyond its borders.

In the light of the data quoted above, we must now come back to a matter discussed before, the problem of the so-called "relative agrarian overpopulation." This very term contains within it the source of many misunderstandings. On the one hand, nobody dare deny the existence of a "land shortage" which by itself indicated a surplus of farm labor in relation to available land; and on the other hand, the fact that a certain number of peasants from Russian *gubernias* migrated for seasonal work to the steppes of Kherson and Tauria gave an opportunity, to those who wished to avail themselves of it, to generalize this phenomenon and to maintain that Ukraine represented a market of unfilled farm labor and high wages where, as the saying went, "the more unfortunate Russian peasants" sought relief from their ill fortune. Those who so argue wish to see facts which allegedly contradict the statements about the colonial position of Ukraine.

[83] *Trudi Kharkovskogo obshchestva selskogo khozyaystva* (*Proceedings of Kharkiv Agricultural Society*), Kharkiv, 1889, I, 19.
[84] S. Ostapenko, *op. cit.*, p. 123.

Even if we were not disputing that such were the facts, they still could not preclude the existence of a colonial status, because, for example, when America was an English colony, its status was in no way altered by the fact that emigrants from the metropolis came seeking a better living. However, the very interpretation of migration of Russian peasants seeking work in the Ukrainian steppe is entirely incorrect. We do not pretend to idealize the position of the Russian peasants, and are far from denying that their fate was hard when compared with that of the peasants of economically developed countries of Western Europe. Here, in the Russian Empire, the formula was even more true than elsewhere that "whoever oppresses other people inevitably oppresses also his own." Particularly since in Russia, subjected nations were included within continuous borders of the state compelling, in large measure, the making of identical legal norms of conduct. We do not pretend that the Ukrainian peasants were badly off, and the Russians well off. What is of essence is that the entire economic development of Russia, whose complexion also included agriculture, differed from that of Ukraine, and the difference was determined by the colonial position of Ukraine.

Agrarian Overpopulation

We have already brought together such basic factors as determine agrarian conditions: land holdings; rent; mobilization of land; density of the rural population; outside income, and localization of the national economy. We have been able to see the much worse conditions under which the Ukrainian peasants came after the reform in comparison with the Russian peasants, because of specially directed measures of the economic policies of the Imperial Government. Further we shall see an economic policy even more flagrantly in the interests of Russia in industry, tariffs, finances, foreign trade, etc.

But let us return to agrarian overpopulation, and see if in this respect Ukraine was also in a position different than Russia. Let us see if at its base we can again see a specifically directed policy.

Illumination on this point is of importance for yet another reason: there is an unconcealed Russian tendency to treat the "relative agrarian overpopulation" as absolute, and to base on this the thesis of the inevitability of a connection between

Ukraine and Russia. Only in this situation, it is alleged, does Ukraine preserve an opportunity to have the necessary *lebensraum* on the peripheries of the Russian territorities for placing the surplus of the Ukrainian population.

First of all we must define the term, "overpopulation." Do we mean the inability of the given territory to feed its own population, or to employ it? Neither the one, nor the other is, as we well know, something that can be measured in absolute figures. As far as the second factor is concerned, the scope of employment of a population is determined by the general tone of the economic development, natural resources of the territory, and, in much lesser degree, its extent. Concerning the first, the ability of Ukraine to feed its population, no one can have any serious doubts about it. The quality of Ukrainian soil, climatic conditions, density of population, and a comparison of all those factors with Western Europe indicate the immense possibilities Ukraine has to increase consumer products and to satisfy the needs, not only of the existing population, but also of the natural increase for a long time to come. In addition, the food balance of a population is determined not merely by the consumer products of that share of the production of a given country in the world division of labor. Hence, any analysis of the overpopulation of Ukraine in this aspect would be superfluous.

The matter is then reduced to the problem of employing the population. But even in this respect we must distinguish between two situations: paucity of natural circumstances which make the development of productive activities of the population difficult, and artificially created social-economic conditions which prevent such development. Only in the first instance, and relatively at that, could we speak of an absolute overpopulation. The second must, in all justice, be analyzed as relative.

It is the latter that we encounter in Ukraine, and in relation to the peasants we consider it to be a relative overpopulation. We must include in this term the absence of a surplus of means of production in relation to agricultural productivity. This came about as a result of: 1) insufficient land holdings of the peasants coinciding with the availability of the necessary land area, 2) compulsive necessity of increasing the holdings of the peasants at the expense of narrowing their production possibilities, 3) preventing the peasants from reorganizing their economy in the direction of absorbing more labor, 4) a one-sided development of the national economy or, more precisely, the absence of a total national economy which would warrant a normal social division of labor and provide a certain part of the natural increase of the population with an opportunity of employment in other branches of socially useful work. We have already indicated the existence of such factors in Ukraine, and only they can explain the existence of a surplus population among Ukrainian peasants. In this, and not in a comparison to the existing life conditions, or of a standard of living, lies the difference between the Ukrainian peasants' life and that of the Russian. This cause of the surplus population was not felt as acutely by Russia, and in a majority of Russian localities was entirely unknown. The difference between Ukraine and Russia cannot therefore be reduced to the fact that Ukraine had an average density of population of 64 people per square kilometre, and Russia only 22, and that in Ukraine 79% of the people were engaged in agriculture compared to 68% in Russia. The gist of the matter is not to what extent the Ukrainian peasant had a harder life than the Russian, but in the fact that the former was unable to utilize the opportunity to live better, and in the fact that conditions made their appearance under which a part of the peasant population could not make a livelihood at all.

It is unnecessary to repeat many illustrations previously given in this chapter, but we wish to provide some additional proof that during the period under discussion the agricultural economy offered opportunities for a considerable increase in employment. Few people know, for example that the geographical boundary of sugar-beet culture extends far into the Southeast, but the spreading of this culture was stymied by an absence of refining establishments. At the same time, rotation of sugarbeets with grain crops triples the amount of labor needed in comparison with grain cultures. The same can be said of viniculture which did not nearly reach its northern boundaries. Wide possibilities existed in Ukraine for such cultures as tobacco, hops, flax and many others providing raw materials for industry, and requiring much more labor per unit of area. We could list many more products for which Ukraine's natural conditions are favorable, cotton for example, widely planted at present.

Thus, it was not a lack of natural opportunities which prevented the increase of the number of employed people, but the level of development of industry based on agriculture, and the peasants' lack of capital indispensable for such a reorganization of production.

This also explains the fact that Ukraine, utilizing the highest percentage of arable land of all territories of the Empire, nevertheless had 24% of it lying fallow, either under *pary*, or *toloka*.[85] Under multi-field rotation and proper eradication of weeds the unexploited area could have been considerably reduced. We could cite innumerable examples of increasing labor per unit of area known to agriculture and to the peasants themselves, but this is superfluous. We must stress again that the "surplus" of the rural population cannot, under any circumstances, be regarded as an absolute overpopulation. It is only the result of conditions created for the Ukrainian economy.

It is impossible to give accurate figures for this "surplus." Different authors take a different approach to make their estimates. We have already noted that S. Korolenko estimated this surplus for the 1890's at 5 million, of whom 2.5 million could find work only beyond the borders of their own territory. Professor Ostapenko wrote in this connection: "On the eve of the revolution, the Ukrainian peasants' agricultural economy had a 'surplus' of 7,778,866 workers."[86] It is not important whether the surplus was 7 or 5 million, or even less, but the very fact that richly endowed Ukraine had millions of peasants who, by virtue of created conditions, could not make a living.

This also caused the mass migration which marks so vividly the differing positions of Ukraine and Russia, the latter not experiencing such phenomenon.

The numbers of peasants who left Ukraine, and migrated in the main beyond the Urals, to the so-called *Zeleny Klyn* (Green Wedge) in the Far East are shown in *Table XLIII*.

TABLE XLIII

1886 to 1890	9,880
1891 to 1895	106,993
1896 to 1900	243,523

[87]

We must note that this migration was spontaneous, and against government orders. In 1894, the number of spontaneous

---

[85] *Para* is fallow ground lying plowed, while *toloka* is fallow ground under stubble left on it.
[86] S. Ostapenko, *op. cit.,* p. 119.   [87] M. Slabchenko, *op cit.,* p. 174.

migrants constituted 78% of the total. But in 1905, the government set up the so-called Central Commission for Resettlement which subdivided land in localities of new settlement, provided aid for transportation, etc. After that, migration assumed greater proportions. *Table XLIV* shows the numbers of peasants resettled during the period between 1906 and 1912.

TABLE XLIV

From the Region of:	Number
Poltava	198,459
Chernihiv	157,622
Kiev	148,157
Kharkiv	127,538
Katerynoslav	69,979
Kherson	85,739
Volhynia	43,287
Podilla	42,355
TOTAL:	873,136 [88]

Professor Vobly estimates the number of emigrants going beyond the Urals during the period between 1896 and and 1914 at 1,600,000. The Poltava region always occupied first place, 23% of all emigrants; then Chernihiv, 17%, and in last place Podilla, 4.5%.[89] These proportions are very telling, because Podilla, as has been stated, had the smallest extent of average land holdings, though sugar-beet culture and a well developed refining industry provided an entirely different utilization of labor per area unit. From the Poltava region on the other hand, during the same period 60% of the natural increase of the population emigrated. (See *Table XLV*).

TABLE XLV

	Among the emigrants were:
Landless	16.6%
Those owning up to 1 desiatyna	12.9%
Those owning up to 3 desiatynas	27.7%
Those owning up to 6 desiatynas	32.0%
Those owning up to 10 desiatynas	7.8%
Those owning over 10 desiatynas	3.0%

---

[88] Feshchenko-Chopivsky, *op. cit.*, p. 47.
[89] K. Vobly, *Ekonomichna heohrafiya Ukrainy* (*Economic Geography of Ukraine*), Kiev, 1927, p. 73.

This proves conclusively that migration from Ukraine was not in the nature of a colonization of new and unpopulated regions, so well known in world history, and which was the nature of the Russian colonization of Siberia during the 17th and 18th centuries. Here we have neither the hazards of enterprise, nor seeking of wider opportunities for utilizing capital and energy which were peculiar to this colonization. Ukrainian migration was simply an escape of the hungry from famine and in search of bread.

In this respect this phenomenon of migration is analogous to those mass movements of peasants within Ukraine in search of wages, involving hundreds of thousands each year. Not an absolute insufficiency of labor in an annual balance, but an accumulation of seasonal work during harvest time, created a lack of labor in the Southern steppes which was filled by migrants from Poltava, Chernihiv, Kharkiv, the Right Bank, and partially from central Russian *gubernias.* In the 1880's an average of 63,205 migrant workers left the Poltava region annually, and later the number grew to 125-150 thousand. In 1884, from Chernihiv region, 43,957 migrants went out; in 1893, 110,334, and in 1896, 148,157.[90] In all of Ukraine the number of migratory workers, not counting local unskilled labor and industrial workers reached the figure of 600 to 700 thousand every year, among whom the Russians constituted an insignificant percentage, smaller than the number of Ukrainian migratory workers in the Russian *gubernias* of Kursk, Orlov, Voronizh, Samara, etc. and, in particular, in Don Military Region.

The statement that Russian migratory workers were attracted to Ukraine by higher wages compared with what they could make locally, is incorrect. If this were true, it would contradict the large surplus of rural population in Ukraine. In reality, a comparison of wages at sowing and haymaking time (meals included) for the years 1902-1906 gives the picture shown in *Table XLVI*[91] (in kopecks per day).

Much more important than migratory workers in the balancing of labor surpluses was local unskilled labor offering itself for hire. This applies both to the number employed, as well as to steadiness of work and locale of work in the peasants' budget.

Hiring of unskilled day laborers by landowners and wealthier farmers was conducted in the immediate vicinity. In Bakhmut

[90] M. Slabchenko, *op. cit.,* p. 263.   [91] P. Maslov, *op. cit.,* II, 181.

TABLE XLVI

Region:	1902-04 Sow-ing	1902-04 Hay-making	1905 Sow-ing	1905 Hay-making	1906 Sow-ing	1906 Hay-making
Kherson	48	73	45	70	55	106
Tauria	63	101	65	73	85	130
Podilla	35	45	35	45	45	65
Volhynia	36	46	35	60	45	60
Poltava	40	63	45	70	50	85
Kharkiv	45	70	50	75	55	80
and compare with the above:						
Volodimirska *gubernia*	68	105	70	110	80	130
Moscow *gubernia*	63	85	70	100	80	90

county, in 1885, among 3,819 annual day laborers, there were only 244 people from other localities; among 2,022 seasonal workers, 69; among 177 monthly workers, 1; and among 3,713 day workers, 86. This is typical. Hence, unskilled day labor became the steady occupation of a certain part of the local population, bestowing on them the badge of a rural proletariat. A system of economic interdependence came into being between this proletariat and the employers. A large number of peasants with little or no land turned to unskilled day labor as a basis of their economy. Hence, their conditions determined the entire economic interest. This explains the appearance of peculiar phenomena, known only in Ukraine during the revolution of 1904 to 1906. Here along with a mass struggle for land, there was a determined struggle of the village proletariat for a change in the legal and economic conditions of work. As early as 1863, at the time of the abolition of serfdom, temporary regulations regarding rural workers were issued. The employer had a right to punish a worker with up to 2 days wages for leaving work without permission, laziness, carelessness, etc. He could discharge for sullenness or insolence. On his part, a worker had the right to leave work if he was beaten, insulted or not paid for his time. In addition, by decree of July 12, 1886 an employer had the right to punish without recourse to a court of justice. It compelled the workers to deposit their passports with the employer, depriving them of the right of free movement. It raised violations of labor contracts by workers to the classification of crimes, punishable under the criminal, and not civil law.[92]

[92] F. Danilov, *op. cit.*, I, 179.

From this we can see that the present Bolshevik classification of labor contract violations to the category of criminal transgressions had a precedent in the former Russian Tsarist legislation.

In differentiation from agrarian revolts which for the most part consisted of seizing lands of the estates, wrecking of estates, etc., the struggle of the village proletariat for a change of legal conditions and wages assumed the proportions of organized strikes with well-defined demands. In the village of Dyakovo, of Haysin county, during a period of five years, the day laborers conducted a boycott of estates. In the town of Sorochyntsi, near Poltava, striking laborers demanded an increase of wages: for men from 75 kopecks to 3 rubles, for women, 50 kopecks to 1.50 rubles; monthly wages from 5 or 6 rubles to 30 rubles, etc. During this period, similar demands assumed mass proportions.

Professor Ostapenko estimates the total number of agricultural workers as of 1916 at 964,000. This is 7% of the number of workers among the rural population between the ages of 20 and 59, whose total at that time was 13,740,000 (6,768,000 men and 6,972,000 women). According to his data, during the same period there were in Ukraine, of the total number of day laborers, 48.5% were employed by small farms, 46.9% by medium sized farms, and 4.6% by large farms.[93]

Wages of day laborers were lower than the average reward for work on the peasants' own farms which Professor Ostapenko estimates at 203 rubles per annum for an able bodied man. A day laborer made 110 rubles and meals (meals cost the employer 20 kopecks per day, or 73 rubles per year), therefore the total was 183 rubles per year. But if we compare these wages with the income of a poor farmer on his own holding, then they appear twice as large. The total sum of the peasants' income in the year 1916 reached 2,235 million rubles, of which 449 million rubles were made by poor farms, 1,341 million rubles by medium farms, and 445 million rubles by the wealthy. This gives a total for each worker in the corresponding class of 91 rubles, 283 rubles and 812 rubles per year.

Thus, the "relative agrarian overpopulation" was characterized not only by the fact that part of the Ukrainian peasants could find no work on their own land and had to leave it, nor only that certain masses of peasants had to move over Ukraine

[93] S. Ostapenko, *op. cit.*, p. 118.

each year in search of work, but also by the fact that some of those peasants had a lower income than the average wages on the labor market.

Common Holdings

As a final illustration of agrarian conditions which came into being in Ukraine following the reform of 1861, we must consider one more factor which played a very important role in the life of the peasants. It was likewise not peculiar to Ukraine, and was imposed on Ukraine by Russia in the interests of the treasury. We have in mind the so-called *obshchyna* or common holding. In Russia it has a history of many centuries. The essence of it is that the land is the property of the community, and it is divided among members of the community not on the basis of outright property, but of temporary individual land use. The basis for the division is the number of people in the family, i.e. a norm in kind. Changes in the composition of families bring about either periodical redistribution, or an equalization of norms by means of subtracting from some and adding to others. Thus, the Russian peasants did not feel tied to a particular piece of land as being their own property and they did not feel that they were acquiring property gradually along with payments for land endowed according to the reform. Their attitude was one of considering land as something to which to apply their labor. This form of land holding was favored by the interests of the government, to some extent also by the interests of the Russian peasants themselves, and was much idealized by the political trend which was most acceptable by the peasants, the *narodniks* or populists.

It gave the government an opportunity to apply the principle of the so-called "community liability" in the interests of the treasury, i.e. the responsibility of the entire community for the payment of taxes by all its members. Individually unpaid taxes were assessed among the remainder and paid by them.

The peasants wished to see the *obshchyna* as guaranteeing an equitable distribution of land, and a safeguard giving them additional distribution when there were more mouths to feed in the family.

Finally, the so-called *narodnitski* (populist) trend in the Socialist political movement perceived, in the principle of *obshchyna* or community property of land, the pattern of a future socialist society.

Ukraine had never known *obshchyna*. In old times, even
before serfdom, there was community property in Ukraine, but
only to a very small extent, and exclusively applicable to lands
of common use: pastures, forests, etc. Community enterprises
were encountered even before the reform of 1861, but this was
an *obshchyna sui generis,* on a contract basis, and not connected
with results of labor. It was simply a cooperative enterprise of
labor and capital. This was not an *obshchyna* of the Russian
type, although in some places immigrants from Russia made attempts "to get organized according to the Russian pattern."[94]

Nevertheless, at the time of the abolition of serfdom, *obshchyna* was widely imposed upon Ukraine. "When peasants received
endowments, 9,056 thousand *desiatynas,* or 53% of usable land
was given to 1,945,000 people (42.7%) as community property,
and the remaining 7,913 thousand *desiatynas* or 46.7% was given
to 2,605,000 people (57.3%) as household property."[95]

Or, if we take into consideration not individuals, but households, then 1,191,643 households (41.5%) were on rights of
obshchyna and 1,683,477 households on household property
rights.[96]

In some *gubernias, obshchyna* then became the dominant
form of land holding. (See *Table XLVII.*)[97] The imposition of

TABLE XLVII

Region:	Obshchyna land	Household land	Total	% of land in household property
Chernihiv	969,238	913,799	1,883,037	48.3
Poltava	239,107	1,639,692	1,878,799	84.1
Kharkiv	2,450,925	121,236	2,572,161	4.7
Kherson	1,915,368	241,678	2,157,046	11.2
Katerysnoslav	2,535,770	92,331	2,628,101	3.5
Kiev	326,864	1,619,967	1,946,831	83.3
Volhynia	480,331	1,690,867	2,171,198	77.9
Podilla	90,606	1,576,058	1,666,664	94.6

such form of land holding upon Ukraine according to the Russian pattern, although "the *obshchyna* was not applicable to the
very nature of the economy, as accepted long before the reform"
(Slabchenko) was exclusively for fiscal purposes; to transfer the

94 M. Slabchenko, *op. cit.,* p. 14.   95 M. Porsh, *op. cit.,* p. 44.
96 *Ibid.,* p. 166.   97 M. Slabchenko, *op. cit.,* p. 29.

guarantee of collecting taxes, even from those households which were unable to pay, to the backs of others as an additional burden, even if they were already overburdened, and applying for the purpose a "community liability." Ukraine did not, as a matter of fact, accept this *obshchyna* imposed on her. "Among the *obshchynas*, a total of 80.2% did not comply with the re-allotment requirements of *obshchyna*."[98]

But the Russian authorities did not take this into consideration, as Professor Slabchenko appropriately says: "One of the most interesting scholars of agrarian conditions in Ukraine, Shymansky, is right when he says that individual enterprise dominated in Ukraine, while the Russian authorities were certain that *obshchyna* existed in Ukraine and erected their financial policy on this. Thus *obshchyna* itself was a fiction, imagined by the central Petersburg authorities; in Ukraine they knew only an individual, albeit a three-field economy."[99]

Nevertheless, although the Ukrainian peasants violated the rules of *obshchyna* and used the land on the basis of household holding, its detrimental results, as of the formally existing form of land holding, laid heavily upon the economy. Even disregarding "community liability" noted above, it presented an insurmountable obstacle to the general effectiveness of land distribution by massing all the land of one farmer within one boundary. Splitting, which had its source in it, augmented by family divisions, became one of the decisive factors which excluded a rational organization of the productive process. The distance separating pieces of land from each other, and from the farmer's abode even reached several kilometres. A large part of the land was thus wasted on boundaries and field roads.

In addition, *obshchyna* forms of land holding frequently compelled the peasants to apply involuntarily forms of crop rotation. For the most part the three-field system was revived (winter planting, spring planting, and then fallow land, *toloka* field covered with the previous year's stubble and grown with weeds which were used for animal pasture). The need for pastures preserved this system, preventing the more developed farms to change over to a many-field system, with grass sowing etc., not to mention the fact that a fallow field with stubble contributed to deterioration of the soil.

[98] *Ibid.*
[99] M. Slabchenko, *Orhanizatsiya khozyaystva Ukrainy (Organization of the Economy of Ukraine)*, Kharkiv, 1925, I, 64.

Another important factor was that *obshchyna* land holding made documentary proof of any household's rights to land impossible. The application of Russian practice, where *obshchyna* encompassed more than 80% of all households, brought about in Ukraine a situation where the peasants were deprived of a legal formulation of their property rights to endowed land. "It is a terrible thought," wrote later Minister Witte, "that farmers, both under household, as well as *obshchyna* land holding, do not have in their hands any documents which would prove their rights."[100]

All this was written, however, in face of the fact of the agrarian revolution, when community liability was being repealed (1903), when endowed land had been paid for, and when the order of the day was the Stolypin reform. But 40 years earlier this *obshchyna* was imposed on Ukraine by force, contrary to the existing situation in Ukraine, and caused the rural economy great harm. Such were the agrarian conditions created in Ukraine following the reform of 1861, and such were its consequences.

It is understood that the colonial policy of Russia in relation to Ukraine was not only mirrored in the area of agrarian policy. Of such nature was the agrarian-economic policy in general. We shall show this in subsequent chapters of this work, where we shall illustrate this policy in connection with other social-economic processes of similar kind.

We here are deliberately not taking into account the reactions of a national and political content which the agrarian conditions produced in the Ukrainian peasants, as did all Russian policy in relation to Ukraine. The social-political processes in Ukraine are complicated, to such an extent, peculiarly revealing in their presentation of a national entity, that they cannot be considered superficially. They demand a separate and independent illustration.

Precisely within the Ukrainian peasantry these processes showed themselves most clearly, often assuming very acute forms. Beginning with the 1870's signs of mass opposition appear, sometimes taking form of fairly well organized peasant movements. The opposition reached its culminating point in 1902 when the peasants of the regions of Poltava and Kharkiv started an agrarian revolution. The revolution spread all over the Em-

[100] Witte, *op. cit.*, p. 221.

pire in 1905 to 1906. No repressions were in a position to break this spiritual opposition, because reality left no alternative, but to fight. The hopelessness of the situation found the most vivid expression in the words of peasant participants of revolts, during the punishment by the whip: ". . . although we shall perish," shouted the peasant Khoma Pr'yadko, a participant of the Chyhyryn revolt, "at least our children will get better land." And Trokhym Shayda, a Poltava insurgent of 1902 yelled: "Slaughter us, beat us, just the same we shall have to die without land."

The thirst for Land and Freedom is not only a revolutionary banner-word around which all the peasantry gathers in struggle, it is not merely a formula of economic and political demands. Land and Freedom is the ideological basis of the entire outlook, of the understanding of the natural right which penetrates deeply into the consciousness of the peasantry, having its roots in religious faith and feeling.

The Stolypin Reform

The revolution of 1902 to 1906, as is well known, ended in failure, although under its pressure the Government agreed to a series of concessions. These included a declaration of the freedom of religious beliefs; repeal of "community liability"; abolition of corporal punishment by judgment of village courts; aid for resettlement; etc., as well as greater civil rights and introduction of population representation in the State Duma. But the most important problem of agrarian conditions, the mainspring of all the peasant movements, the problem of land, remained unsolved. It was not solved by the State Duma in all of its four sessions, although a new land reform bill was the center of all of its legislative programs. The first Duma was dissolved precisely because of its radical attempt to solve the land problem, and it called upon the people to continue their fight.

Of the 458 legislative demands that were served upon members of the second Duma, 297 demanded a solution of the land problem, and even the rightist, monarchist circles saw the danger of any further procrastination in this matter, and the threat to the preservation of the Tsarist Empire itself. The electors of the Stavropil county demanded: "1) Autocratic government with participation of representatives of the people; 2) Preservation of the entirety and unity of the Russian State on condition of equalizing all the rights of nations constituting it, but in no event should any land or nation be permitted to separate in an independent political government; 3) All the land should be proclaimed common state property, etc."[101]

The idea of "nationalization of land" had wide support among a majority of the deputies from the central Russian regions, but it "created *sui generis* separatist trends among the representatives of the borderlands, because to those who had experienced the decrees of the central government in the matter of 'unifying the nationalities' the danger of nationalizing the land was clear." [102]

As far as the demands of peasants are concerned, and these came from all nine *gubernias* of Ukraine, their content can be reduced to the invariable demand of the free transfer of all Ukrainian lands to the Ukrainian peasants, a reduction of the tax burden and a guarantee that the people would have a right to determine their form of life.

Having conquered the revolution which threatened not only Tsarist autocracy, the gentry's landownership, the integrity of the Empire, and still preventing the State Duma from a legal solution of the agrarian problem, at least to the extent of blunting its acuteness, the Government nevertheless understood that some changes were inevitable, and that it was imperative to take the initiative in this matter away from the stormy peasants. This is where Stolypin's law came in.

Credit for this law should properly go not to Stolypin, but to his predecessor, Count Witte. In 1904, in his *Zapiski po krestyanskomu delu* which was based on resolutions of 11,000 meetings held in this matter, Witte posed the problem of abolishing the compulsory form of community land holding under *obshchyna*. Even the decree of 1861 foresaw the possibility of quitting an *obshchyna*, and the compulsion to remain within it was tied only to the final payment of installments for land. Article 165 of the Payment law stated: "If a peasant, who desires to separate will pay to the county treasury the entire amount due for land from him, then the community is obliged to separate for this peasant the appropriate part of land, if possible in one location." This article was repealed in 1893, however, because by that time the fiscal interests, and not land payments, demanded the preservation of *obshchyna*. One cannot say therefore that the negative properties of *obshchyna*, from the viewpoint of agricultural

[101] P. Maslov, *op. cit.*, II, 379.   [102] P. Maslov, *loc. cit.*

production, were not clear even at the time of the abolition of serfdom. In *Materyali Redaktsionnoy Kommissiyi* (materials of the editors' committee) of the law of 1861, we read the following: "In the further economic development, the community structure will change into a burden on the peasants themselves. A change of community land holding will, most probably, be inevitable."[103]

Thus, Count Witte's proposal, expressed in the above cited *Zapiske po krestyanskomu delu,* of facilitating an exit from *obshchyna* was foreseen long before. He argued for his proposal in the following manner: "Such an order of land holding kills the main stimulus of any economic culture, the consciousness and certainty that the fruits of his labor will be enjoyed by the worker or people close to him by blood relationship; a member of a community cannot have such certainty by virtue of a temporary use. Economic expectations, the initiative and energy of individuals are futile, and in many instances cannot be realized. Such main carriers of any material culture encounter insurmountable obstacles under conditions of community structure."[104]

The law of Stolypin (Nov. 9, 1906) gave nothing above the opportunity to acquire private property over endowed land. Article 9 of this law stated: "Every head of a household, who holds land according to community right, may demand any time that it should be determined as his individual property, or property in common with other members of his family." Article 32: "Every head of household whose land holding is determined has a right to demand that the community give to him, in place of separate pieces of land, an appropriate piece of land, if possible in one location." This land will become outright private property without any restrictions (Article 47).[105]

Stolypin's law did not, therefore, completely abolish *obshchyna.* It only facilitated avoiding it, and made possible the establishment of farm enterprises, either so-called *otruby* (all the land in one piece, but the home of the farmer is in the village) and *khutirs* (the land and home all in one location, much like an American farm). With this law, as has already been noted, the operations of the Land Bank were authorized to facilitate the sale of land to peasants.

[103] *Materyali Redaktsionnoy Kommissiyi* (*Materials of the Editing Commission*), St. Petersburg, 1876, IV, 45.
[104] S. I. Witte, *Zapiske po krestyanskomu delu* (*Notes on Peasant Affairs*), Stuttgart, 1903, p. 87.
[105] V. Voznesensky, *Deytvuyushche zakony o krestyanakh* (*Binding Laws Pertaining to Peasants*), Moscow, 1910.

This law was dictated by far-reaching political aims, and by no less important economic reasons. The year 1905 proved that the government had very weak support in society. Even the industrial bourgeoisie, including that of noble origin, joined in the opposition to the government. And the landed gentry, weakened by its parasitic existence, was unable to create any strong political force. This created the idea of favoring the establishment of such a social force, which by its nature would be conservative, and on which the throne could rely. The law was constructed in such manner as to favor such a class, with its credits for land, *khutirs* and *otruby*, in other words, a landed middle class. In addition, for the Russian peasants, where 80% of them were within *obshchyna*, facilitating their quitting *obshchyna* and becoming an industrial proletariat. *Obshchyna* land holding and in this respect Stolypin's law provided a certain relief to the tension resulting from the agrarian revolution. Under the conditions of a well developed industry in Russia, the peasants with small land holdings had long since been leaving the land and becoming an industrial proletariat. *Obshchyna* land holding, prohibiting the alienation of his land as his own property, bound the peasant to the land artificially and tied him as a proletarian to the land. The new law made it possible to become an outright owner of the land and to sell it, thus improving his financial position without changing the basis of his livelihood, i.e. hiring out as labor. Such a sale of land by the proletariat, the former small holding peasants, was at that time very widespread in Russia. In this respect the Stolypin law gave the Ukrainian peasants no benefit at all. The liquidation of *obshchyna* forms of land holding hardly introduced anything new into the lives of peasants with small holdings. As has been noted, the institution of *obshchyna* was in general alien to the Ukrainian peasantry. In that degree in which it had been imposed on Ukraine by Russia it did not take deep root, remained a fiction, therefore its removal was nothing very significant. The main thing is that, with an undeveloped industry which could not provide for the employment of peasants with small land holdings, these peasants, as before, remained affectionately tied to their piece of land as their sole means of subsistence.

The Stolypin law had, however, a deep significance for Ukraine in a different aspect, which was, undoubtedly, one of its most important political aims. The revolution disclosed in

Ukraine more than the will of the Ukrainian peasants for a change of the existing order. In no less a degree it indicated a unity of the peasant masses in the struggle and a welding of all its social strata. This gave the revolution the character of a national deed. In the slogan "Land and Freedom" the term Freedom spread to include an introduction of "our own order in our own land." This contained the gravest danger to Russia that the peasant revolution in Ukraine offered.

It was clear that suppression by arms did not halt the process of the revolution. And it was not the intention of the government to solve it by means of a change of agrarian conditions. Hence there arose the need to change the nature of this process, to deprive it of the hallmark of a national movement, to break the unity of the national community by way of planting and spreading within the peasantry social controversies, thus creating a cleavage between the wealthy and the poorer peasants. As we shall see, subsequently, the Bolsheviks made use of this device to the fullest extent.

It must be admitted that in and of itself, the form of farm enterprise is in the highest degree commensurate with the spirit of the Ukrainian peasantry, it is therefore not surprising that in this respect the Stolypin law found favorable acceptance among the better off peasants. Nowhere else were *khutirs* and *otruby* as widespread as in Ukraine. The wealthier peasants began to consolidate their lands into single units in a mass movement, determining thereby in large measure a more rational farm economy. Likewise all land purchased through the bank assumed the form of *khutirs* and *vidruby*. During the period from 1906 to 1913 this land was divided according to the form of use as shown in *Table XLVIII*. [106]

TABLE XLVIII

Gubernia	% of khutir land	% of vidruby land
Chernihiv	48.9	51.1
Podilla	25.1	74.9
Kiev	59.1	40.9
Poltava	36.0	64.0
Volhynia	21.9	78.0
Kharkiv	21.9	78.0
Kherson	28.2	71.1
Katerynoslav	18.1	81.9
Tauria	21.2	78.8

[106] "Sils'ke hospodarstvo . . .," p. 24.

Such a transformation of the wealthy group of peasants in Ukraine constituted the economic object of the law. The decline of the Ukrainian agrarian economy, under pressure of land conditions and of general economic circumstances faced Russia with great difficulties. Grain crops of Ukraine constituted 23% of the entire Russian crops,[107] and in exports of grain Ukraine participated to the extent of almost 80%. This grain of Ukraine was a basic export product, at the cost of which Russia covered in large measure her payments of foreign loans. Therefore the maintenance of a production level of grain in Ukraine and of its export goods part was an absolute necessity to Russia.

Without a change of agrarian conditions, with a general impoverishment of the peasant masses, and under a general decline of agricultural productivity, Russia sought a solution of the problem at the expense of the wealthier peasants.

The material condition of the Ukrainian peasants was, including also land taken under lease, as is shown in *Table XLIX*. But

TABLE XLIX

Poor peasants (0 to 3 desiatynas of land)	61.7%
Middle peasants (3 to 9 desiatynas of land)	33.4%
Wealthy peasants (9 to 50 desiatynas of land)	4.9%

the top echelon of those in the middle and of the 4.9% of the wealthy held over 60% of all peasant land and were the chief producers of commercial grain.

Favoring this part of the Ukrainian peasantry, the Stolypin law had as its objective the preservation of a source of income for Russia. Hence, the new Stolypin reform did not change agrarian conditions in Ukraine created by Russia.

The acuteness of the agrarian problem, as well as of the general economic conditions, not only did not subside by 1917, but grew even worse as a result of the war.

[107] B. Dzinkevych, *Produktsiya khliba v Ukraini (Grain Production in Ukraine)*, Kharkiv, 1923, I, 19.

CHAPTER 3

UKRAINIAN INDUSTRY: CONDITIONS OF ITS EXISTENCE AND DEVELOPMENT

Explanation of Colonial Dependence

TWO SHARPLY DIFFERENT periods must be distinguished in Ukrainian industry following the land reform: the period of decline to the 1880's, and the rapid growth since the 1880's and in particular since the 1890's. We can accordingly discuss two stages of Russian economic policy in relation to Ukrainian industry.

At this point, we take the liberty of making a slight digression from the main subject in order to concentrate on the idea of colonial dependence. The concept of colonies, as we know, is given various meanings, especially with reference to conditions in industry. We make this digression, however, not to refute various extreme concepts, nor to lecture on the subject. This work is an analysis of Russian-Ukrainian relations, in the economic sphere, during the time of Tsarism. The subsequent, second part of this work is devoted to Ukraine's position under Communist Moscow. The latter professes to be continuously fighting against colonialism. The main emphasis of Moscow's foreign policy is upon this point, particularly in the recent, post-war period. Much space in Soviet works on politics and economics is devoted to colonialism. They all refer to countries of Asia and Africa which, until recently, had been colonies of western empires, or remain even now in some relation of dependence.

There was a time, however, prior to the seizure of power by the Communists in Russia, when they similarly evaluated the position of nations conquered by Russia: Ukraine, Turkestan, Georgia, etc., defining the position as colonial. In support of this, they cited in the literature of that and of the subsequent period, definitions of the very concept of colonialism and of those manifestations which determine the position of one or another country as being in the category of a colony. These definitions provide in general a fairly accurate definition of the concept of a colony. Therefore, our object being to shed further light on the colonial nature of Ukraine's economy of that period, we believe it would be proper, before coming to the analysis of the position in the branch of industry, to state how a colonial nature of an economy is to be understood when confronted with it as understood by the Communists themselves. Then, in an analysis of the present position of Ukraine, we shall only have to continue to stay with those definitions which the Communists themselves applied earlier to Ukraine as a colony of the Russian Empire.

We have done this advisedly in the chapter devoted to industry because development of industry in a country is most frequently the cause of a confusion of the real nature of the economy inasmuch as the center of attraction then becomes development as such, and its nature is ignored.

There are many authors who treat the rapid industrial development in Ukraine as proof of equality between Ukraine and Russia. The location of different forms of industry over the territory is, these say, the Empire, a result of a social division of labor within a single economic body. The high level of industry in Ukraine reached at the beginning of the 20th century is, in their opinion, higher than in many regions of Russia proper, and would of itself disprove the condition of colonial dependence of one economy upon the other. They would inject into the term "colony" a content applicable to that term in old times: of an industrially and culturally backward land whose economy is an annex to the economy of the metropolis, and the latter drawing products of consumption and raw material for its industry from the colony, and supplying it in turn with its manufactured goods.

Such an understanding of the term colony is correct when applied to relations between old Western European empires and their overseas possessions. But these relations changed as time went by, and the subsequent process of imperialist conquest of new terrains also assumed different forms. It is not surprising therefore, that two terms made their appearance in literature for the designation of colonies, i.e. colonies of the so-called "Asian" type and of the "European" type. The respective adjectives denoted not their geographic location, but a different form of economic dependence.

The direction of industrial development, not its level, is the determining characteristic of a colony of the modern type. In other words, whether the development of industry, its extent and form, is dictated by the interests of the metropolis, rather than the demands of the total complexion of a national economy. The main characteristic of a colonial condition is the enforced accumulation of a major part of the national income beyond the borders of the national economy.

The product of society is the result of the labor effort of the community, and ought to be used for the satisfaction of the needs of the particular society. There is the realization, however, that among such needs there is also the necessity of providing work for coming generations, and a drive to broaden the satisfaction of the needs of the present community. All parents have a natural desire to provide by their own labor an existence for their children, either in the form of giving them professional intelligence or skill, or in the form of creating new enterprises for them. These desires of each generation of parents accumulate in society and contribute toward the exclusion of a certain part of production from consumption, adding to the amount of accumulated capital goods.

Likewise in the satisfaction of their own needs, both of those that exist already, of those which are created by invention and the production of new articles of use, and to shield themselves from complications of all sorts, people try to restrict their everyday consumption, thus nearing these goals. In this case, also part of society's production is saved.

Therefore, the presence of a national reserve (production created in the process of society's labor, but excluded from direct consumption within the given productive circle, either for the purpose of increasing the tools of production, or increasing the satisfaction of personal needs) is a phenomenon common to every society. We have gone into these common tenets to recall matters logically connected with our study of Ukrainian economics.

We wish to emphasize, that by the term "national reserve" we mean part of the national product but do not identify it with the Marxist "surplus production." We reject the Marxist theory of "value of labor," already discarded by life, and the theory of "surplus value" emerging therefrom, as well as its understanding of surplus product.

In the process of creating values the market is, to a large extent, an independently acting factor, as is also the so-called "law of widening renovation of capital" of Marx, which is far from encompassing the entire process of industrial capital accumulation. In this, an essential part is played by that part of the national product which is created by excluding from current consumption of a part falling due to men as the equivalent of their labor. This is a conscious act on the part of man which is effected by means of personal savings, social undertakings (insurance, union funds, etc.), stock participation in enterprises and so forth. The significance of these kinds of sources for creation of capital can be observed from the fact that, in the United States, out of 240 billions of bank deposits, nearly one-half constitutes personal savings and communal funds.

Hence, in the given instance, we should not speak of the accumulations which are created within the process of production, but of that part of the entire national income which is excluded from consumption in the form of savings, profits or compulsory curtailment of consumption, and is not used up in the national economy.

This accumulation of a part of personal income takes place, during the very process of creating the given goods as a manufacturing profit, in the process of exchange as a commercial profit, in the form of savings of the community, and in the form of taxing the people to a greater extent than the expenditure budget requirements.

The disposition of these resources, and directing its location is the most distinct indication of the mutual relationship of two complexions of a national economy. Whenever these resources leave one national economy to join another, be it in greater or lesser degree, we have sufficient evidence to make a statement that there exists a colonial dependence of the former upon the latter, regardless of the degree of their industrial development.

In this instance there is a violation of the very root of human action which stimulates this exclusion of part of the national product from consumption in the interest of further development of the national community. All, or a major part of accumulation of this kind, then goes beyond the circle of this community's living organism, and this automatically creates a cleavage between the causal purpose of the phenomenon and its effect.

This acts with equal force upon all countries regardless of their degree of colonial dependence, be it, "Asian" or "European."

"All the confusion arises from the fact that it is considered the rule for a colony to be more backward than the metropolis, and that colonial policy is confined only to the 'exploitation of the colony's backward economy.' "[1]

"The shape of relations between a metropolis and colonies of a 'European type' is undoubtedly different from its relations with 'Asian type' colonies. Colonies of the 'Asian' and 'European' type are not separated by any insurmountable barrier. There are many transitional forms between the one and the other, and a 'European type' colony is merely a glimpse into the future of its 'Asian' counterpart, provided its economic development will continue to proceed on the basis of colonial dependence . . . The exportation of capital, being the most important form of exploitation of an economic terrain during periods of imperialism, by means of decomposition of pre-capitalist forms of the economy and favoring the development of the productive forces of a colony in capitalistic form, transforms such an 'Asian' colony into a 'European.' "[2]

Thus, any characteristic of the economy of Ukrainian industry cannot, by any means, be confined to a finding of its "stormy development" toward the end of the last, and the beginning of the present century, as is frequently done by those economists who deliberately refuse to consider the true nature of such development. They fail to consider the basic element: the draining of the national income which comprises the most essential feature in describing the position of Ukrainian industry, "because in relation to Ukraine, no other but a colonial policy was conducted, as a result of which surplus values were siphoned to go beyond the borders of the colony, and this started a general impoverishment of all classes."[3]

Let us take one facet which we shall consider in more detail: "The value of Ukraine's annual exports was 1,022,780 thousand gold rubles, and imports were valued at 647,900 thousand gold rubles. It is clear from these figures that the dragon

---

[1] M. Volobuyev, "Do problemy Ukrainskoyi ekonomiky" ("On the Problem of the Ukrainian Economy"), *Bolshevyk Ukrainy* (*The Ukrainian Bolshevik*), Kharkiv, 1928. Quoted from a reprint.
[2] *Ibid.*
[3] M. Slabchenko, *Materialy do ekonomichno-sotsialnoyi* . . ., p. 373.

of capital, which ventured into Ukraine, drained away into its centers, for the purpose of capitalist "accounting," an annual sum of 374,820 gold rubles, or the equivalent of the annual labor of 1,874,000 Ukrainian workers."[4]

"The matter becomes more clear when we compare the exchange of goods between Ukraine and all the lands of the former Empire. Ukraine delivered to different lands of the former Empire goods of the value of 551,760 thousand rubles which constituted 54% of Ukraine's total exports . . . All the lands of the former Empire exported to Ukraine—a total of 291,320 thousand rubles, or 45% of all imports of Ukraine . . . We have here therefore, a difference between exports and imports amounting to 260,440 thousand rubles, or 70% of the entire difference . . . In general, this difference can either be caused by the fact that 'foreign' capital dominated Ukraine, with the aid of which the Ukrainian worker was exploited, or by the fact that Ukraine was simply being robbed, as they say by 'highway robbery'; to pay for wars, or for borrowings for such wars, or for both. But one may state at the outset that in this case both foreign capital and highway robbery are of equal force."[5]

"This condition cannot under any circumstances be dimmed by the fact that the development of Ukrainian industry, as we later shall see, took place at the expense of Western European, and not Russian, capital. This did not change the nature of Ukrainian economic dependence upon Russia . . . There were wide discussions among us, as to whether Russia was a colonial land, or not, whether we had a colonial type of development, or not. They took into consideration that Russia was itself a colony for Western European capital. But they did not pay any attention to the other side of the question, that Russia itself is one of the greatest colonial states in the world . . . . Regarding the area of Russia's colonies, Russia held first place. . . . But if we understand the term 'colony' to mean what it means to all literate people, i.e. . . . such a land which serves the latter (metropolis) as a source of raw material, and in modern times as a place from which capital is exported . . . then all these lands (Siberia, Central Asia) appear as the most typical colonies."[6]

[4] S. Ostapenko, "Kapitalizm na Ukraini," p. 114.
[5] *Ibid.*, p. 207.
[6] M. Pokrovsky, *Marksizm i osobennosti istoricheskogo razvitya Rossiyi* (*Marxism and Peculiarities of Russia's Historical Development*), Moscow, 1923, p. 47.

The development of industry in Ukraine and the growth within Ukraine of productive forces, not only did not weaken her colonial dependence, but on the contrary, brought about an even deeper entrenchment of that dependence and a greater accentuation of differences existing between Ukraine and Russia. It could not be otherwise, as both the nature of this industrial development, its direction and its economic results, all this on the one hand, defined more clearly in the minds of the Ukrainian community the meaning of the national economy. On the other hand, it made that community feel the dependence on a will and interests alien to them. "The gigantic development of industry affected only the mining and smelting branch, which concentrated its enterprises in the Southern Left Bank region. Other branches of industry, first of all light and artisan industry, were far behind heavy industry, and were also far behind Russian industry of the same categories. The reason for this backwardness of Ukraine in this line of economic development was that Russian competition diligently guarded its colonial privileges in Ukraine from the mass consumer."[7]

This is the only criterion applicable to an analysis of the condition of Ukrainian industry, if we are to understand the nature of the telling contradictions which appeared in its development throughout the post-reform period. M. Volobuyev is right when he says: "The essence of the results of colonial dependence in the case of colonies of the European type lies primarily in a divergence of the development of productive forces in favor of the economy of the metropolis. For an analysis of the degree of colonial dependence of such a colony, the following elements are of importance: the level of development of manufacturing industry which indicates the extent to which the colony has left its position of raw material market for the industry of the metropolis, further (and this ties in directly with the aforesaid) such changes in the economic structure which imported capital brought with it (of special importance is the problem of what kind of capital was imported, in loan, or industrial investment form); of no less importance are data which indicate the direct, preying exploitation of the colony (even if it is only the equalization of imported and exported goods.)"[8]

---

[7] M. Yavorsky, *Ukraina v epokhu kapitalismu* (*Ukraine in the Era of Capitalism*), Odessa, 1924, III, 17-18.
[8] M. Volobuyev, *loc. cit.*

Volobuyev is also right in his statement that the particular form of colonial dependence which is understood under the connotation "European type" does not occur as a mutation following the prior "Asian" form, but is only its supplement or further stage. As a rule the old form keeps its place, and they both exist together. Ukraine is a prime example of this. Precisely all that is connected with the modern system of colonial relationships, i.e. investment of capital in the colony and the development of industry on the colony's territory, are characteristics of the economic position of Ukraine during the period of about twenty years before World War I. They related in the main to the mining and smelting industry. In all other respects that system of conditions was maintained and spread which combined to make for the political dependence of Ukraine on Russia during the entire period of such dependence and which basically had their origin in such political dependence.

Ukrainian Industry Within the System of Russian Industrial Capitalism

It has been stated in the introductory part of this work that from the time of the Treaty of Pereyaslav of 1654, Ukrainian industry, which at that time was far ahead of the Russian, was subjected to a ruthless political and economic oppression, not only by means of granting Russian industry and commerce a series of privileges, and imposing legal restrictions upon the Ukrainian, but also by means of direct destruction of Ukrainian industrial enterprises (e.g. the Pochep textile plant and others). The aim of Russian economic policy was not merely to shield their industry and commerce from dangerous Ukrainian competition, but also the transformation of Ukraine into a source of supply of raw material and a market absorbing their production. Simultaneously Ukraine was being turned into a market completely isolated from economic relations with the rest of the world, with which it heretofore had had ties by reason of its geographic position, natural resources, and historical economic development. The climatic moment of this isolation was the above mentioned tariff law of 1822 which virtually stopped the flow of any goods to Ukraine except Russian. Russian goods were not barred by any customs border, because with the loss of statehood in the form of the Hetmanate, and even earlier, Ukraine had been deprived of any tariff rights.

Up to the time of the land reform, which, as has been stated, signified the transition to modern forms of capitalist development, Ukraine did not, as a matter of fact possess any large industry of her own. Only in sugar-refining, distilling, milling and coal-mining were there enterprises of more or less considerable size. But we must remember that the process of centralized production, even in these enterprises, occurred at a later period. In addition we must note that a greater part of these enterprises were not owned by Ukrainians.

The basic form of industrial enterprise of that period was the *votchinna* factory, a factory owned by the landowner as part of his inherited estate. The "*votchinna* factory was based on its own raw material, it was many-sided, and used local serf labor." But even then "the city factory appeared as its competitor, having been established by an alien Russian or Jewish merchant-entrepreneur."[9]

During 1857 the average number of workers employed by an enterprise was: (regions of) Kiev, 107; Poltava, 93; Kharkiv, 148; Kherson, 70, and Chernihiv, 62. Considering the very low level of mechanization of that period, manual labor predominating, such numbers are indicative of a semi-artisan nature of these industrial enterprises. The value of goods produced attests to the same facts. In Volhynia the value was measured in the amount of 984 thousand rubles, which gave an average of 2.2 thousand rubles per enterprise, and corresponding figures for other regions are: Katerynoslav, 813 thousand and 10 thousand; Kiev, 4,107 thousand and 21.3 thousand; Podilla, 1,078 thousand and 5.3 thousand; Poltava, 671 thousand and 7.5 thousand Kherson, 806 thousand and 8.8 thousand; Kharkiv, 868 thousand and 6 thousand, and Chernihiv, 1,688 thousand and 8.5 thousand rubles.[10]

At that time the production of the factory industry of the entire Russian Empire reached 224,332 thousand rubles. Of that figure 116,769 thousand rubles or more than half, were contributed by four *gubernias*, Moscow, Petersburg, Volodimir and Perm.[11]

By the time of the land reform the value of this production grew considerably, but its concentration in the same regions

9 M. Slabchenko, *op. cit.*, p. 205.
10 *Ibid.*, p. 200.
11 *Statisticheskiye tablitsi Rossiyskoy imperiyi za* 1856 g. (*Statistical Tables of the Russian Empire for the Year, 1856*), St. Petersburg, p. 275.

did not change. According to data for 1865 and 1866, for example, out of the total value of the cotton industry's output of 72,104 thousand rubles, 70,800 thousand rubles, or more than 98%, came from the *gubernias* of: Ryazan, Moscow, Petersburg, Volodimir, Kaluga, Kostrom, Tversk, Yaroslavl, and only an insignificant percentage from Livonia and Estonia.[12]

In addition, in the *gubernias* around Moscow, a putting-out cotton industry was very widespread. It employed 350,000 workers while the factories themselves employed only 80,000. A similar concentration of industry in the Russian *gubernias* can be also observed in other branches, particularly those of a mass consumption nature. "Out of a total of 28,517 thousand rubles value of products of cotton goods, the *gubernias* of Volodimir, Moscow, Ryazan, Petersburg and Tversk contributed 28,036 thousand rubles, or more than 98%. Out of 46,137 rubles worth of woolen goods, 39,700 thousand rubles, or 88% came from the *gubernias* of Moscow, Grodno, Symbirsk, Kaluga, Petersburg, Penza, Tambovsk and Livonia, while Moscow *gubernia* alone accounted for 53%. Out of 13,815 thousand rubles worth of flax and hemp products, 11,956 thousand rubles or 86.5%, again came from the *gubernia* of Tversk, Volodimir, Yaroslavl, Kostrom, Vologda and Petersburg. Moreover, in the processing of flax there were, at that time, engaged in the same *gubernias*, in putting-out industries, 3 million spinners and 500,000 weavers. Out of a total of 3,736 thousand rubles' worth of silk goods, 3,645 thousand rubles, or 97.5%, fell to the Moscow and Petersburg *gubernias;* in gold-weaving goods of 2,090 thousand rubles worth, Moscow *gubernia* alone produced 2,039 thousand rubles worth, or 97.5%. Out of 3,267 thousand rubles worth of chemicals and dyestuffs, Petersburg and Moscow *gubernias* produced 1,957 thousand rubles or 60%. The machine building industry produced 16,571 thousand rubles worth of products and Petersburg alone participated to the extent of 13,292 thousand rubles, or 80%.[13] The same is noticeable in other branches of industry. Copper manufacturing plants were also centered in the Northern part of the Russian Empire, on Russian territories. More than half of the copper products came from the *gubernias* of Moscow, Petersburg, Tula and Volodimir.[14]

[12] *Sbornik Svedeniy i Materyalov Ministerstva Finansov za 1867 god. Yun' (Collection of Reports and Materials of the Ministry of Finance for the Year, June, 1867)*, St. Petersburg, pp. 381-398.
[13] N. Yasnopolsky, "Ekonomicheskaya buduchnost . .," p. 292.
[14] *Vyestnik Evropy (European News)*, St. Petersburg, Nov. 1870, p. 138.

Even such activities as processing tobacco and distilling spirits were better developed in the North than in the South. Out of 14.5 million rubles' worth of processed tobacco, 9 million rubles worth, or 62%, came from the *gubernias* of Moscow, Petersburg and Livonia. Similarly, out of a total of 6,771,394 barrels of spirits produced in the Empire in 1862-63, 4,045,000 barrels, or nearly 60% came from the *gubernias* of Petersburg, Moscow, Vilna, Grodno and Kaunas. (Some non-Russian *gubernias* are included here, such as Livonia, Vilna, etc, but the extent of their production, compared to that of the Moscow and Petersburg *gubernias,* was quite insignificant.)[15]

Such disproportion in the industrial development and industrial concentration, mainly in the central Russian regions, was by no means the result of natural conditions prevailing in these regions, of abundance of raw materials nor of sources of energy. It was all the result of a deliberately directed economic policy of the Imperial Government, according to which the "borderland" was destined to be the source of supply of raw material for Russian industry, and markets for Russian goods. This policy had its most vivid illustration in tariffs, details of which will be discussed later.

Ukraine played the role of one of the most important suppliers of raw material. As has already been stated, 88% of the woolen industry was located in central Russian *gubernias.* At the same time "out of a total of Spanish (fine wool) wool produced in the Empire, 21,667,800 pounds (cleaned), the South produced 14,986,885 pounds. This total amount of wool was allocated in the following manner: exports abroad, 36,113,000 pounds ;to Petersburg and Moscow, 10,300,544 pounds; to Bialystok, 3,791,865 pounds; to Riga, 1,986,215 pounds; to Minsk, 650,544 pounds; to Chernihiv, 1,986,215 pounds; to Kiev, 650,-034 pounds; to Podilla, 722,260 pounds; to Volhynia, 252,791 pounds. (The figures are for 1867.)[16] Thus only 25% of the wool produced in Ukraine remained in Ukraine, while Moscow and Petersburg received 70% of it.[17] During that year a total of 16,-106,398 pounds of all kinds of wool (Spanish and common) was exported from Black Sea and Azov Sea ports. Baltic ports sent

---

[15] Material taken from *Yezhegodnik ministerstva finansov* (*Annual Report of the Ministry of Finance*), St. Petersburg, 1869 (1st ed.), 3rd. dept.
[16] N. Yasnopolsky, *op. cit.,* pp. 281, 282. The weight unit used in the original is *poods,* translated into pounds at the rate of 36.113 pounds per *pood.* [17] *Ibid.,* pp. 281, 282.

4,947,481 pounds. "It must be noted that a major portion of the wool, hides, lard, and other goods which went abroad through Baltic ports, originated in the South of Russia." (The author quoted here means Ukraine for South Russia.) "Similarly, hides, over and above the quantity exported abroad, were directed to leather manufacturing plants of Moscow and of the central gubernias, and came back from there in the shape of a variety of manufactured leather goods . . . Also 1,805,650 pounds of high quality porcelain clay from Hlukhiv county went hither, out of which 90% of all porcelain goods of the Russian Empire were manufactured."[18]

A large portion of cotton arrived in the Black Sea ports of Ukraine, but not for the purpose of assuring a place for Ukrainian industry. With tremendous outlay for transportation, this cotton went to Russia, to return again to Ukraine in the form of expensive manufactured goods.

"To what extent this land (Ukraine) is poor in plants and factories, can be seen from the fact that in the Katerynoslav region in 1866 the total of locally produced goods amounted to 2 rubles, 71 kopecks per inhabitant," while the corresponding figure "for Petersburg *gubernia* was 51 rubles; for Moscow *gubernia*, 41 rubles, 47 kopecks, for Vladimir *gubernia*, 25 rubles, 25 kopecks."[19]

"It is evident that such a preponderance of the Russian light manufacturing industry over the Ukraine . . . delivered the Ukrainian market into the absolute power of Russian industrial capital, which could peacefully continue its colonial policy in Ukraine, a policy already existing since the 18th century, and introduced by Russian commercial capital . . . this proves unequivocally that Ukraine was as yet unable to satisfy her needs out of her own manufacturing industry, and was compelled to import manufactured goods from Russia." [20]

This was the position of Ukrainian industry after the abolition of serfdom, on the threshold of the era of industrial capitalism in the Russian Empire. Such disproportion could not go unnoticed, both in relation to the number of population (at that time the population of Ukraine was 22.6% of the Empire's entire population), and, what is even more important, in relation to her natural resources. It was a fact that even then, Ukraine

[18] *Ibid.*, p. 283.
[19] N. Yasnopolsky, *op. cit.*, p. 294.
[20] M. Yavorsky, *op. cit.*, p. 118.

had very good prospects of developing her coal-mining industry, being already an important supplier of coal.

"An abundance of cheap hard coal as fuel has, at all times and in all places, been of the highest importance to manufacturing. Therefore, naturally, a question arises: why should not the South now utilize this mineral wealth, and would it not be more profitable to process raw materials on the spot, which have heretofore been dispatched to a distance of thousands of miles."[21]

The opening of the Suez Canal in 1869 added to the economic importance of the Black Sea considerably, and made possible a wide scale development of Ukrainian industry, in accordance with the existing natural wealth. It is therefore not surprising that even people, whose ideas were entirely free from any thought of a partition of a single Russia, as for example, Professor Mykola Yasnopolsky, could not ignore the fact of the impoverishment of Ukraine which was the result of a deliberately directed economic policy of the Government. Guided by the thought of a rational organization of the state economy, and far from any admission of the colonial nature of the existing phenomena, Yasnopolsky began his work on the economic backwardness of the South with a paragraph which is worth quoting here in its entirety: "Until this time, the South of Russia constituted a land extraordinarily endowed by nature, but it lacks any improvements of civilization. Thus far the economic progress is disproportionately more marked in Northern Russia. There, since the time of Peter the Great, much energy has been spent to aid its development: canals were built, roads improved, credit institutions established, private enterprise was favored and helped, and finally in 1822, an uninterrupted development of factories was guaranteed. In brief, much was done of such nature as would influence the fortune of the North. A land without natural wealth, covered for the most part by forests, marshes and sand, with poor soil (it would be more appropriate to say: a land which neglected to develop its own wealth because of a more profitable exploitation of annexed lands—*Author*). It has become at the present time a factory for the far-flung Russian Empire, and for that reason, under a favorable tariff, capital from almost all parts of Russia began to flow there in the form of overpayment for products of the factories which could be brought from abroad for much less. Now an 80-million person

21 N. Yasnopolsky, *op. cit.*, p. 270.

114   *Ukraine and Russia*

market is surrounded by a tariff wall in the interests of the
manufacturing region, and the latter, it might be stated, developed at the expense of other regions of Russia. Our two capitals,
are located in ᵗhis region which, as capitals of a centralized
state, draw unto themselves the wealth of the most widely extended state in the world . . . But even for these successes our
industrial regions with both our capitals are to a great extent
indebted to other parts of widespread Russia. The agricultural
half of our state served, and continues to serve, as a provider
for the industrial region for both our capitals, and pays for it
by its backwardness in respect of its economy."²² Even M. V.
Wolf, who entirely rejected the thought of the existence of any
colonial conditions in Ukraine, was compelled to admit: "It
would be a great mistake to look for the causes of the development of the Central-industrial region (Moscow and adjacent
gubernias—Author) to its natural resources, i.e. to a wealth of
raw material and fuel. Local fuel and local raw material is used
by only an insignificant part of the industry of the land; the
most important manufacturing is dependent on imported fuel
and raw material. On first glance the metal divergence of the
industry of the Northwestern region (Petersburg) may appear
to be somewhat incomprehensible. Having neither iron, nor fuel
suitable for a metallurgical industry . . . the region was compelled to import both the metal, and the fuel, either from
abroad, or from the South and the Urals. Therefore, the development of a strong metallurgical industry in such a region may
appear to be irrational."²³

Wolf wishes to find in Moscow's central location a justification of the first region's development and in the second instance,
Petersburg, in the abundance of qualified labor. There were
also attempts to explain this phenomenon by the fact of the development of communications in these central regions. Regarding
the Moscow region, whose basic branch of industry is the textile, the statement with respect to its alleged central location
bears no relation to the truth either with regard to fuel or raw
material. As has already been stated, a large amount of cotton
went to Moscow from Black Sea ports, in transit through
Ukraine, a land of abundant fuel. Even in relation to Turkestan

²² *Ibid.*, p. 269.
²³ M. V. Wolf, *Geograficheskoye rozmyeskcheniye Russkoy promishlennosti* (Geographic Distribution of Russian Industry), Moscow, 1925,
p. 27.

cotton, Moscow cannot under any circumstances be called "centrally located."

Concentration and development of communications is not a factor of spontaneous appearance, only a consciously directed effort for the realization of a certain goal. Therefore, in this case, the basically important question is: why did the development of transportation take a direction safeguarding the interests of Moscow? The resulting influence of transportation upon industry can be moulded by adopting a certain course of policy.

The same goes for an abundance of industrial labor. This factor plays a role in the development of industry, but it does not appear as a gift of nature. It is only the result of the existence of industrial plants which teach the appropriate skills. Petersburg did not become an industrial center because it possessed cadres of qualified labor, but it had cadres of qualified labor because it was an industrial center. Therefore M. Volobuyev is right when he says: "The basis of the errors of those economists, as well as of many others, lies in a misunderstanding of the importance of the role which the colonial policy of Tsardom played in the geographical location of industry within the borders of Russia."[24]

An explanation of the causes of industrial development, like that of any other economic phenomenon, requires calculation and analysis of the whole gamut of factors which determined, favored, or hindered certain processes. A correct illustration of our theme, the nature of economic conditions in Ukraine and in Russia, requires an insight into the official course of the economic policy, into those norms of a legal nature which determined the direction of the economic process. Such economic policy reaches far beyond mere enforcement. It should embrace an appropriate direction of policies of tariffs, customs, money credit, market conditions, etc., which give rise to immutable economic impulses and create a certain economic climate, and most important, causes the absorption of the surplus production of the national income.

We shall be more detailed later. Here we shall only analyze the Government's tariff policy in relation to the textile industry in order to illustrate the catastrophic backwardness of Ukraine in industry during the period of the first decades following the land reform. We are considering this branch of industry not only

[24] M. Volobuyev, *op. cit.*

because Ukraine was the most backward in this branch, but also because the textile industry provides a product of mass consumption offering great opportunities for a colonial exploitation of the population.

"The customs tariff of 1822, proposed by Minister Kankrinin, introduced a system of protectionism. Very high import duties were imposed on foreign goods and many goods were prohibited entirely. Exports of products of the Empire were facilitated . . . The tariff of 1822 was very detrimental to the Ukrainian economy. Its first repercussions were upon Ukraine's foreign trade."[25]

Ukrainian protests were of no avail, because the precise object of the tariff act was to free Muscovite industry from foreign competition, to give it monopolistic privileges on the internal market and to facilitate the securing of excessive profits. The interest of that industry were looked upon as the interests of "the whole" which had to have a priority over "local interests." The *Komercheskaya Gazeta* editorialized in 1826: "Southern Russia complains about the prohibition of importing goods and about high tariffs. They say that nothing can be sold because we do not want to buy anything from foreigners, and that everything is either prohibited, or burdened with a customs duty in excess of any measure . . . Such complaints are of a local nature, which show a lack of understanding of the interests of the whole . . . Even the official organ of the Ministry of Finance had to admit that if the tariff of 1819 were restored . . . the ports of the Black Sea would certainly gain a great deal. A huge amount of goods would come here, commercial profits and the income of the population would be generally excellent in this case."[26]

But the Government was not concerned with the interests of Ukraine: certainly not at the expense of a loss of income from customs duties that were creating artificial conditions for the development of industry in central Russia. "The prohibitive system, introduced in Russia in 1822, awoke the national energy in almost all branches of factory, plant and trade industries and contributed to the establishment of many factories and plants; but the accomplishment was made at huge expense, on the one

25 O. Ohloblyn, "Problema Ukrains'koyi ekonomiky v naukoviy i hromadskiy dumtsi" ("The Problem of the Ukrainian Economy on Scientific and Community Thought"), *Chervony Shlakh (Red Path)*, Kharkiv, 1928, No. 9-10, p. 167.
26 *Ibid.*

hand of the Government, on the other, of the consumers; the whole state became, for a period of several decades, vassal of a certain number of industrialists. As a result of this, common and widely used goods were sold to the people at prices 60% to 100% in excess of normal for the benefit for the manufacturers."[27]

In and of itself, a protective tariff system is nothing unusual. It was applied by other states wishing to shield their undeveloped industry from ruthless competition. Hence we wish here to underline not the mere fact of a protective tariff, but of the peculiarity of its application. In the first place it strengthened an artificially created industrial center at the expense of an industrial development of other terrains which were more suitable. Under such conditions these non-Russian terrains were transformed into markets for compulsory consumption of the products of Russian industry, and the above mentioned 60% to 100% overcharges for these goods became nothing else but colonial exploitation. In the second place, the application of customs duties as a protective measure was of a unilateral nature. While prohibiting or hindering the importation of machines essential to the Ukrainian economy (e.g., farm machinery), the importation of weaving machines was entirely free of customs duties. What is more, not only in the act of 1822, but in its subsequent changes of 1847, 1850, 1857, 1868 and later, one principle was constantly adhered to, disproportionately high duties on ready textile goods (e.g. fine woolen cloth, 60%; medium, 100%, and coarse 200% *ad valorem*) and very low duties on raw material and semi-manufactured goods. Whenever the interests of two forms of industry clashed, spinning and weaving, of which the former was interested in high duties on yarn, and the latter, just the opposite in low duties, the Government would step in to protect both. During discussions on the tariff of 1850, the weaving industry demanded a lowering of the duty on yarn from 6.50 rubles per 36.11 pounds (1 *pood*) to 5.75 rubles, because, it was alleged, this duty, together with additional expenses, amounts to 8.50 rubles, equal to 50% of the value of the yarn. They wrote that "a continuation of this duty will benefit only a small number of spinners, because the Moscow spinners, who do not feel the competition of English yarn, will be able to raise the price of yarn as much as they please."[28] In their turn, the spinners wrote

[27] M. Sobolev, *Tamozhennaya politika Rossiyi (Russia's Customs Policy)*, Tomsk, 1911, p. 22.
[28] *Ibid.*, p. 39.

that they are not in a position to compete with England, where
yarn was half as cheap as in Russia. The State Council complied
with the request of the former, lowering the duty to 5 rubles
per pood, but compensated the latter by leaving unchanged the
duty on cotton at 25 kopecks per *pood,* against the wishes of the
Treasury which wanted it increased to 1 ruble, for the following reason: "As far as cotton is concerned, the Tariff Committee
thought it desirable to leave it untaxed by any duty; but due
to the fact that the duties on cotton constitute a considerable
item of the Treasury's income, it has agreed to leave the present
duty at 25 kopecks per *pood,* calling, however, the Government's attention to the desirability of, if not a complete abolition, then at least a reduction of the duty to 5 kopecks.[29] After
1863 cotton was, for a considerable time, entirely free of duty.
But such meticulously attentive attitude to industrial benefits
in the same textile industry is quite absent when it comes to
matters concerning Ukraine, because the objective was to deprive Ukraine of any influence upon the monopolistic rule of
Moscow over the textile market. As has been noted, at the beginning of the 19th century Ukraine was well advanced in fine-
wool sheep ranching, and was a large supplier of wool to Russia.
Wool, like cotton was taxed very lightly, and by the tariff of
1850 the duty on wool was reduced from 1.90 rubles to 20 kopecks which was a heavy blow to Ukrainian sheep ranching,
unable to compete with British exports of wool, mainly because
of the lack of communications. Nevertheless frequent endeavors
of Ukraine to have the duty on wool increased produced no
result. During discussions on the 1877 tariff act "representatives
of the Kharkiv corporations trading in wool indicated that the
fine-wool sheep ranching industry of Poltava, Kharkiv and Katerynoslav regions is at a standstill because of the considerable and
almost duty-free importation of foreign wool.[30] They requested
that the duty be increased to 3 rubles per *pood* and that the
importation of wool substitutes should be prohibited. The same
request was made by the Rural Economic Congress in Kharkiv
in 1874 and in Odessa in 1878. At a Congress held in Kharkiv in
1886, the regions of Poltava, Kharkiv, Katerynoslav, Tauria and
Kherson again requested that the duty be raised to 2.50 rubles
or even to 4 rubles, but Moscow was always against it. The
duty was raised only in the late 1880's but not out of considera-

[29] *Ibid.,* pp. 38 and 447.
[30] *Ibid.*

tion for the Ukrainian economy, only in the interests of the Treasury which was compelled to find a way out of the unfavorable trade balance. But by this time the Ukrainian fine-wool sheep ranching industry was already completely ruined.

Thus, the development of industry, in this case of the textile industry in the central Moscow region, was, from the very beginning, dictated by the interests of Russia as the metropolis, and based on the solid support of the Government, with a deliberate disregard and rejection of the interests of the so-called "borderlands." And in spite of the fact that this monopolistic situation on the internal market and the high prices of textiles caused losses to all consumers, the Russian consumers included, this was compensated for by the extension of the labor market, and by the fact that the accumulation of industrial and commercial profits went toward strengthening the Russian economy. On the other hand, Ukraine became from all this a real "vassal of Russian industry," giving up a large part of its national income for the benefit of its development.

Noteworthy are the motives expressed by the industrialists on the desirability of high duties on ready textiles during discussions on the tariff act of 1850. It was alleged that not only industrialists were interested in the development of this industry, but also the peasants, because they make wages on it. Therefore the protective policy is justified, because it is directed "in the interests of the textile industry, mainly the weaving industry, which employs hundreds of thousands of the peasant population without taking them away from their family life. Therefore it deserves a more favorable attitude on the part of the state than does the spinning industry."[31]

Concerning regions which had no textile industries, such as Ukraine, it was maintained that "the peasants of agricultural regions will not suffer from high prices on the internal market because they have no money, don't buy and wear home-spun clothes."[32]

The impoverishment and primitive life which came in the wake of colonial exploitation were treated as conditions which justified a further exploitation!

From the motives mentioned above we have been considering the textile industry in more detail, as a leading industry of the time and as most clearly illustrative of the colonial condi-

[31] *Ibid.*, p. 111.
[32] *Ibid.*, p. 150.

tions. But the same thing existed in other branches of industry. Until the end of the 19th century even at a time when foreign capital began to flow into Ukrainian industry freely, it was incomparably weaker than the Russian. And as of old, the Ukrainian market was under the complete domination of Russian industry.

"In the Ukrainian economy of the period following the reform, we were able to note a continued growth and strengthening of the dominant position of the Russian manufacturing industry. In *Table L* are telling data, illustrating this dominant position (the figures refer to the year 1904).

(The total of consumption goods is missing from the column referring to Russia. We have computed it as the result of the difference between the sum total and the addition of single items in the table.)

The first thing that strikes us upon closer analysis of the above table is the conspicuously unilateral development of industry. Processing of consumption goods constitutes 66.1% of Ukraine's total industrial production, and together with metallurgy, mining and processing of minerals, 88%. All other branches of industry add up to only 12% of the total, and some, like textiles, chemicals, processing of animal products are virtually lacking. Every national economy is characterized by a comprehensive industrial development. One or another branch of industry may be lacking, because its development would, due to natural conditions, be unprofitable, but we never encounter a normal situation where only two or three branches of industry would prosper, and in all other respects a national economy would make itself dependent upon an outside economic body. Such a situation gravely contradicts the economic interests of a national community and can only exist under circumstances wherein these interests are subject to some other interests, whenever in other words, an economic system is merely an adjunct of another, dominant system. It is the most convincing sign of a colonial position.

For a better illustration of this disproportionate development of industry, we give in *Table LI*, another variation of the previous table, i.e. a compilation of the relative importance of each branch of industry in Ukraine and in Russia.

It must be noted, for a proper evaluation of the above table, that although in the manufacture of cotton goods both Ukraine

TABLE L

Branch of Industry	Number of enterprises			Production total in thousand rubles		
	Ukraine	Russia	% Ukraine	Ukraine	Russia	% Ukraine
Manufacturing of cotton	13	986	1.3	475.0	928,496.6	0.5
Manufacturing of wool	48	1,037	4.6	9,461.3	225,346.7	4.2
Manufacturing of silk	..	277	0.0	......	34,549.4	0.0
Manufacturing of linen-hemp	40	175	22.8	6,567.7	93,491.4	7.0
Manufacturing of other textiles	28	384	7.3	733.6	49,632.5	1.5
Paper manufacturing	232	1,333	17.4	11,389.4	128,889.3	9.0
Mechanical woodworking	290	1,900	15.3	10,604.3	119,510.9	8.9
Metal working shops and machine building ..	197	916	21.5	60,442.6	347,371.3	17.4
Repair shops	59	323	18.2	1,388.5	13,644.3	10.1
Other metal manufacturing	86	712	12.1	5,010.8	67,345.8	7.3
Railroad shops	36	176	20.4	22,543.4	71,466.4	31.6
Shipbuilding yards	6	17	35.2	451.6	43,800.3	10.3
Manufacturing of minerals	278	1,521	18.3	15,600.6	97,726.0	16.0
Manufacturing industry of mining products.....	13	186	7.0	84,483.7	214,841.5	39.4
Processing of animal products	91	1,153	7.9	11,035.6	159,241.5	6.9
Processing of consumption goods under internal tax	1,968	7,948	24.8	503,482.2	1,515,513.3	33.3
Chemical industry	80	801	10.0	18,514.6	387,812.6	4.8
TOTALS:	3,465	19,845	17.4	762,184.9	4,498,679.8	16.9

[33] M. Volobuyev, loc. cit.

TABLE LI

Relative Importance of Branches of Industry

Branch of industry	% Ukraine	% Russia
Manufacturing of cotton goods	0.05	20.6
Manufacturing of woolen goods	1.2	5.0
Manufacturing of silk goods	0.0	0.8
Manufacturing of linen-hemp	0.9	2.1
Manufacturing of other textiles	0.1	1.1
Paper manufacturing	1.5	2.8
Mechanical woodworking	1.4	2.9
Metal working and machine building	7.9	7.7
Repair shops	0.2	0.3
Other metal manufacturing	0.7	1.5
Railroad shops	3.0	1.6
Shipbuilding	0.05	1.0
Processing of minerals	2.0	2.0
Processing of mining products	11.1	4.8
Processing of animal products	1.4	3.5
Processing of consumption goods	66.1	33.7
Chemical industry	2.4	8.6
	100.0	100.0

and Russia lacked their own raw material yet in relation to sources of supply (Egypt, India) Ukraine was situated closer and in direct contact by sea. We must not look therefore to natural conditions to find an answer to the query why Ukraine's cotton industry was 412 times smaller than Russia's. The same applies to the four times smaller wool manufacturing industry which is absolutely unjustified when we consider that Ukraine was a large supplier of wool both to Russia, and to foreign lands. Even the equal figures in such an industry as metal working are not normal, because, at that time Ukraine was supplying 57.2% of all the ore extracted in the Empire, and the Urals only 20.8%. In the production of pig iron Ukraine stood at 52%, in ready iron and steel, 44.7% against the Urals' 22.4%. Coming back to the indices of the totals of production we must not overlook the fact that the total production of Ukraine amounted to only 16.9% of the Russian Empire (see table on p. 189), at a time when the population of Ukraine was 22.6% of the Empire's total, and 40% of the population of Russia. The figure of 16.9% is only due to the large extent to which Ukraine participated in the processing of food products. Without that item the participation of Ukraine would fall to a mere 8.7%.

Let us consider the food processing industry of Ukraine. Out of the wide variety possible in this line, Ukraine had only three comparatively strong industries: sugar refining, milling,

and distilling. All other industries, even those like tobacco processing and wine making for which Ukraine possessed ample
raw material, were very insignificant. Out of the three territorial
parts into which the Ministry of Commerce and Industry divided
Ukraine-Southern agricultural, agricultural industrial, and mining industrial (a division which did not exactly correspond to
the borders of Ukraine), only two were really producers of
food products. In the third, food accounted for only 9.1% of its
total industry. The other two above mentioned parts produced
87% of all processed food and 68% of the sugar.[34]

Thus, the above mentioned figure of 503 million rubles for
the food processing industry in Ukraine creates an imaginary
conception of a high stage of development of that industry when
in fact over two-thirds of that figure applies to the sugar refining industry. On the contrary, on closer analysis, the low level
of the development of the food processing industry becomes
obvious, and in any event is nowhere near the natural possibilities. If we consider only the agricultural-industrial part which
takes in the regions of Kharkiv, Chernihiv, Kiev, Podilla and
Poltava, regions with the highest level of that industry (329
million rubles out of a total of 401 million of all industrial products of the regions, or 82%), then the division according to
branches of production is characterized by the figures of values
and percentages in *Table LII.*

TABLE LII

Branches of industry	Thousands of rubles	%
Sugar refineries	237,121	72.0
Milling	47,679	14.4
Distilling	18,441	5.5
Tobacco	11,729	3.6
Oil pressing	2,944	0.9
Confectioneries	2,514	0.8
Grits and cereals	1,991	0.6
Baking	1,754	0.5
Sausage-making	732	0.23
Distilling-cordials	247	0.07
Slaughterhouses	196	0.06
Starches-molasses	156	0.05
Cooling drinks	125	0.04
Others, not specified	4,250	1.25
TOTAL	329,405	100.0

[35]

---

[34] Minister Torgovli i Promyshlennosti (Minister of Commerce and Industry), *Torgovla i promyshlennost Yevropeyskloy Rossiyi po rayonam*
(*Commerce and Industry of European Russia by Districts*), St. Petersburg, 1912, VIII-XII, pp. vii-17.
[35] *Ibid.*, pp. x-16.

As we can see from the above, all industrial enterprises with the exception of the first four categories produced such insignificant amounts and participated in such small fractions of percentages that one should rather speak of their absence than presence. The one indisputable fact is that the sugar refining industry of Ukraine was highly developed, but its growth did not come about without many obstacles created by the nature of economic relations with Russia.

The Sugar Industry

The concentration of the sugar-refining industry in Ukraine was caused primarily by factors of an objective nature, the main one being that the transportation of sugar-beets over long distances is economically unprofitable. This industry is in the category of localized industries where the raw material is processed at the place of its production. The geographic line of sugar-beet cultivation almost coincides with the Northern border of Ukraine, encompassing Southern parts of Russia's Voronizh and Kursk *gubernias*. Farther north, the beet loses its percentage of sugar. In Ukraine, one *desiatyna* under beet cultivation gave 971.4 pounds of sugar, against 657.2 pounds from neighboring regions of Russia. One *berkovets* of beets, between 356 and 396 pounds, yielded 13.72 pounds of sugar in Ukraine, and 10.29 pounds in Russia.

It would seem that such favorable natural conditions in Ukraine should have precluded any doubts as to the desirability of concentrating the sugar refining industry in Ukraine. But such was not the case and Ukraine had to exert itself to secure a position of primacy, and still this industry, as opposed to the textile industry of Russia, experienced severe handicaps. When the pharmacist Bindheim originally proposed, in 1800, that a sugar industry should be organized, the Emperor Paul I favored it and began to endow his favorites with land for the purpose. But the first refinery did not become established until after the Napoleonic Wars, in the 1820's. From that time on, refineries began to appear at a fast pace, but in South Russia, not Ukraine. The first sugar refinery in Ukraine was established in the Kiev region in 1827. By 1840 there were eight of them in the Kiev region and about forty-five in all of Ukraine, less than one-third of the number in the whole Russian Empire. Nevertheless, favorable conditions gave Ukraine so much superiority that the industry's rate of development always kept ahead of Russia. By 1852, Ukraine had 229 sugar refineries, half the Empire's total. Subsequently, beginning with the 1880's, the growth of this industry in Ukraine took the shape not so much of an increase in the number of establishments as an increase of their productivity. In some localities there was even a decline in the number of refineries. For example, in Sumy county near Kharkiv, there were half as many refineries in 1880 as in 1859, but the production of sugar had risen nine-fold. On the eve of World War I, compared with 1890, production of sugar increased 2.5 times, and the number of plants by only 29%. According to average production figures per refinery, Ukraine occupied first place among all countries of Europe. In Ukraine one refinery produced 16,034,172 pounds; in Austria-Hungary, 11,556,460 pounds; in Russia, 9,281,041 pounds; in Poland, 8,883,798 pounds; in Germany, 8,739,346 pounds; in Belgium, 6,536,453 pounds, and in France, 4,478,012 pounds.[36]

And although Ukraine had at that time only 62% of all the refineries of the Empire, 75.8% of sugar beet cultivation and 68.4% of the industry's employees, Ukraine produced seven times as much sugar as Russia, together with Russia's part of Poland (the Kingdom of Poland). According to the amount of sugar produced, Ukraine occupied, in 1910-1911, second place among all the capitalist countries of the world: (in millions of pounds). For data, see *Table LIII.*

TABLE LIII

Country	1900-01	1905-06	1910-11
Germany	3,914,649	4,745,248	4,037,437
Ukraine	1,487,855	1,563,696	3,690,748
Austria-Hungary	2,148,723	2,964,877	2,470,129
France	2,181,225	2,134,278	1,592,583
U.S.A.	325,017	624,755	1,000,330
Belgium	635,588	650,034	491,137
Poland	249,179	332,239	444,190
Holland	343,907	408,077	386,409
Switzerland	227,512	241,957	249,179
Spain	......	180,565	234,734
Italy	......	162,508	166,120
Denmark	101,116	133,618	130,006
Russia	25,279	25,279	86,671

[37]

[36] S. Ostapenko, *op. cit.*, p. 197.
[37] *Ibid.*, p. 199.

During 1914-15 Ukraine had 241 sugar refineries, 731 thousand *desiatynas* of land under sugar beet cultivation and produced 3,900,212 million pounds of sugar.

We have considered the development of the Ukrainian sugar refining industry at considerable length in order to emphasize the great opportunities which Ukraine had for an all-round growth of this industry. The opportunities were far from realization because "it can be stated with certainty that with the development of electric power near the Dnipro rapids, at least half of the agricultural activities could be turned to the sugar industry."[38]

Neither can we underestimate the tremendous importance of this industry as one of the most important labor markets for the Ukrainian peasants, who always felt a need for employment. Nor can we lose sight of the fact that sugar beet cultivation contributed to significant changes in the agricultural economy of the villages. The industrial cultivation of sugar beets necessitated a break with the conservative and backward three-field system, greatly increased the amount of labor per unit of land and thus the income from land, aided in the cleaning of fields of weeds, contributing to its fertility, and finally it created a fodder basis for the development of productive animal husbandry.

These circumstances make it obvious that the Ukrainian interests demanded the widest possible development of opportunities and special considerations. But Russia's approach to the matter was entirely different.

When the idea of centralizing this industry in Russian regions encountered defeat because of the unsurpassed natural conditions in Ukraine, and when it became quite clear that in this branch priority would have to be conceded to Ukraine, Russia transformed this industry into a source of her enrichment and put it in the service of her interests. First of all, Russia put sugar, an article of universal consumption, into the category of goods subject to excise taxes, like spirits, tobacco, etc. "The Moscow Government held a really heavy hand on this department. In 1881 the excise tax on sugar was established at 50 kopecks per 1 *pood* (36.113 pounds); in 1884, 60 kopecks; in 1885, 75 kopecks; in 1890, 1 ruble and in 1895, 1 ruble, 75 kopecks. During the fiscal year 1911-12, the Moscow Government collected

[38] *Ibid.*, p. 195.

131.8 million rubles in excise taxes on sugar, plus seven million
in the form of a direct, so-called industrial tax."[39]

The excise tax was over 40% of the sale price. But the problem cannot be confined merely to this burden. It had far-reaching economic consequences: the high price of sugar, by reason
of the tax burden, narrowed the internal consumer market considerably, and in this manner sugar was artificially compelled
to become an export article. The Government was interested
in this phase, desiring a favorable foreign trade balance. Although the population of Ukraine increased its consumption of
sugar somewhat, Ukraine remained in second place in production and in last place in consumption. Producing over 3.5 billion pounds of sugar, the Ukrainian peasants were deprived
of an opportunity of consuming it. The average annual consumption of sugar per capita in Ukraine in 1850 was 2.2 pounds; in
1887, 7.5 pounds, and in 1914, 17.7 pounds, while figures for
the corresponding years for other countries were: England,
100 pounds, U.S.A., 97 pounds; Denmark, 89 pounds; Germany,
50 pounds, etc. "If that excise tax were taken off, then the price
of Ukrainian sugar at home would be 6 to 7 kopecks per pound,
that is, it would be sold . . . at the same price at which Ukrainian sugar was sold abroad."[40]

Pursuant to a 10-year Russo-German trade agreement of
1904, concluded during the Russo-Japanese war, Ukrainian
sugar was exported to Germany at 5 kopecks per pound, and
Germany, the largest producer of sugar in Europe, considered
it profitable to import that sugar as feed for hogs!

But the excise tax was not the end of the subjection of the
Ukrainian sugar refining industry to the interests of Russia. A
customs policy also exerted its influence, aimed at favoring an
artificially created refining industry in Petersburg, and partially
Moscow.

It has been noted before that Moscow, and in a larger measure Petersburg, without possessing any natural requirements
for it, developed a sugar refining industry. Moscow received
the necessary raw material, semi-refined sugar, mainly from
Ukraine, especially after the construction of the Kursk-Kiev
railroad which connected Moscow with mass producing sugar
regions of Ukraine. Petersburg's refining industry was based on
colonial white and yellow cane sugar mainly imported from

[39] *Ibid.*, p. 197.   [40] *Ibid.*, p. 198.

England. This situation determined the position of the Government with respect to imposing a duty on imported sugar. The Petersburg refineries were interested in getting the imported raw material duty-free, and exerted pressure upon the Government. It openly admitted that otherwise it would not be able to compete with Ukraine. The Moscow refining industry was also interested, although it ran in the main on semi-refined Ukrainian sugar, because it created a convenient position under which it could depress prices, bringing out the threat of competing prices of English sugar which came in through Baltic ports.

The Ukrainian sugar refining industry suffered from the fact that the customs policy favored the interests of these Russian refineries by cutting off the path of Ukrainian sugar northward and placing Ukraine in an awkward position in exports of sugar.

In 1849, the importation of raw sugar was permitted under a duty of 3.80 rubles, while refined sugar was under a prohibitive tariff. When the Committee of Customs Tariffs spoke in favor of permitting the importation of refined sugar, arguing that refineries were concentrated exclusively in Petersburg and that the population was suffering because of high prices for sugar, the Ministry of the Treasury expressed itself against the proposition, and defended the interests of the Petersburg refiners. It stated that "the refining industry aids many branches of industry connected with it."[41]

The problem of customs duties came under discussion many times, always with the object of a further reduction in order to aid Petersburg refineries. The motive was not only to permit them to continue taking profits, but also to facilitate their competition with the Ukrainian industry and no secret was made of it. "Here the contradictory interests of Southern owners of sugar refineries and Northern refiners clashed."[42]

The Government wished to hinder rapid development of the Ukrainian sugar industry. In 1854 the Minister of Finance introduced in the State Council a project of reducing the duty on raw sugar . . . "The arguments for such a reduction ran thus: 1) A noticeable decline in imports of raw sugar; 2) An excessive growth of the sugar industry in Russia (what was meant was Ukraine—*Author*); 3) The extraordinary growth of the sugar beet industry causes an apprehension that imports of foreign sugar

[41] M. Sobolev, *op. cit.*, p. 29.   [42] M. Sobolev, *op. cit.*, p. 98.

will fail off further, and might stop entirely." The Minister of Finance believed that the existing high import duty on colonial (imported) raw sugar was entirely unnecessary for the protection of the Russian (i.e. Ukrainian—*Author*) sugar industry," because "under the existing duty the refiners of the Northern *gubernias* pay 7.55 rubles for sugar (*per pood* or 36.113 pounds) and refined sugar is sold locally for 9 rubles per *pood*. Therefore the refiners get for their cost of refining, labor and interest on capital only 1.45 rubles per *pood*. At the same time Southern refiners who make the end product from their own material, which costs them, including the excise tax 3.30 rubles, therefore selling the refined product locally at 8 rubles leaves them 4.70 rubles. Under such circumstances the northern refiners will not be able to stand up against the southern." Therefore, they argued "by making the colonial (imported) raw sugar cheaper, the excessive development of the sugar beet industry could be halted."[43]

This makes it clear how different the tariff policy in relation to the Russian textile industry was from that policy in relation to the Ukrainian sugar industry. In order to benefit the artificially created and economically unprofitable refining plants of the North, the order of the day was, by application of a customs policy, to hinder the further development of the Ukrainian industry, and to prevent Ukrainian sugar from capturing the internal market. "Thanks to it (customs policy), northern refiners will be in a position to compete at least partially with those of the South in marketing sugar in the central *gubernias*."[44]

The Minister of Finance, set on accomplishing this did not hesitate to violate the basic principle of the Russian customs policy, i.e. its fiscal nature. Out of a total income from customs duties in 1852, 48.2 million rubles, the duty on sugar amounted to 7 million and was the largest single item among all others. After the tariff was reduced, this item fell to 2.7 million for 1856.

Such policy quite understandably produced an appropriate reaction on the part of Ukrainian industrialists. At the request of 23 owners of refining plants, the Kiev Governor Prince Vasilchikov sent a protest, demanding a change of attitude toward the interests of Ukrainian industry. He wrote: "The sugar industry requires much capital, proper knowledge and labor; in addition it provides work for the rural population, and the cul-

[43] M. Sobolev, *op. cit.*, pp. 86-87.   [44] *Ibid.*

tivation of sugar beets, which aids new industries, is extraordinarily profitable to the land." Polish sugar refiners also wrote that the tariff support of Petersburg refiners who run their plants on imported raw sugar is without merit, inasmuch as such plants "cannot hope to prosper because of the fact that the home industry has advanced so much that competition with it cannot succeed."[45]

The figures of the Minister of Finance were also proved wrong: refined sugar sold in Petersburg in 1856 not for 9 rubles, but for 12.80, and the manufacturers' cost of sugar in Ukraine was not 3.30 rubles, only 4.71 rubles and the refined product sold for 8 rubles. But the protests were of no avail: the duty on foreign raw sugar was reduced many times. Even at a time when the tariff policy of the Government in the 'seventies and 'nineties embarked upon a path of a general increase of duties, raw sugar, like other industrial raw materials, was affected only in a reduced proportion.

If Ukrainian sugar was finally able to win, and largely pushed foreign sugar off the market, it was only because of high profitability. But even then, at the cost of special railroad rates, the Petersburg and Moscow refineries were kept alive. Ukraine sugar was hauled almost 1200 miles, in order to return to internal Russian markets and, partially, to Ukraine.

The fight for the subjection of the Ukrainian sugar industry to the interests of the metropolis did not end with this. As has been noted, this industry became a source of considerable income to the treasury by way of huge excise taxes collected on sugar, and it contributed to foreign exchange balances through exports. Subsequently, as we shall indicate, the Ukrainian sugar industry itself was taken over by Russia through banking cartels.

We thought it worth-while to dwell on this phase of Ukrainian industry a little longer and dispell many impressions such as: the large amount of "processed food products," 503 million rubles, of which sugar constituted the major part, are proof that industrial development went on in accordance with the true interests of Ukraine, and in this matter no colonial dependence of Ukraine is noticeable. As we have seen, even in this branch of industry, given Ukraine by nature itself, there was no freedom from Russian subjugation.

To study other branches of this industrial group would be to repeat the same story: oppressive excise taxes; Ukraine's interests ignored in tariff policies; obstacles on the internal market, etc. Thus, for example, the well developed distilling industry was much hindered by the law *O piteynom sbore* (*Alcoholic Beverage Tax*). As a result of this law, the number of distilleries in Northern Ukraine declined between 1863 and 1883 from 180 to 52.[46] In the regions of Kiev, Poltava and Katerynoslav there were 887 distilleries in 1863 with a production of 4.2 million barrels of spirits; in 1864, only 678 distilleries with a production of 3.4 million barrels; and in 1866, 499 distilleries with 2.7 million barrels.[47]

The only reason this industry did not fail, and by means of increasing production per plant still gave a considerable output, was that the price of potatoes and grain was extremely low locally, and processing them into alcohol was still profitable. But here too, the main profit went into the treasury as excise tax. In 1913 Ukraine paid into the state treasury 182.7 million rubles in excise taxes on spirits.[48]

Low duties on wines, imported from Hungary and Greece hindered the development of Ukrainian viniculture, and the treasury did not wish to part with the income from this source in order to favor the Ukrainian economy. The same can be said of tobacco of which Ukraine was a major raw-stage supplier though processing was done in Petersburg.

The Coal Industry

Different conditions developed in the coal-mining, metallurgical and metal working industries. The factors contributing to the situation were many, but the most decisive of them were: 1) Huge natural deposits of coal and iron ore, easily and conveniently extractable. [Coal deposits of the Donbas are estimated at over 6.5 billion tons suitable for coking. Iron ore deposits of Kryvyi Rih are estimated at 56 million tons (recently revised to 1.5 billion tons) of 50% to 62% iron content, and of Kerch at 175 million tons of 35% to 45% iron content. Deposits of manganese ore in the Nikopol region are estimated at 500 million tons of a 35% to 48% manganese content.][49] 2.) The fact that these large

46 M. Slabchenko, *op. cit.*, p. 191.   47 N. Yasnopolsky, *op. cit.*, II, 74.
48 S. Ostapenko, *op. cit.*, p. 193.
49 *Bolshaya Sovietskaya Entsiklopediya* (*Great Soviet Encyclopedia*), Vol. 55, 1947. Title: Ukrainian Soviet Socialist Republic. Also Feshchenko-Chopivsky, *op. cit.*, and P. Fomin, *op. cit.*

iron ore deposits in Ukraine were discovered at a late date. 3) Russia's protracted lack of interest in Ukrainian coal due to a complete lack of rail communications, the isolation of the coal fields from the sea and a narrowly limited market for coal. 4) A sudden change of this attitude toward both coal and iron when Russian began large railroad construction. 5) Tariff policies of the Russian Government aimed at protecting the Russian metallurgical and metal working industries. 6) The Ukrainian population's acute need for employment, and the consequential cheap labor and acquiescence of the workers to the most primitive standard of living.

During the last decades of the 19th century, as a result of these influences, Russian and Ukrainian capital, active in the development of the Ukrainian coal industry, was joined by a third force, foreign capital, which contributed to a special system of economic conditions in this branch of industry. But notwithstanding the stormy growth of industry since that period, Ukraine did not come out of colonialism, and now the consolidated and organically related Russian-foreign factor became the proponent of colonial exploitation. By its influence it penetrated into other branches of industry, as well as into transportation, administration of municipalities, etc.

Although coal deposits were known to exist in the Donets basin early in the 18th century, yet until the late 19th century, the extraction of coal was in the nature of a semi-trade. Even in 1840 the amount of coal mined equalled only 4,000 tons. By 1855 it was 72,000 tons, and in 1860, 96,000 tons. After 1870 coal mining developed very rapidly, and along with it the participation of Ukraine in the total amount of coal mined in the Russian Empire.

The dynamics of that increase are shown in *Table LIV*.

The great jump in coal mining made in the 1870's (from 240 thousand tons to 1,376 thousand tons per year within ten years) was connected with the possibility of the coal mining industry supplying the Black Sea shipping with coal. For that reason the amount of anthracite, which was the grade preferred by steamships, accounted for more than 50% of all the coal mined. But within a few years prospects of supplying shipping dwindled because of British competition. An important factor in this connection was the fact that prohibitive tariffs caused exports from Black Sea ports to be much higher than imports

TABLE LIV

The figures, stated in original sources in millions of poods, have been converted into tons at the rate of 1,000,000 poods = 16,000 tons. The figures are in thousands of tons.

Year	Ukraine	Poland Dombrova basin	Ural	Moscow region	Caucasus	Turkestan	West Siberia	East Siberia	Total	Percent Ukraine
1885	1,838.4	1,748.8	174.4	340.8	3.2	6.4	38.4	8.0	4,158.4	44.1
1890	2,931.2	2,412.0	242.2	208.8	9.6	4.8	19.2	14.4	5,842.2	50.0
1895	4,601.8	3,596.8	281.6	163.2	17.6	8.0	22.4	19.2	8,710.6	53.7
1900	10,749.2	4,028.8	363.2	281.6	62.4	9.6	150.4	137.6	15,782.8	68.2
1905	12,564.8	3,483.2	481.6	209.6	28.8	38.4	428.8	1,001.6	18,236.8	69.1
1910	16,300.8	5,451.2	688.0	222.4	48.0	54.4	505.6	1,076.8	24,347.2	67.1
1912	20,347.2	6,312.0	920.0	220.8	68.8	96.0	691.2	1,289.6	29,945.6	68.6 [50]
1913	24,700.8	6,820.8	1,176.0	292.6	70.4	134.4	857.8	1,147.2	35,200.0	70.3
1914	26,940.8	3,697.6	1,347.2	320.0	65.6	150.4	968.0	1,320.0	34,809.6	77.4
1915	26,025.6	....	1,259.2	433.6	60.8	164.8	1,251.2	1,294.4	30,489.6	85.4
1916	27,816.0	....	1,268.8	676.8	57.6	196.8	1,257.6	....	....	... [51]

[50] D. Shary (ed.), Statistichesky Yezhegodnik na 1914 god (Statistical Yearbook for 1914), St. Petersburg, p. 147.
[51] M. Golman, "Russkiy Imperyalizm" ("Russian Imperialism"), Priboy (The Surf), Leningrad, 1926, p. 444.

into them, and for that reason foreign ships arrived empty at
these ports with coal for ballast. Ukrainian coal at that time,
was deprived entirely of rail lines, had very sparse connection
with the seaboard, and suffered high railroad tariffs. Under
such circumstances, Ukraine could obviously not successfully
compete. The largest shipping concern in the Black Sea "Russ-
koye Obshchestvo Parokhodstva i Torgovli" (ROPIT) used
55,344 tons of British coal and only 10,656 tons of Ukrainian
coal in 1878, and the corresponding figures for 1880 were:
51,492 tons and 22,768 tons.

Under conditions of very limited home consumption of coal,
there being then no Ukrainian metallurgical industry, and weak-
ly developed rail communications (the railroads would not only
aid in widening the market, but would themselves become a
large consumer), the Ukrainian hard coal mining industry was
faced with a serious crisis in the late 1870's. There was a catastrophic decline of prices, and coal fell from 7.32 rubles per ton
to 1.22 rubles. Large stocks piled up at the mineheads with no
customers in prospect. In seeking a way out of this impasse, the
Ukrainian coal industrialists faced two basic problems: either
to lower railroad tariffs within Ukraine and in the direction of
the seaports, or, in view of the light demand for coal on the
part of Ukrainian industry, to push coal into the industrial centers of Russia. But the latter way out faced the obstacle of imports from abroad. In 1876 a special railroad tariff rate applicable to coal was introduced which was openly contrary to
the interests of Ukrainian industry. "The coal industrialists
urged lowering railroad rates within the state. The railroad
tariff was set up in the interests of Russian plants. Analyzing the tariff of 1876 one can easily see that for example in the
Southern sector of the Kozlov-Voronizh-Rostov railroad, from
Shakhty to Rostov (in the direction of the Oziv Sea) the charge
per *pood-verst* was one-thirty-sixth of 1 kopeck, while in the
Northern sector of the same railroad (in the direction of Moscow) the *pood-verst* charge was only one-sixty-first of 1 kopeck.
. . . Even if we take the rate to be one-fortieth to one-sixtyieth
kopeck, still the coal industrialists would have to lose against
English coal which went to Moscow and the Moscow industrial
region at the freight rate of one-seventh of 1 kopeck per *pood-
verst.*"[52]

[52] M. Slabchenko, *op. cit.,* p. 216.

Only those conditions, imposed upon Ukraine prevented her from successfully competing against British coal, at least on the Black and Oziv Seacoast, because otherwise both the quality and the location would work in favor of Ukrainian coal. In Odessa imported coal was sold at 10.37 to 10.98 rubles per ton, and Ukrainian coal, under such high freight rates at 10.93 to 11.51 rubles per ton. Even Odessa, one of the largest consumers of coal (annually 320,000 tons) which also derived benefits from the importation of coal (that is why the people of Odessa were against introducing an import duty on coal) maintained that "Donets coal could push out foreign coal, if only freight were cheaper and a sufficient number of coastal ships were available."[53]

The fight against duty-free importation of coal began at the very outset of the crisis. The problem of imposing a duty on coal was raised at the Second Congress of Mining Industrialists of "South Russia" in 1877. Even earlier Ukrainian businessmen tried to convince Moscow of the advantages of converting her industries from wood to coal, and the coal coming from Ukraine. "In Petersburg, a ton of foreign coal costs 9.76 rubles; in Riga, 17.08 rubles and in Moscow between 18.91 and 21.35 rubles. At the same time a ton of Donets anthracite equals one cubic *sazhen* (eight cubic metres) of wood, and even at a price of 2.40 rubles per ton (as we have noted, the price at that time fell to 1.22 rubles per ton—*Author*) coal would cost locally 2.40 per ton while wood at Ivanov (near Moscow) cost 20 rubles per *sazhen*."[54]

The Sixth Congress of Mining Industrialists of Ukraine again raised the question of duty-free importation and approached the Ministry of Finance with a request: "in order to provide a market for Donets coal in the Northwestern and Moscow regions, a duty on coal should be introduced in the following amounts: coal coming into Baltic ports, 1 kopeck per *pood* (about 60 kopecks per ton); coal in transit to points inside Russia —2.5 kopecks per *pood* (1.50 rubles per ton); coal coming through inland points on the Austrian and Prussian border 3 kopecks (1.80 rubles per ton) and through Black Sea ports 3.5 kopecks (2.10 rubles per ton)." But the Minister of Finance, although interested in raising revenues from duties, stood, as usual, pri-

[53] M. Sobolev, *op. cit.*, p. 524.
[54] N. Yasnopolsky, *op. cit.*, p. 95. (References to *poods* in the original have been converted to tons.)

marily in defense of Russian industry, whose interests were always above those of the tariff policy of the Empire. He wrote: "Revenue from duties will in no event compensate for the damage done to our industry and the national economy through an increase in the cost of fuel, particularly in the North of Russia where many branches of shop and manufacturing industries, consuming much fuel, would not be able to operate under the smallest duty burden imposed on coal."[55]

Insistent demands of Polish coal industrialists were partially satisfied, and a duty of 1 kopeck per *pood* of coal was introduced on the western border of Poland. The Seventh, and in 1883 the Eighth Congress of Ukrainian Mining Industrialists brought up the matter. They indicated that 33% of the coal consumed in the Empire was foreign at a time when, in 1883 in the Donets basin 2,112 thousand tons of coal were mined, of which 240 thousand tons were used locally, 960 thousand tons were sold, and 912 thousand tons remained unsold.[56]

The manager of the Kharkiv Commercial Bank, Alchevsky, told the Eighth Congress: "Defending the interests of Moscow manufacturers, the interests of our land should also be considered; if there were no favorable tariff policy in relation to goods which our land receives from Moscow, then many branches of Moscow's manufacturing industries would not reach that stage of high development which they now enjoy."[57]

Thus, as we can see, the other basic Ukrainian industry—coal, just like the sugar industry, cannot boast of a favorable attitude of the Imperial Government. On the contrary, everything possible was done to serve Russian industry at its expense. The Government quite openly tried to hold the price of Ukrainian coal at the lowest possible level by putting it into a position of having to fight heavy competition.

Only in 1884 was a law introduced which imposed a duty of 2 kopecks per *pood* on coal, coke and peat in the ports of the Black and Oziv Sea; 1.5 *kopecks* on inland border points in the West, and 1.5 kopecks in ports of the Baltic Sea. In 1887 the duty was raised to 3 kopecks in Black Sea ports, and to 1 kopeck in Baltic ports.[58]

But it would be a mistake to think that this denoted any change in the Government's attitude toward the Ukrainian coal industry. It was caused by a complete change which took place

[55] M. Sobolev, *op. cit.*, p. 438.   [56] M. Sobolev, *op. cit.*, p. 514.
[57] *Ibid.*, p. 512.   [58] *Ibid.*, p. 529.

in Ukraine at the time, the rapid development of a Ukrainian metallurgical industry which became a large consumer of fuel, as well as the construction of railroads, also creating a demand for coal. This contributed to an immense increase of the local market, strengthened the position of the coal industry, drew foreign capital investments in it, and facilitated organized marketing of coal. Subsequently, a syndicate for the marketing of coal "Produhol," was established, which almost monopolized the market, but by that time Ukrainian capital had already been squeezed out of the coal industry. This high prosperity of the coal market permitted the Ministry of Finance to utilize the opportunity of increasing revenues from this item, and that is why an import duty was introduced on coal, but privileges were nevertheless reserved for the Petersburg industry.

Later, between 1901 and 1906, when the production of coal was almost stabilized, the prices always rising and the industrial centers of Russia feeling a dependence on Ukraine, the duty on coal was reduced. In 1913, it was abolished entirely.[59] From 1908, the annual import of coal was 400 thousand tons. The leading position of Ukraine in the coal industry of the Empire brought about a condition where Ukraine's place was becoming more and more important in the Empire's fuel balance. Although most of the coal was consumed in Ukraine, "a tendency became noticeable in the direction of capturing distant markets: transportation of Donets fuel increases faster than cost of freight to the Southern market, closer to its source."

Regions of destination of coal hauled by railroads (in thousands of tons) are shown in *Table LV*.

TABLE LV

	1904	1913	% of increase
Southern region (railroads within Ukraine)	7,824	13,872	77
Central Russia and Volga region	848	8,576	343
Other regions	656	1,504	131

[60]

And yet, in spite of a growing consumption of Donets coal beyond the borders of Ukraine, the internal market grew even more, taking over 50% of the total production. The metallurgical industry became a reliable customer, contributing in large meas-

[59] M. Golman, *op. cit.*, p. 353.
[60] P. Fomin, "Ekonomichna kharakterystyka Ukrainy," p. 69.

ure to the independent action of the Donets basin. In addition, the leading position of the Ukrainian coal industry in the Empire fuel balance changed the nature of the consumption of its product beyond the borders of Ukraine. Not only did the railroads become organically dependent on it, but many other branches of the Empire's industry also. This added to the importance of the Ukrainian coal industry. In 1912 the fuel balance of the whole Empire, railroads excepted, was characterized by the figures in *Table LVI* (in thousands of tons).

With the exception of Poland and the Urals which had their own coal deposits, only the Northwestern region (the industries of Petersburg), under the protection of an official tariff policy, relied on foreign coal. In all other regions Ukraine gained a dominant position in the supply. The Donets basin played an even greater role in supplying the railroads. The railroads' coal consumption reached 4,123.2 thousand tons in 1913, of which 2,416 thousand tons were used by the railroads of Ukraine. At that time the production potential of the Ukrainian coal industry was already much greater. Beginning with 1905 the "Produhol" coal syndicate, in order to keep prices up, stabilized the extraction of coal at an annual level of 24,000 to 24,600 thousand tons. In view of that the Government, favoring the industries of Petersburg, reduced and later abolished the duty on foreign coal. Thus, during the period of the last few years before the outbreak of World War I, a situation arose under which the coal industry had made a great sweep and had grown strong economically, yet was restricted in the utilization of its full potential. Many factors which contributed to this situation will be discussed later. The railroad rates, determined by the Government, played no small part in this. For example, a distance of only 800 kilometres (500 miles) would double the cost of coal, in spite of the fact that the rates were lower than North-South rates. The excessively high freight rates toward Black Sea ports as well as high ocean freight rates, and a limited freight fleet, excluded the possibility of extending the Ukrainian coal export market to lands of the Near East where British coal reigned unchallenged. What is significant, is the fact seen from the above table, that Ukraine (to be exact, the ships of the Black Sea) consumed 152 thousand tons of foreign coal. Exports of Ukrainian coal amounted to: 1911, 28.8 thousand tons; 1912, 16 thousand tons, and 1913, nothing.

TABLE LVI

Categories of Fuel

Regions of Consumption	Donets coal	Polish coal	Coal of other regions	Foreign coal	Petroleum	Wood	Peat
Baltic and Northwestern gubernias	272.0	64.0	4.8	3,723.2	176.0	1,001.6	81.6
Poland	56.0	3,934.4	....	1,688.6	24.0	161.6	240.0
Central Russia and Volga region.....	2,268.8	30.4	75.2	30.4	3,112.0	7,059.2	731.2
Urals	30.4	....	398.4	8.0	72.0	2,148.8	152.0
Ukraine and Don	8,963.2	142.4	3.2	152.0	192.0	480.0	22.4
Caucasus	248.0	....	32.0	....	480.0	19.2	....
TOTALS	11,838.4	4,171.2	513.6	5,602.2	4,056.0	10,870.4	1,227.2

[61]

[61] P. Fomin, op. cit., p. 73.

It must be admitted, however, that the Ukrainian coal industry overcame in large measure all the difficulties which had stood in its way and, within a comparatively short time reached a position of considerable importance. It grew into a basic source of fuel, contributing 77.4% of all the coal of the Empire before the outbreak of World War I.

The coal industry also grew strong as an organized body. A close network of railroads was developed in the Donets basin, whose density in that area exceeded that of Germany. The coal industry acted as a unit in its approach to matters of marketing and a fairly lively process of combining the coal and metallurgical industries in trusts was begun.

The essential fact is, however, that the more successful the Ukrainian coal industry became, the less Ukrainian it became. It was dominated completely by Franco-Belgian capital which was tied with Russian banks. The influence of this foreign capital played a major role in the very development of this industry.

Whereas in the beginning the position of the coal industry was determined by the colonial dependence of Ukraine upon Russia, subsequent changes did not touch the system of colonial management. The changes merely introduced more modern forms, appropriate to the new nature of exploitation. The only difference was that during that period and in that branch of industry, Ukraine was no longer an object of exploitation by Russia alone, but also of foreign capital.

The matter of complete domination of Ukrainian industry not only in coal, but elsewhere will be discussed later.

The Metallurgical Industry

We have already noted that Ukraine is a land rich in high-quality iron ore deposits. According to latest research and estimates by the Soviet authorities iron ore reserves of Kryvyi Rih are estimated at 1.5 billion tons with an iron content between 50% to 62%. The Kerch reserves are even larger. In addition, Kryvyi Rih and other regions have huge deposits of iron quartzites (over 21 billion tons). Magnetic anomalies northeast of Kryvyi Rih also indicate the presence of iron. There are also magnetic anomalies around Kremenchuk, Chortomlyts'ko-Verkhotsevsk, Orikhovo-Ilyanivs'ka (near the Donets basin), Konkinsl.a, Volhynia, and Western Ukraine.

The main iron ore base of Khyvyi Rih is located close to the Donets coal basin which has 6.6 billion tons of coal suitable for coking. It is also close to the Nikopil region of manganese ore, one of the richest in the world with deposits of over 500 million tons. These regions, tied organically to each other in the metallurgical industry, form a tight triangle whose longest side is only about 300 miles long.

It is not surprising that such conditions contributed to the fact that, shortly after the beginning of iron smelting in Ukraine, it occupied first place in the production of pig iron in the Empire, and became the main center of the iron-ore industry.

But all this happened only in the last decades of the 19th century. It happened only as the result of a stubborn struggle, and acquired peculiar features, as with other branches of Ukrainian industry. How odd that the German traveler Kohl should write about this land in 1841: "In all of the South of Russia there is not one place where one could find any metal. This huge area of Europe is deprived of metals; not enough iron can be found to make a single nail."[62]

Actually, the smelting of Kryvyi Rih ore did not start until 1871. Prior to that time, the iron industry of Ukraine depended upon the importation of Russian pig iron. The Luhansky Works, which served primarily the military, used Ukrainian coal, but pig iron from the Urals.

The history of mining iron ore, and the increase of the part which Ukraine played in the Empire is shown by the figures in *Table LVII* (in thousands of tons).

TABLE LVII

Year	Ukraine		Poland		Urals		Moscow Region	
	Quantity	%	Quantity	%	Quantity	%	Quantity	%
1870 ..	20.8	2.6	105.6	13.6	456.0	58.5	134.2	17.9
1880 ..	43.2	4.3	144.0	14.4	611.8	61.5	140.8	14.1
1890 ..	366.4	20.9	212.8	12.1	989.2	51.4	195.2	11.1
1900 ..	3,360.0	56.0	474.0	7.9	1,619.2	27.2	377.6	6.3
1910 ..	4,160.0	73.9	161.6	2.9	1,171.2	20.6	123.2	2.2
1913 ..	6,420.0	72.2	302.4	3.2	1,747.8	18.9	513.1	5.5 [63]

Within twenty-three years the amount of ore mined in Ukraine increased almost twenty times, while the increase in the old Russian ore center of the Urals merely doubled. Ukraine became the main source of iron ore, contributing close to 75% of

62 O. Ohloblyn, *op. cit.*, p. 171.   63 S. Ostapenko, *loc. cit.*

the Empire's total. During the same period, Ukraine surpassed Austria-Hungary, although Ukraine was still far behind countries with a highly developed metallurgical industry. In 1913, the production of iron ore in thousands of tons was: Austria-Hungary, 4,800; Sweden, 8,608; Great Britain, 15,872; France, 21,600; Germany, 35,200, and USA, 54,848.

The growth of Ukraine's participation in the Empire's production of pig iron was equally stormy. Production of pig iron is shown in *Table LVIII* (in thousands of tons).

Production of iron and steel (in thousands of tons) is shown in *Table LIX*.

We must not be led to believe that such fast growth of Ukrainian metallurgy and the accession to a leading position in the Empire is explained merely by the presence of rich iron ore deposits. It is true that the quality of the ore and its geographic location in Ukraine surpassed all other regions of the Empire, but as to the quantity of deposits, the position of Ukraine in the Empire is nothing exceptional. According to data of Professor Bohdanovych, iron ore reserves and the amount of iron in them are characterized by the figures in *Table LX* (in thousands of tons).

It was therefore not the presence of rich iron ore deposits alone then which determined the leading position of Ukraine in the iron ore and metallurgical industries. Many factors con-

TABLE LVIII

Year	Empire total	Ukraine (Quantity)	Ukraine %
1860	313.6	0	...
1875	398.4	14.4	3.6
1890	883.2	214.4	24.3
1900	2,828.8	1,464.0	51.8
1910	2,972.8	2,020.8	68.1
1914	4,225.6	2,979.2	70.6

TABLE LIX

Year	Empire total	Ukraine	Urals	Ukraine %	Urals %
1860	197.9	...	161.7	...	81.9
1870	232.0	...	148.1	...	63.9
1880	565.9	25.9	211.0	4.5	37.0
1890	2,149.7	953.7	477.6	44.4	22.2
1900	2,947.2	1,582.4	592.0	53.6	20.1
1914	3,835.2	2,302.4	649.6	60.0	16.8

[64]

[64] P. Fomin, *op. cit.*, pp. 89, 90.

TABLE LX

	Ore	Iron in the ore
Ukraine	523,136	227,800
Urals	275,100	132,400
Central Russia	771,360	307,400
Poland	288,000	117,120
Caucasus	13,600	8,096

65

tributed to this, a major one of them being the high technical production level. The plants of Ukraine were established from the beginning with all the technical improvements. They were established on the pattern of concentrated enterprises of Western Europe. The production capacity of the plants of Ukraine, compared with plants in other regions of the Empire shows the *Table LXI* figures of pig iron production in 1891 and 1900 (in thousands of tons per annum, plant capacity is also indicated in thousands of tons per annum):

Therefore, Ukraine surpassed all other metallurgical regions as far as concentration of production was concerned. In 1900, in Ukraine, 66.5% of all pig iron production came from plants with a capacity of 80 to 160 thousand tons, and over 160 thousand tons per annum, while in the rest of the Empire outside of Ukraine 54.6% was produced in plants of a capacity below 16,000 tons. By the 20th century Ukraine was approaching such a land of highly developed metallurgy as Germany. The average plant of Ukraine would have an average of 2 ovens, 345 workers and would work 74.8 thousand tons of ore per oven, the corresponding figures for Germany are: 2.5 ovens, 322 workers and 86.1 thousand tons. The technical and productive superiority of Ukrainian metallurgy is even more obvious when we compare it with that of the Urals, the most developed region in Russia. This superiority must be emphasized because of the role it played in the relationship between Ukraine and Russia in this field. (See *Table LXII.*)

Such incomparably higher production indices were the result of a more perfect technique and organization of production: hot blast furnaces, use of mineral fuel, Martin ovens, Bessemer and Thomas converters, etc. Thus, from the very beginning, the Ukrainian metallurgical industry developed as an industry of high capital investment. For this, a source of supply of capital was necessary, as well as conditions favoring the influx of such

65 P. Fomin, *op. cit.*, p. 89.

TABLE LXI

Plants with a production capacity of:

Year	Total pig iron	Over 160		80 to 160		48 to 80		16 to 48		Under 16	
		Ukraine	Rest of Empire	Ukraine	Rest of Empire	Ukraine	Rest of Empire	Ukraine	Rest of Empire	Ukraine	Rest of Empire
1891 ...	953.8	...	...	80.7	...	151.6	50.8	...	127.0	...	543.7
1900 ...	2,828.8	474.3	...	496.3	94.8	353.7	111.2	111.0	441.2	...	746.6

66 N. Vanag, "Finansoviy kapital v Rossiyi nakanune mirovoy voyny" ("Finance Capital in Russia on the Eve of the World War"), *Proletariy*, (*The Proletarian*), *Moscow*, 1930, p. 17.

TABLE LXII

	1890		1900	
	Ukraine	*Urals*	*Ukraine*	*Urals*
Production of pig iron per plant (in thousands of tons)....	23.8	4.0	51.1	6.9
Power of plant in HP	1,530.0	135.0	6,159.0	244.0
Number of workers per plant..	1,505.0	1,281.0	1,841.0	1,496.0
Production per oven (in thousands of tons)...	15.3	...	32.5	5.4
Production per worker (in tons)	15.8	3.1	27.4	4.7
Ore mined per worker (in thousands of tons)...	171.2	38.4	308.8	52.8

[67]

capital, such as good market conditions and a high margin of profit.

The source of these investments was foreign capital, in organic relationship with the already existing financial oligarchy of Russian banks, centered mainly in Petersburg. In an unequal struggle against this strong Government-backed faction, local capital was either ruined, or completely subjected. This happened not only in the metallurgical, but in all other important industries of Ukraine, coal, sugar, etc.

Favorable market conditions for the metallurgical industry were created primarily by a great demand for metals, caused by the mass construction of railroads. But this did not happen suddenly The initial "skeptical attitude toward the ore wealth of Kryvyi Rih dominated both Government and scientific circles almost until 1880," in other words, we have here to deal with another aspect of Russia's desire to hold on to an industrial monopoly. "This historical conflict of the region of Kryvyi Rih and the Urals was resolved by the interference of foreign capital, contrary to the interests of national Russian capital."[68]

Until that time, even the developing railroads' acutely felt hunger for metals was powerless against the negative attitude toward the development of industry in Ukraine. A solution was being sought in facilitating the importation of metals from abroad, but in such degree only, as not to hurt the interests of the Urals. During discussions of the proposed tariff act of 1857, the well known economist Tengoborskiy, who was chief speak-

[67] I. Glivits, *Zhelezodelatelnaya promyshlennost' Rossiyi* (*The Iron-Working Industry of Russia*), Moscow, 1911, p. 114.
[68] M. Wolf, *op. cit.*, p. 42.

er, said: "The prohibition of the importation of iron and pig iron should be repealed, and the duty on these essential metals should be lowered to 20 kopecks from 1.03 rubles for pig iron, and to 60 kopecks for iron coming by sea and 40 kopecks for iron coming by land from 1.38 rubles." The need for such reductions was argued as follows: 1) Iron is one of the most essential products for all branches of industry, and all are interested in getting it cheap. But the existing tariff does not permit it to become cheap because its importation by sea is prohibited, and importation by land is prohibitively high. Transportation of metal from the Urals to industrial centers costs more than the metals themselves; 2) The amount of iron manufactured in Russia is at a standstill, regardless of the growing demand for it; 3) Competition between Russian and foreign iron is quite possible thanks to the high cost of freight from the seaboard to inland points."[69]

The State Council went even further. They repealed the importation by sea (with the exception of Black and Oziv Sea ports, Odessa excluded) and set up a rate of duty: pig iron— 15 kopecks, bulk iron—50 kopecks, sheet iron—60 kopecks etc.

This brought a radical change in the extent of imports: "the annual import figure of pig iron and iron increased from 3,168 tons between 1851 and 1856 to 312,000 tons between 1867 and 1871, and to 470,400 tons between 1877 and 1881.

" . . . Even for the construction of railroads in the Urals, the center of black metallurgy, not only locomotives and rails were imported, but also various small metalware like screws, bolts, etc."[70]

"The total value of imported iron goods and iron for the construction and servicing of railroads during the ten-year period between 1870 and 1880 reached one billion rubles."[71]

Such a solution of the iron supply problem obviously went against the interests of Ukraine, whose productive capacity was thus automatically ignored.

"The Kharkiv Committee of Commerce and Manufacturing, representing the interests of the Donets region, pointed to the existence of huge deposits of iron ore in this region." This Com-

[69] M. Sobolev, *op. cit.*, pp. 33-34.
[70] B. Brant, *Inostranniye kapitaly* (*Foreign Capital*), St. Petersburg, 1899, III, 20.
[71] P. Lashchenko, *Istoriya narodnoho khozyaystva SSSR* (*History of the National Economy of the USSR*), Leningrad, 1952, II, 110.

mittee th ught it wise to solve the problem of the supply of
iron in the development of Ukrainian metallurgy which "has
been halted in its development, and duties should be kept in
force in order to aid it. The growth of the mining industry in
the Donets land will provide a large amount of wages for the
peasants, heretofore restricted to a single agricultural pursuit."[72]

These just and understandable claims of Ukraine did not
meet with a positive response. On the contrary, two years later
came another proposition to lower the duty on pig iron to 5
kopecks (from 15 kopecks) and for assorted iron to 45 kopecks.
It was carried into effect. Moreover, on motion of the Minister
of Finance, duty-free importation of iron and pig iron on special
request of individual plants was allowed. This duty-free importation was considerably high even in the 1870's, and constituted
a large percentage of the total. *Table LXIII* shows these figures
in thousands of tons. Thus, the economic policy of Russia regard-

TABLE LXIII

Year	Pig iron	Of that, duty-free	Sheet and assorted iron	Of that, duty-free
1875	56.1	44.3	85.6	42.6
1876	47.4	38.8	80.5	30.6
1877	51.6	47.4	50.5	28.4
1879	181.1	122.5	96.5	30.8 [73]

ing metals was not determined by the interests of the Ukrainian economy, nor of the development of the metallurgical industry of Ukraine which, as has been noted above, was soon
to rise to a leading position. Russia ignored those interests entirely. Russia's colonial policy toward Ukraine required a continuance of it as an agricultural economy. But the extremely
favorable market conditions and the growing demand for metals
created an interest on the part of foreign capital, in investing
in Ukrainian industry. The opportunity to balance foreign trade
compelled Russia to substitute for the antiquated colonial system
a more modern one, which offered much higher returns not only
to the metropolis as such, but also to this metropolis' still shaky
finance capital.

In 1871 an Englishman, Hughes, built and put into operation two metallurgical plants in Ukraine. He was not actually

[72] M. Sobolev, *op. cit.*, p. 567.
[73] *Ibid.*, p. 198.

an independent entrepreneur. He had the backing of English financial circles and of some high-ranking Petersburg personages. Following Hughes, the Moscow industrialist Pastukhov became active in the black metal industry of Ukraine. The development of the metallurgical industry assumed wide proportions in the 1880's, when the large-scale influx of foreign capital came legally.

As has been noted, initially Ukrainian industry relied mainly on the railroads' demand for iron. Even at that time the railroads required annually between 800 and 1,000 engines, 20,000 to 25,000 freight cars, between 320,000 and 368,000 tons of rails, etc. Converted to terms of pig iron, this required annually 640,000 tons a year. "If we take into consideration the fact that in 1890 the entire metallurgical industry produced only 960,000 tons of pig iron, and in 1895, 1,388,800 tons, and its production reached 2,828,800 tons only in 1900, it becomes clear to what extent the great demand for metals by the railroads was decisive for the metallurgical industry."[74]

On the average, the railroads' demands for metal reached 68.8% of the total production figure. Some plants (Pruzhkovsky, Novorossiysky) worked for the railroads 87% to 100% of production time.

This was the decisive factor in the development of the Ukrainian metallurgy (See *Table LXIV*).

We can see from the above that Ukraine was the supplier of goods in great demand: rails, beams, telegraph wire, etc. But in the production of goods in mass demand for mass consumption, such as roofing steel, hardware and universal iron goods Ukraine was behind other regions. This is clear if we take into consideration the amount of these goods produced in proportion to the total amount of metal goods manufactured. Even such a branch of metal manufacturing as nails which would appear to be closely tied with the manufacture of wire, was underdeveloped when compared with other regions.

This one-sided aspect of the metallurgical industry imposed upon Ukraine was dictated by the desire to conserve the wide consumption market for the Urals. It was the cause of Ukrainian industry's continued dependence on railroad construction which, as we shall see later, facilitated its domination by foreign and Russian finance capital. And to the extent that railroad con-

[74] P. Lashchenko, *op. cit.*, p. 125.

TABLE LXIV

Rolling-mill products (in percentages):

Product:	Years	Ukraine	Urals	Central Industrial Region	Volga	North (Petersburg)	Poland
Beams and bars	1903	81	8	..	1	2	8
	1912	88	5	..	1.4	1.6	4
Rails	1903	82	18	..	..	..	..
	1912	79	21	..	..	..	..
Wire	1903	24	15	16	..	21	24
	1912	56	5	6	..	18	15
Roof iron	1903	12	80	3	1	2	2
	1912	24	61	5	6	1	2
Light sheet	1903	36	31	..	7	1	25
	1912	41	16	0.5	9	4.5	29
Heavy sheet	1903	54	6	8	12	10	10
	1912	63	7	9	8	7	6
Assorted	1903	35	19	5	9	9	23
	1912	47	13	5	8	8	19
Universal	1903	39	0.5	0.5	3	8	43
	1912	46	..	..	5	8	41 [75]

Total rolling-mill production (in thousands of tons):

	Years	Ukraine	Urals	Central Industrial Region	Volga	North (Petersburg)	Poland
	1903	1,102.4	496.0	212.0*		126.4	273.6
	1912	2,051.2	630.4	320.0*		244.8	393.6
	1903	50.8	20.9	10.0*		5.8	12.5
	1912	56.4	17.3	8.9*		6.7	10.7 [76]

*These figures pertain jointly to the Central Industrial and Volga regions.

[75] M. Golman, op. cit., p. 436. [76] Ibid., p. 433.

struction was mainly, and particularly during the 19th century, undertaken at Government cost, the size of that construction depended upon budget means of some fiscal year. The length of newly opened rail lines in the Russian Empire is shown in *Table LXV*, for five-year periods between 1861 and 1915, the last item being for a ten-year period (in miles).[77] In addi-

TABLE LXV

Years	Miles	Years	Miles	Years	Miles
1861-1865	1,295	1876-1880	2,340	1891-1895	4,294
1866-1870	4,349	1881-1885	2,038	1896-1900	5,289
1871-1875	4,922	1886-1890	1,899	1901-1905	4,324
				1906-1915	18,932

tion to these circumstances which determined the market for the products of Ukrainian metallurgy to a large extent, imports also played an important part in this respect. These also were subject to the will of the Imperial Government, primarily to its tariff policy.

This provides a clue as to why exports and imports of metals never achieved an equilibrium. One, or the other showed marked fluctuations, and there was no lack of such instances where imports, thanks to lower customs tariffs increased, with a concurrent increase in exports, although the latter, because of the high railroad freight rates could never be as profitable as selling at prices prevailing on the markets of the Empire. Profits of the Russian industry on cheap imported metals went hand in hand with losses of the Ukrainian industry on exports, from which Russia drew the exchange to pay for imports. These conditions prevailed, as we shall indicate later, until the time when, Russo-French syndicates were set up for the Ukrainian coal and metallurgical industry. This subjected the home market to a monopoly, and the Imperial economic policy conformed with the interests of that monopoly, even to the extent of making the tariff policy follow its needs. The process did not get into its full stride until after 1905.

Until that period of monopoly the imports of metals and metal goods into Ukraine were as shown in *Table LXVI* (in thousands of tons).[78]

[77] P. Lashchenko, *op. cit.*, p. 123.
[78] P. Fomin, *op. cit.*, p. 69.

TABLE LXVI

Years	Pig iron	Pig iron products	Iron and steel	Iron and steel products	Tools and machinery
1860-69 ...	9.45	5.74	78.58	21.05	3.07
1870-79 ...	66.57	15.27	279.98	45.68	42.10
1880-89 ...	199.76	5.24	121.62	26.81	34.38
1890-99 ...	113.75	6.97	239.89	32.82	89.63
1900-09 ...	16.64	5.28	67.8	46.35	138.47

Thus, along with a gradual and systematic increase in the importation of tools and machinery, we are able to note sharp fluctuations in the importation of pig iron and iron. And this was at a time of simultaneous and rapid increase of the production of these goods in Ukraine which even resulted in a surplus after demands of the home market had been met. Thus, the extent of imports was not determined by the home market balance of metals, only by Russian industrialists' conjectures in the matter of commercial profits. For example, the sharp increase of imports of pig iron during the 1880 to 1889 period was the direct result of the 1880 repeal of duty on this item. And although a major part of the imports was not absorbed by the economy of Ukraine going merely in transit to Russia, nevertheless the existence of such considerable imports with simultaneous exports of the same kind of goods from Ukraine is indicative of the subjection of the industrial interests of Ukraine to the interests of Russian industrial centers.

This one-sided aspect of the Ukrainian metallurgical industry and its dependence on the demand by the railroads which were under the control of the Government (the factor determining the legal regulations in the area of economic policy) was the main reason for the fact that this industry, in spite of an acute shortage of metal goods in the land and a great demand for them, nevertheless had to go through a hard marketing crisis in the 1890's, and an even harder one in 1904-05. As a result of these crises and the artificial decline of the price of stock of this industry on foreign exchanges which followed the crises, Ukrainian capital was almost entirely forced out of this industry, and it came under the domination of Russo-French capital.

This was the cause of the various fluctuations in the exportation of pig iron and iron, alongside an almost unchangeable level of exports of manufactured metal goods.

Table LXVII illustrates the export situation in metals during the 1902-1912 period. Even after the crisis of 1904 Ukraine con-

TABLE LXVII

(The figures are in thousands of tons.)[79]

Year	Pig iron	Iron and steel	Pig iron products	Iron and steel products	Tools and machinery
1902	53.61	6.40	. . .	. . .	. . .
1903	.35	8.75	1.07	5.44	2.88
1904	.80	6.16	1.16	4.51	1.63
1905	.94	13.87	1.00	4.62	1.36
1906	20.38	31.63	1.10	11.98	3.36
1907	72.78	167.63	.91	6.14	2.20
1908	10.38	109.80	1.10	6.35	1.71
1909	1.15	162.16	1.10	7.36	1.84
1910	2.00	89.47	.89	9.79	1.66
1911	1.07	77.55	.89	6.76	2.51
1912	.38	28.43	1.15	12.32	3.10

tinued to export rails in considerable quantities because the home market was restricted in order to keep prices up. Exports of rails amounted to: 1905, 7,184 tons; 1906, 8,480 tons; 1907, 89,280 tons; 1908, 86,232 tons; 1909, 140,320 tons, and in 1910, 66,880 tons.[80]

Obviously, under such circumstances the productive capacity of the Ukrainian metallurgy always exceeded actual production, and because of that, mined ore was exported in large annual quantities abroad, in spite of the fact that there was an acute need for industrial employment among the local population. This is typical in a colonial land. The amounts of ore exported are shown for the period between 1901 and 1912 in *Table LXVIII* (in thousands of tons):[81]

TABLE LXVIII

1901	3.52	1907	878.48
1902	38.43	1908	564.43
1903	285.63	1909	505.58
1904	246.70	1910	827.44
1905	211.15	1911	865.39
1906	460.24	1912	647.77

[79] G. Kasperovich, *Zhelezodelatelnaya promishlennost v Rossiyi za 1903-13 g. g.* (*The Iron-Working Industry in Russia during the Years 1903-1913*), Moscow, 1914, p. 41. In his table, the author includes rails in the "Iron and steel" column.
[80] P. Fomin, *op. cit.*, p. 72.   [81] *Ibid.*, p. 70.

The main consumers of this export item were Germany, Great Britain and Holland, countries which were simultaneously exporters of pig iron and iron for the Petersburg industry. Ukrainian ore went through the Black Sea ports to England and Germany, and later in the form of pig iron and products it went through Baltic ports to nourish the metalworking plants of Petersburg. In 1913 Germany alone took 400,000 tons of Ukrainian ore, 6% of the total mined.

Much light is shed on the position of the Ukrainian metallurgical industry by data on the home consumption of metals. Statistics of carloadings provide a real insight. If we group the stations of loading metals and stations of destination of the entire Empire, then we will get the following picture for the year 1911. Out of a total of 1,660.6 thousand tons of pig iron and semi-manufactured metal goods, Ukraine accounted for 973.8 thousand tons, or 58.7%. But of the latter amount, only 461.3 thousand tons, or 46%, of Ukrainian carloadings were for internal Ukrainian destination. The remainder went beyond Ukraine. It was the same with iron and steel. Out of a total of 1,997.1 thousand tons of carloadings, Ukraine accounted for 1,134.6 thousand tons, or 56.7%, of which 465 thousand tons, or 41% went for internal Ukrainian consumption. The following table shows us to what regions of the Empire the metals were destined. Carloadings in 1911 are shown in *Table LXIX* (in thousands of tons).[82]

According to these figures Ukraine delivered to the central Moscow regions 57% of their pig iron and 49.4% of their iron and steel. Similarly to the Petersburg (Baltic) region went 47.2% of its pig iron and 43.4% of its iron and steel. And to European Russia in general, Ukraine delivered 44.4% of the pig iron and 46.8% of the iron and steel. The fact that Ukraine alone was consuming only 46% of the pig iron produced, and only 41% of iron and steel does not by any means prove that the Ukrainian market's needs were fully satisfied. On the contrary, Ukraine, satisfying more than 50% of Russia's metal consumption, imported over 32,000 tons of iron from the Urals. The Ukrainian population was supplied with iron and its products on a starvation level; 98% of the peasants' homes were straw-thatched, all utensils were earthenware not only in the villages, but also to a large

[82] P. Fomin, *op. cit.*, p. 75.

TABLE LXIX

Regions of destination	Pig iron and semi-manufactures Regions of loading			Iron and steel		
	Ukraine	Urals	Empire total	Ukraine	Urals	Empire total
Northern ..	....	....	....	1.5	0.25	5.53
Baltic	109.40	49.30	227.10	115.60	41.20	266.80
Central Asia	....	0.32	0.32	3.18	4.78	7.98
Moscow Central ..	112.83	25.90	196.90	153.40	46.00	319.10
Central Volga ...	89.80	3.82	97.40	47.07	25.28	79.60
Central Chernozem	54.14	0.99	57.02	106.27	17.14	142.35
Poland ...	111.88	0.21	279.88	62.40	3.13	313.40
Ukraine ...	461.37	14.99	486.37	465.02	35.34	525.70
Urals	3.95	271.28	276.25	7.50	101.95	109.68
Southeastern.	....	....	....	1.39	0.67	2.10
North Caucasus..	2.29	....	2.29	65.82	5.54	71.41
South Caucasus..	5.39	....	5.39	63.98	1.73	66.00
	951.05	366.81	1,628.92	1,093.13	283.01	1,909.65

extent in the cities, carts had wooden axles, gates and doors were hung on wooden hinges. All this speaks eloquently as to whether or not the people's needs in metal were satisfied. True enough, the insignificant consumption of iron can be explained to a large extent by the low purchasing power of the population, impoverished by colonial exploitation. But a large part was also played by the nature of the Ukrainian metallurgical industry, whose efforts, as has been pointed out, were concentrated on the manufacture of such products as rails, beams, bars, etc. with a very limited production of universal consumption articles. The entire industry was looking not toward the satisfaction of the needs of the national economy, only toward satisfying Russia's needs for products of black metals and of supplying Russian metalworking industries with raw materials and semi-manufactured products. The very nature of manufacturing thus compels us to delegate Ukrainian metallurgy to the category of a colonial industry.

Ukraine did not possess any metalworking industry with the exception of farm machinery manufacturing and a railroad equipment industry. Any other metalworking did not go beyond the stage of crafts on a level of black and lock-smithing.

On the eve of World War I Ukraine had 17 smelting plants and 6 mills, of which half were rolling mills, and one served the shipbuilding industry belonging to the Mykolaiv Shipbuilding Company.

We have been considering three basic branches of Ukrainian industry: sugar refining, coal mining and metallurgy. We have been making only cursory remarks about others because it is not within the scope of this work to draw a statistical and economic characteristic of the the pre-revolutionary position and development of industry of Ukraine. Our task is to discover the real nature of those social-economic conditions in Ukraine, and in Russia, which were decisive in the development and direction of that industry, and which formed the essence of economic processes in Ukraine. We have deliberately paused to consider these branches, which were the basis of Ukrainian industry and in whose development Ukraine met with considerable success, achieving a leading position in the whole Empire in these branches. Another reason for considering them in detail was that they are all based on natural wealth and by reason of this fact possessed a solid foundation for further development. It would seem that this natural wealth gave Ukraine the right to expect favorable conditions for rounded development of these branches of industry. But, as we have seen, even here Russia's attitude was characteristic. It treated Ukraine's economy as that of a colony.

The central purpose of Russian economic policy all along, was to keep Ukraine in a position of a supplier of raw material produced by agriculture, and a market for Russian industrial products. Conforming to this plan, Ukraine should have remained in a stage of merely rudimentary industrial development. This was the object of the early ruination of Ukraine's industry, and its transfer to, and concentration in Russia. As we have noted, in many branches of industry, particularly in the production of goods of mass consumption, the scheme succeeded almost 100%.

The first stages of development of the three industries herein analyzed were met with a desire to apply the same principle to them; to prevent their coming into existence by setting up against them appropriate branches of Russian industry. We have seen that such was the case with sugar refineries which were being established in Russia; such was the case with coal, where other mining regions, wood as fuel and imported coal were used as means of preventing the emergence of a Ukrainian industry, and such was the case in metallurgy, in the struggle of the Urals against Kryvyi Rih.

When, however, economic conditions appeared to be stronger than such desires, Russia would begin putting obstacles in the way of the growth endeavoring to make them adjuncts of and subject to Russian industries.

And finally when Russia was faced with the prospect of an irresistible superiority of these branches of Ukrainian industry over the respective branches of Russian industry, and when their growth was dictated by the economic needs of all of Russia, there began the conquest of these industries with the aid of foreign capital. Then came the introduction of a modern system of colonial exploitation, peculiar to the so-called "European" type of colonies.

But here we encounter a very special process of financial expansion into the economy of a colony. The process is special not only by reason of the fact that foreign capital was drawn into participation, and not only because Russia did not have too much capital. The peculiarity of the situation lies in the fact that economic struggle does not suit Russian colonial imperialism. Russian expansion was always based on armed force; on brutal compulsion, and on cementing her political rule by completely depriving subjected people of all rights. The clearest illustration is provided by imperialist expansion conducted by Russia during the very same period in lands of the Middle and Far East, whither Russia wanted to extend her colonial holdings.

In 1896, Russian financiers of the "Discount-Loan Bank" gave Persia (Iran) a loan in the amount of 1 million pounds sterling. At the same time the Government imposed a treaty upon Persia, according to which Persia was obliged to negotiate all further loans only through Russian banks. There was a new loan in 1900, and in 1902 a treaty granting Russia profitable concessions and trade facilities. In 1907 there was a treaty with Great Britain concerning the division of spheres of interest in Persia, and finally in 1908 military occupation of Northern Persia. There was an analogous situation in Afghanistan. The same thing in China: in 1895-96 a loan for the payment of China's reparations to Japan; and in return, the right to construct the Eastern Chinese Railroad through Manchuria, and huge concessions in

Manchuria. In 1901 military occupation, the lease of Port Arthur and Dalny, and a complete conquest of the oil, sugar and grain market through the Russian-Chinese Bank and the Siberian Bank. In 1903, huge lumber concessions in Korea followed the establishment of military bases, and this finally led to the Russo-Japanese War of 1904-1905.[83]

Always and everywhere, Russian colonial imperialist expansion was in the nature of compulsion by force of arms and of political subjugation.

Russia's policy of the so-called "financial imperialism" was conducted by devious ways. It was not a policy of financial investment in the Ukrainian economy, nor a development of industrial enterprises of the metropolis in the territory of the colony. The heart of the process was that Russia, in cooperation with foreign capital, by means of various "reorganizations" and of direct pressure, appropriated Ukrainian industry, and in 1917, following the Bolshevik upheaval, extended the expropriation also to foreign capital invested in that industry.

This process of appropriating Ukrainian industry and of thus conquering the entire Ukrainian economy disclosed the system of colonial exploitation of Ukraine most clearly.

We shall now proceed to illustrate that process.

---

[83] According to material in M. Golman's "Russkiy Imperyalizm," pp. 347 ff.

CHAPTER 4

FINANCE CAPITAL IN UKRAINIAN INDUSTRY

Western European Capital

THAT PERIOD IN UKRAINIAN economic history which brought a mass influx of foreign capital into industry, evokes in people unacquainted with the real nature of these processes a distorted picture of the Ukrainian economy at the time. There are also some, who deliberately utilize the situation in order to distort the true picture. Some, like M. Wolf, K. Pazhitnov and others, perceive in it a colonial dependence of Ukraine not upon Russia but upon foreign capital. Others, like M. Balabanov, M. Hurevych, and partially Peshekhonov, making their point of departure the leading position of Ukrainian metallurgy and coal mining as main branches of industry which determined the entire industrial level, and particularly from the fact of a monopolistic domination of the imperial markets by syndicates established in these branches, attempt to treat the matter in such manner that they allege that Ukraine was not the object of colonial exploitation, but on the contrary, the whole Empire was economically dependent upon, and subject to Ukrainian industry. The most prevailing attitude is, however, to ignore the specific nature of foreign capital investments in the Ukrainian economy, and to dwell upon the semi-colonial dependence of the whole Empire upon Western Europe, and upon the reparation and localization of labor within the entire Imperial economic body.

Such distortion of the real nature of affairs, along with the true impact of foreign capital upon the direction and nature of the development of industry in Ukraine requires a separate analysis. This is all the more necessary, inasmuch as industrial conditions created in that time played a definite, and no small part, in the subsequent economic relations between Ukraine and Russia during Soviet times.

We shall begin with the characteristics of foreign (Western European) capital in Ukrainian industry, its origin, specific gravity, and dominant role in places of its highest saturation. There is no complete summary of foreign investments in Ukraine, because available figures refer mainly to industrial corporations. Neither are there accurate figures available as to the territorial repartition of foreign capital in commerce, transportation, or municipal enterprises. Nor is there any summary of other forms of capital accumulation, except corporate. And most important, there cannot be a determination made of that part of capital which flowed into Ukraine through Russian banks.

Direct investments of Western European capital in industry are a phenomenon of only the last decades of the 19th and of the beginning of the 20th centuries. In addition, foreign capital played an important part in the industrial development of Russia, but mostly in the form of Government borrowing. Even during the time of Finance Minister Vishnegradsky, there was a conversion of internal loans, placing them abroad, which gave the Government almost 1.5 billion rubles, used almost exclusively for the construction of state railroads in Russia. Later, foreign loans were of tremendous importance in the so-called "extraordinary budget" which made it possible, as we shall indicate later, to appropriate large sums of money for the Ministries of Communications and of Finance, of which Russian railroads and industry took good advantage.

The participation of Western European capital in industrial corporations of the whole Empire totalled, in the year 1870, only 26.5 million rubles. By 1880 the amount had increased to 97.7 million rubles, during the next ten years to 214.7 million rubles, and by 1900 it had reached 911 million rubles.[1]

The influx of foreign capital increased its tempo even more from that time on. At the time of World War I the nominal value of stock owned by foreign capital equalled 1,532 million rubles, plus 300 million rubles worth of bonds.

In 1917 out of a total of 3,185 million rubles representing stock and bond capital of industrial corporations in the Empire, 1,595 million rubles, or 50.1% were the property of foreign capital, and out of 470 million rubles worth of stock in banking corporations, 237 million or 49.9%, were foreign held. The total of 3,655 million rubles in the two groups was about evenly divided

[1] P. Lashchenko, *Istoriya narodnoho khozyaystva SSSR*, II, 156.

between foreign and domestic capital, the latter owning 1,832 million rubles, or slightly over 50%.[2]

The percentage of foreign capital in corporations was steadily increasing, and surpassed the rate of increase of capital accumulated from domestic sources. In 1901, foreign capital held only 39.5% of the stock in industrial corporations (608 million out of 1,548 million) and in banking corporations only 6% (11.4 million out of 188.4 million). But prior to the outbreak of the revolution this percentage had grown to 50%. This does not mean that all corporations in the Empire were under an absolute domination of foreign capital, because its distribution among the various branches of industry and among the territories was very uneven. "This is very clear from a comparison of the South with the Urals. Foreign capital displayed no desire to go into the Urals, where remnants of conditions of serfdom still existed, and for this reason domestic capital reigned there. The enterprises were on a small scale with a low technical level of production and, besides the region did not possess its own hard coal. Later, during the period of Imperialism, the predominance of foreign enterprises which entered into monopolistic associations or combines with the largest Russian enterprises, made a very marked appearance."[3]

"In the light (manufacturing) and in the food industries, particularly in cotton, milling, oil, leather, woodworking etc. Russian national capital was in the majority, and in some regions and branches (the central regions and in textiles) it reigned supreme. Separate from this group of light industry enterprises stood the sugar and the tobacco industry. Because of the nature of its manufacturing (particularly refineries), the sugar industry felt an acute need of production and turnover credits, and for this reason it was the first to fall under the control of banks, at first of special local banks (Ukrainian—*Author*) and later banking monopolies of Petersburg banks."[4]

Thus, with the exception of railroads and banks, the bulk of foreign capital was concentrated in Ukraine, and the two main branches of light industry, sugar and tobacco, were, in contrast to the Russian, also captured by foreign capital. Therefore the statement that Russia herself was a semi-colony of Western

---

[2] M. Golman, "Russkiy Imperyalizm," p. 330.
[3] P. Lashchenko, *op. cit.*, p. 151.
[4] P. Lashchenko, *op. cit.*, pp. 376-377.

European capital, does not conform to reality. Ukraine, and Azerbaijan with its oil were almost exclusively with object of this kind of exploitation, with the possible exception of gold mining in Siberia. It is true that Russia proper consumed a large slice of foreign capital in the form of state loans, but, as we shall see later, the payment of these loans fell in large measure upon Ukraine.

Taking all corporations in the Empire, foreign capital was invested in them, according to the various branches of industry, during the ten-year period 1890 to 1900, in the amounts shown in *Table LXX* (in millions of rubles).[5] Thus, the participation of

TABLE LXX

Industry	1890			1900		
	Total corporate capital	Of this foreign	%	Total corporate capital	Of this foreign	%
Coal mining	85.7	70.1	81.6	492.2	437.9	89.0
Metal	27.8	14.0	50.4	257.3	145.3	56.5
Chemical	15.6	6.4	41.0	93.8	29.3	31.2
Ceramic	6.7	0.2–	3.0–	59.0	26.3	44.7
Textile	197.5	26.0	13.2	373.7	71.4	19.1
Food	87.6	7.6	8.7	153.1	11.4	7.5
All branches of industry...	580.1	186.2	32.1	1,742.3	911.0	52.2

European capital in the most highly developed branches of industry in Russia was relatively low, in any event such that could not gain a dominating position. And if we consider that the majority of enterprises in these branches of industry were not corporate in form, it is quite futile to speak of any domination over Russian industry. Domination of foreign capital applies then only to non-Russian territories and primarily to Ukraine.

Out of a corporate capital, the property of foreign investors, according to the status in 1913 of 1,343.5 million rubles was: investments in Ukrainian industry, 465.7 million; in Polish industry, 126.9 million; in Latvian, 45.4 mllion; Lithuanian, 5 million, and in Estonian 2.5 million. Hence the amount remaining for the rest of the Empire is 703 million. But of this, 200 million was invested in Azerbaijan oil and 250 million in banks which, in their turn, owned stock in industrial corporations of non-Russian

[5] *Ibid.*, p. 157.

territories. Finally, 100 million was invested in railroads serving both Russia proper and non-Russian terrain. Thus, the direct participation of foreign capital in corporations of Russian industrial enterprises did not exceed 10% to 15% of the total amount of such investments.[6]

The best illustration is provided by the repartition of French capital in two such industries taken over by it, as coal mining and metals. Out of 102 million rubles of such capital in the coal industry in 1903, 81.9 million was invested in the Donets basin, 18.8 million in the Dombrowa basin (Poland), and only 2.3 million in the Kuznetsk and Moscow regions (Russia). The same applies to metals: out of 158.4 million rubles, 111.8 million were invested in Ukraine; 10.4 million in Poland, and 16.9 million in Russia.[7]

The most important role in the investment of capital in Ukrainian industry was played by Franco-Belgian banking syndicates, first place being held by three French banks: Banque de l'Union Parisienne, Banque des Pays Bas and Societe Generale. Participants were also: Credit Lyonnais, Comptoir National d'Escompte, and others. Worthy of mention is the Belgian Societe Belge du Credit Industrial et Commercial German. (Mendelsohn, Disconto Gesellschaft, etc.) and British banks played only a secondary role in foreign capital investment in Ukraine, although Germany occupied first place in Ukraine's foreign trade.

Among the foreign financial industrial enterprises there were about 20 which were governed by French and Belgian by-laws, and one (Spilka chornoyi metalurgiyi: Black Metallurgy Company) had German by-laws. Many of them conducted their business records in French. Thus, even as to form, these were completely alien businesses located on Ukrainian territory.

According to data published at the time in such periodicals as "Yezhegodnik Finansov," "Torgovo-Promishlenna Gazeta" and "Vestnik Finansov," the distribution of foreign capital in three industrial groups of Ukraine was, in the year 1911, as is shown in *Table LXXI* (in thousands of rubles).

The 16,367 thousand rubles under the title of unknown capital could certainly be included in the Franco-Belgian capital group, because the majority of the associations in this group consisted of enterprises governed by foreign by-laws. Thus,

---

[6] P. Fomin, "Ekonomichna kharaterystyka Ukrainy," p. 93.
[7] *Ibid.*, p. 92.

TABLE LXXI

Industrial groups	Total foreign capital	Unknown	Out of this capital total			
			Franco-Belgian	British	Franco-German	German
1. Metallurgical smelting (16 industrial associations)	204,523	....	170,546	11,352	15,400	7,225
percentages	100	....	83.4	5.6	7.5	3.5
2. Pig iron and metal working (8 associations)	20,492	14,492	6,000	....	....	....
percentages	100	70.7	29.3	....	....	....
3. Iron-ore (4 associations)	5,437	1,875	3,562	....	....	....
percentages	100	65.4	34.6	....	....	....
Total of 3 groups	230,452	16,367	180,108	11,352	15,400	7,225
Percentages	100	7	84.1	5.3	7.2	3.4

[8] N. Vanag, "Finansoviy kapital v Rossiyi nakanune mirovoy voyny," 1930, p. 213.

about 90% of all foreign capital invested in Ukrainian metallurgy was provided by French and Belgian banks.

This proportion did not undergo any change until the time of the revolution. And it must be further emphasized that at that time France also occupied first place among the Russian Government creditors, because these two circumstances are, as we shall later indicate, to a certain extent related to each other.

French capital also occupied first place in financing of the coal mining industry. Out of 139 million rubles foreign capital invested in this industry, in the branch which was controlled by metallurgical associations: 106 million (75.5%) was Franco-Belgian capital; 5 million (3.6%), German; 5 million (0.4%), British, and 26.5 million, unknown.[9]

The role of foreign capital, and, by the same token, of the Franco-Belgian part in it will become even more clear, if we consider not the sum of investments, but the production totals of the enterprises which were under complete control of this capital, and of the Russian banks connected with it.

Production of smelting corporations of Ukraine in 1913 (in thousands of tons)[10] is shown in *Table LXXII*.

TABLE LXXII

a. Pig Iron Smelting

Total	Franco-Belgian	British	German	Franco-German
3,025.6	2,526.4	270.4	160.0	68.8
In percentage relation to total imperial production:				
66.8	55.8	5.9	3.6	1.5
In percentage relation to total Ukrainian production:				
99.6	83.2	8.9	5.3	2.2

b. Iron Ore Mining

5,070.4	4,806.4	214.4		
In percentage relation to total imperial production:				
54.4	51.6	2.3	0.5	
In percentage relation to total Ukrainian production:				
75.4	71.5	3.2	0.7	

c. Coal Mining

6,248.0	4,870.4	1,377.6		
In percentage relation to total imperial production:				
17.7	13.8	3.9		
In percentage relation to total Ukrainian production:				
25.00	19.5	5.5		

[9] *Ibid.,* p. 209.   [10] *Ibid.,* p. 216.

The figures referring to coal do not give a complete picture, because the table contains only data of such mines as belonged to metallurgical corporations. Another 36% should be added to account for the production of mines not owned by smelters, but which were also under control of foreign capital.

Thus, almost the entire metallurgical industry, three-fourths of the iron ore mining industry, and more than half the coal industry can be called Ukrainian only in the sense that they were located in Ukraine and were based on its natural wealth.

Even the part of these industries that was not under foreign capital control did not belong to Ukraine. It was in the hands of Russian banks which also played a large part in enterprises controlled by European capital.

The last factor is of essential significance. It refutes the statement that from the time of a mass influx of foreign capital into Ukrainian industry, Ukraine ceased being a Russian colony, and became the object of colonial exploitation by Franco-Belgian capital, and included in the colonial system of the West. Such a conclusion is the obvious one to arrive at, considering the preponderance of foreign investments in the basic industries of Ukraine. Even M. Volobuyev, who painted the most clear picture of the colonial position of Ukraine in the Russian Empire, wrote: "Its (foreign capital's) influx into Ukraine made sharp changes in the economic-geographic map of Ukraine, favoring a rapid development of productive forces in the region of mining and industry. Foreign capital was not directly concerned with centralistic, great-power desires of Russian capitalism. It was as though it had relegated Russian capital to second place, including the Ukrainian economic territory within its system of exploitation."[11]

M. Yavorsky went even further, saying: "In this manner Ukraine became, thanks to the great demand for her pig iron, the first-ranking producer of it, delivering its products to all corners of Russia regardless of distance, pointing in no dubious language to the future centralization of supply, which the Russian economists began to fear so much."[12]

An impression is being created that foreign capital, gaining control of industry in Ukraine, cancelled the latter's colonial ties with Russia, broke the centralistic system, and assumed

[11] M. Volobuyev, "Do problemy Ukrainskoyi economiky."
[12] M. Yavorsky, *Ukraina v epokhu kapitalismu*, III, 27.

the place of Russia in continued colonial exploitation of Ukraine. It would seem from the words of Yavorsky that from that time Ukraine became a separate body which threatened Russia with centralization and with domination of Russia's metallurgy. We have here, undoubtedly, a confusion of terms and ideas, of which many scholars were guilty, some of whom were able to clearly see the true nature of the relations between Ukraine and Russia. In spite of themselves they mechanically interchange the social-economic category with the territorial.

Foreign capital not only did not break the Russian centralistic system in economic life, but, relying on that system and strengthening it, joined in the colonial exploitation of Ukraine. This new exploitation did not force out the old Russian, but facilitated its increase. And what on first glance appeared to be a struggle of the Ukrainian metallurgical and coal industry with the Russian, was nothing more than a struggle within Russian capitalist industry. It was a fight between the modern and more profitable segment which was located in Ukraine, and which took advantage of Ukraine's colonial status, and the remnants of the antiquated, semi-feudal system in Russia proper. This struggle, which contributed to the rehabilitation of Russian industry which had been halted in its development by the privileges extended to it by government policy, resulted again in large losses to Ukrainian national economy.

The whole matter becomes quite clear when we analyze the process of penetration of Western European capital into Ukraine's economy and the part played in this process by Russian banking monopolies.

Anyone becoming acquainted with the economic history of Ukraine in that period quite naturally raises the question: why did not Ukraine, with all the economic advantages, embark upon the clear path of creating a national capital? The main role in this respect was without doubt played by the fact that any production surplus, the basis on which capital is created, was excluded from the Ukrainian economy because of Ukraine's colonial position. Nevertheless, why did not at least some part of the capital surplus become invested into Ukrainian industry, which offered such tempting opportunities? Why was it that the large amounts saved by the peasants for land acquisition, were not deposited in banks, and then become utilized for industrial investment? Why did not Ukraine produce more of such types of businessmen like Kharytonenko and Tereshchenko, and why did not the management of Ukrainian industry find its way into their hands? These are all very proper questions and require an answer. And the only answer complying with the real truth is that there were external forces which prevented all these things from being done.

Ruination of National Capital

All processes of creating capital, although slow because of the position of Ukraine, were present and discernible. Foreign capital did not come into a vacuum. The Russian Minister of Finance, Kokovtsev, wrote a letter to the chairman of the Paris Bourse, Verneuil. [Verneuil had proposed to set up "with the aid of friends a financially strong group which would be ready to study commercial and industrial enterprises existing in Russia (i.e. in Ukraine—*Author*) that could be developed with the aid of French capital."] He wrote: "I am very happy that you are not establishing a new enterprise, but have in mind helping to develop those existing ones which, healthy by nature, suffer from a lack of capital."[13]

In the 1870's to 1890's the process of capital creation in Ukraine was already under way within the national boundaries and within the aspects of Ukrainian interests. Hence the heavy influx of foreign capital was preceded by a period of ruthless struggle against the, as yet, weak Ukrainian industry, resulting in its ruin.

The ruination of Ukrainian capital in industry took place against the background of the crisis of the 1890's. In commenting upon that crisis, we have already noted that it came about as the result of abnormal conditions of industrial development imposed upon Ukraine: the unilateral direction of the metallurgical industry; its complete dependence upon railroad construction; artificial restraints of the market for Ukrainian coal, etc. The crisis of inventory accumulation was simultaneous with an acute desire for iron among the wide masses of the population. The crisis hit the, as yet, financially weak structure of the young industry very painfully. In addition, there came a catastrophic decline of prices of stocks representing Ukrainian industrial enterprises on foreign exchanges.

[13] N. Vanag, *op. cit.*, p. 129.

Exchange values of stocks of Ukrainian industrial corporations, quoted on the Paris and Brussels Bourse (in thousands of
francs) were as shown in *Table LXXIII*.

TABLE LXXIII

	Oct. 15, 1899	Oct. 15, 1901	% of decline
50 metallurgical corporations	868,043	298,069	65
18 coal mining corporations	347,148	185,957	46
6 glass corporations	17,987	3,632	79

[14]

The crisis deepened by accelerated preparations for the
currency reform of 1897. They not only increased the tight financial situation of industry, but had even more detrimental repercussions upon the whole Ukrainian economy. This, in turn,
had an effect on the position of industry: a setback in railroad
construction had an effect upon the purchasing power of the
population; losses on exports of grain fell upon its basic producers, the peasants; bank deposits did not grow at the expected
rate, and the like.

Prior to the currency reform of 1897 there were two types
of currency in the Empire: silver and treasury notes called *assig-
nats,* and the exchange of the latter for silver was suspended
following the Crimean War. The continued issuance of notes
(from 713.5 million rubles in 1862 to 1,121.3 million rubles on
the eve of the currency reform)[15] without regard to the decline
of the price of silver on world markets, brought about a continual decline of the value of the *assignat* ruble in relation to silver. Only in the 1880's did the Finance Ministry begin to take
measures in order to curtail the excessive issuance of paper
money. In the mid-1890's the rate was pegged at 1 *assignat*
ruble or 37 kopecks silver. Nevertheless the internal value of silver in the Imperial currency system was higher than its value as
a commodity. During that period the value of silver per ounce
on the London market was: 1873, 59.2 pence; 1881, 51.7 pence;
1890, 47.75 pence, and 1895, 29.8 pence.[16]

[14] P. A. Khromov, *Ekonomicheskoye razvitiye Rossiyi v XIX-XX v.v.
(Economic Development of Russia in the 19th and 20th Centuries),*
1950, p. 309.
[15] M. Koshkarev, *Denezhnoye obrashcheniye v Rossiyi (Money Circulation
in Russia),* Moscow, 1898, I, 72-73.
[16] N. Ratzig, *Finansovaya politika Rossiyi s 1887 goda (Russia's Financial
Policy since 1887),* St. Petersburg, 1903, p. 47.

For this reason the determination of silver and gold by weight produced an agio. In 1877 this agio amounted to 48%. And to the extent that the Russian Government, in order to accumulate gold for the currency reform and for the liquidation of foreign balances, decided in 1876 to collect customs tariffs in gold, to that extent this agio inevitably produced a decline of the price of export goods. In order to compensate himself for the gold ruble the exporter wanted to get a greater quantity of goods that he purchased for exportation. Thus the determination of internal prices in paper currency falsely altered the currency's real value. "During a period of over 30 years, agio for gold in Russia fluctuated to such an extent that exporters who were selling grain abroad had to get exchange rate insurance. This guarantee cost money and lowered our grain prices."[17]

The basic export commodity was grain, and its chief producer Ukraine. Therefore the losses on currency exchange rates fell in the largest degree upon Ukraine, and had repercussions on Ukrainian industry which, under pressure of the crisis had to embark upon the exportation of its products. In a memorandum on currency reform, Minister Witte wrote: "Following the fluctuations of the exchange rate (of money), our grain prices fell when they rose on the world markets, and vice versa, i.e. these fluctuations falsified grain prices and gave a mistaken direction to our exports, increasing and lowering them in a direction contrary to the proper course which should have been taken, and drawing us into suffering double damages: nudging us towards exports when prices on world markets were detrimental, and curtailing our exports when prices were advantageous. From this the agricultural economy suffers most" (i.e. primarily Ukraine—*Author*).[18]

But Witte fails to mention that in order to get favorable balance of exports over imports, the Government used all available means, primarily through its agrarian policy, to compel the Ukrainian peasants to sell as much of their grain as possible. All these currency conditions, we repeat, became the most grievous during the first years of the crisis and deepened it.

Bank credits could not save Ukrainian industry during that period not only because the crisis impeded the banks themselves,

---

[17] *Ibid.*, p. 52.
[18] A. Bukovetsky, (Ed.), *Materyaly po denezhnoy reforme 1895-97 g. (Materials on the Currency Reform of 1895-97)*, Moscow, 1903, p. 19.

but mainly because Russian banks, clearing the path to Ukraine for their own and foreign capital, led a determined attack against those Ukrainian banks which were still independent of them.

In this respect the history of the Kharkiv Commercial Bank is most illuminating. It was established by a millionaire Ukrainian businessman Alchevsky, who was at the same time a director of the Kharkiv Land Bank and organizer of the Oleksiev Mining Industry Association in 1879. Alchevsky made determined demands that Ukrainian industry should be permitted to develop independently. He used all sorts of business methods to accumulate millions of rubles for the establishment and aid of mining-industry enterprises, which he foresaw as being able to yield "a pot of gold." He estimated the opportunities of Ukrainian industry very highly and used all his power to aid it in surviving the crisis. Nevertheless, he was unable to withstand the common Russo-French financial front. His bank failed and Alchevsky himself committed suicide. "What is the significance of this death in a capitalist community?" asks Professor P. Khromov. He answers: "It means that weaker capitalists, capitalists of 'the second grade' are pushed out by stronger millionaires. The Moscow millionaire, Ryabushinsky, took the place of the Kharkiv millionaire, Alchevsky."[19]

The failure of the Kharkiv bank hit the connected industrial enterprises very hard, among them one of the largest, the Donets-Yurievsky Association. After this, Ukrainian industry was helpless to ward off the appetite of Russo-French financial concerns.

A similar fate befell the Oleksiev Mining Industry Association founded by Alchevsky. It fought for its independence for some time, although "during the crisis it came under some degree of control of Russian banks, the Volga-Kama Bank becoming one of its larger stockholders in 1900. Nevertheless until 1905 it did not lose its national character."[20] When foreign capital established the syndicate "Produhol" in 1904, this Oleksiev Association was its chief stumbling block, since at that time it held first place in production with 780.8 thousand tons. In 1908 the Franco-Belgian banking syndicate purchased the stock in this association from the Volga-Kama Bank and brought it under its control.[21]

[19] P. Khromov, *op. cit.*, p. 308.   [20] N. Vanag, *op. cit.*, p. 124.   [21] *Loc. cit.*

Similar occurrences took place in Kiev, in connection with the second-largest bank, the Kiev Commercial Bank which worked with capital of Ukrainian sugar refineries. The Azov-Don Bank in Petersburg, using French capital, began extending credits to the sugar refining industry on easier terms, and bought up shares in the Kiev Commercial Bank from sugar refineries. "With the aid of French banks, by 1913 the Azov-Don Bank had bought up a majority of stock in the Kiev bank, and had become one of the principal monopolists in financing the sugar industry."[22]

Such warfare against national-territorial banks went on not only in Ukraine, but in Russia's other colonies as well. Thus, in 1908 for example, the French banking syndicate underwrote a new issue of stock of the above mentioned Azov-Don Bank for the specific purpose of buying up of the stock of the Minsk (Belorussian) Commercial Bank. Thus, there was a flow of foreign capital into more than Ukrainian industry. At the same time, against the background of the economically inexplicable crisis, a process of destroying the national financial credit system and of bolstering the financial monopoly of Russian banks, primarily of Petersburg, went on. This too was in the interest of foreign capital.

The matter did not end in complete control of banks. There was a simultaneous attack against industry itself. After wrecking the financial basis of an enterprise, (depreciating its stock capital, favoring its creditors, etc.) and thoroughly ruining it, it would revive with a new complement of shareholders—foreign and Russian banks. Under the term "financial reorganization," such alterations were so widely applied to Ukrainian industrial enterprises that they became routine. In all justice, this period in the history of Ukrainian industry should be called a period of mass and deliberately organized financial bankruptcy which had no justification either in production conditions of the industry itself, or in objective market conditions. In this period the few remaining enterprises whose national designation was Ukrainian, perished. Since then Ukrainian industry in its main branches ceased to exist as such, and became the industry of the metropolis in colonial territories.

How very far real conditions of manufacturing and sales were from causing any crisis and decline of Ukrainian industry is attested to by the evaluation of conditions by French capital

[22] *Loc. cit.*

itself, the same which took an active part in organizing the
bankruptcies of these enterprises. In 1907, the French periodical,
Le Financier International, said: "France has never considered
that by underwriting Russian loans it was thus engaging in any
charitable work. France considered, and still considers, Russian
securities a very convenient, safe and wonderful location of capital. Russia represents a most reliable and remarkably convenient
debtor. Suffice it to recall the uncounted natural wealth of Russia (here they had in mind Ukraine—*Author*), the profitable exploitation of which cannot be doubted. France should never
wish to lose in the future the convenient position in the exploitation of these immense riches which she is now occupying."[23]

It is clear from these words that the principle underlying
these "financial reorganizations" was not any attempt to cure
an existing evil by providing capital which was lacking, but
rather the conquest of such "very convenient positions" which
had to be captured from Ukrainian national capital by destruc-
tive means. This had its repercussions on the nature of such
"reorganizations." The reorganizations "consisted of writing off
a part of the initial capital (depreciation of stock—*Author*), satisfying the main creditors, banks (and depreciating loans of other
creditors—*Author*), and financing enterprises by issuing new
stock which was purchased by such bank or a banking syndicate which conducted this credit operation."[24]

A good example of such "reorganization" is that of the
Donets-Yurievsky Metallurgical Association carried out in 1907.
The Banking House of Telman & Co. delivered the following
ultimatum to the association in the name of French banking interests: "1) It is proposed that the association reduce (re-evalu-
ate—*Author*) its present capital from 8 million rubles to 3.2 million; 2) The association will then undertake a new issue of
shares in the amount of 12 million rubles; 3) If these proposi-
tions are accepted by the shareholders meeting, then after 4 days
Telman & Co. will advise whether it will purchase from the
Donets-Yurievsky Association all such stock of the new issue
which will remain undistributed among the present shareholders."[25]

---

[23] N. Vanag, *op. cit.,* p. 23.
[24] N. Vanag, "Finansoviy kapital v tyazheloy industriyi" ("Finance Capital
   in Heavy Industry"), *Proletariy* (*The Proletarian*), 1930, p. 19.
[25] *Ibid.,* p. 23.

French banks went into negotiations with all the creditors of the Donets-Yurievsky Association and guaranteed payment of these debts. For this they got 6.15 million rubles worth of preferred stock of the new issue at 7%. Cash from the sale of the remaining shares the association undertook to use for the acquisition of coal lands of the Oleksiev Mining Industry Association (the same which resisted the "Produhol" syndicate for a long time, fighting for its independent existence).

Almost all "reorganizations" were carried out according to this pattern: in 1906, the South-Dniprovske Metallurgical Company; in 1905, the Tahanrih Metallurgical Company; in 1908, the Nikopil-Mariupil Metallurgical Company etc. "Reorganizations" often brought along, besides, changes in the financial structure, as well as administrative changes. A new number of directors would be established, such directorships being given mainly to officers of Russian banks. Thus, new directors Balabanov, Pfeiffer, Burchardt and Mikhailov, of the Russian International Bank, were appointed to the Nikopil-Mariupil Company.

The most essential characteristics of the financial expansion of Western European capital in Ukraine were its two goals: join in the exploitation of the national economy of Ukraine, and strengthen the colonial dependence of Ukraine upon Russia. It was not satisfied with the high profits derived from the development and financial strengthening of industry. It further aimed at eradicating all remnants of any signs of a national character of the Ukrainian industry by introducing Russian management. This is the real cause of the terrible ruin inflicted upon Ukrainian industrial enterprises during the process of influx of foreign capital.

By its nature, this capital invested in Ukraine should be fully described as colonial, but there is still no basis for maintaining that since that time Ukraine became a colony of Western Europe. European capital made it possible for a handful of Russian banks to monopolize Ukrainian industry and to increase tremendously Ukraine's colonial exploitation, making larger profits available to both. Without realizing this we could not understand the true role played by Russian banks in that time and in that connection.

Russian Banks

It is not hard to guess why Western European capital chose
the path it did. The decisive factor was that colonial capitalist
expansion was carried out in a territory without any political
ties with Western Europe. In such situations, capital always desires to take out insurance in the form of legal guarantees, or,
to put it more precisely, to cloak its activities with legality. A
partnership with Ukrainian banks could not give foreign capital
adequate protection, because these banks worked within a system of economic dependence on Russia. Moreover, foreign capital could foresee that in spite of a temporary complacency, the
Ukrainian banks would inevitably oppose any excessive colonial exploitation. Such a partner would always defend the interests of the land and would strive to shake free of any foreign
domination.

Russian banks presented a different picture. Their interests
were parallel to those of Western European capital. Any
differences that would arise would only be on the plane of a division of profits. Foreign capital then sought satisfactory opportunities of expansion in territories politically independent of its
control. This capital could not have ignored the prospect that
even under a complete subjugation of the Ukrainian economy,
political prerogatives, without which it could not continue, will
still be in the hands of the Russian Government. Hence the decision to form ties with the Russian political system. The symbiosis with Russian banks provided a way out of the impasse, because in their Ukrainian activities, the Russian banks had not
only the opportunity to rely on a favorable policy of the Government, but were also an organic part of the official system.
"Commercial banking corporations had strong ties with the
state apparatus. Russian ministers of finance nominated directors of banks (frequently from among their own officials)
through the credit bureau, authorized payment of millions of
subsidies to banks, etc. Such subsidies reached as high as 800
to 1,000 million rubles."[26]

The Russian Government took an active part in the realization of this symbiosis of Western European capital with Russian
banks for the purpose of gaining control over the industries of
colonies, because in this manner it facilitated the floating of

[26] P. Khromov, *op. cit.*, p. 370.

state loans abroad. ". . . Interested in the success of state loans, the Government opened the doors wide for the influx of foreign capital into the Russian banking system and industry . . . The Minister of Finance delivered the controlling portfolio of stock in the Russian-Azov Bank to French banks in order to interest French capital in Far-Eastern enterprises of the Tsarist Government."[27]

The participation of Russian banks in capital stock of Ukrainian industrial corporations, and even more their role of middlemen in the financing of these enterprises by foreign capital, were, for the most part, the result of a deliberate policy, dictated by the motives discussed above.

Eloquent testimony on the artificiality of the participation of Russian banks in financial activities of foreign capital is provided by the following excerpt from a letter by Minister Kokovtsev to his deputy Ya. Utin who was at that time, conducting negotiations with French banks: "These (claims of Russian banks to participate) mean that either the profits of the French capital will have to be cut, or the treasury's expenses to compensate the banks (Russian) will have to be increased, the latter having joined a matter in which they have no real participation."[28]

Similarly the participation of foreign capital in capital stock of Russian banks was in large measure organically connected with the role which they played in the common cause of exploiting colonial territories. In this manner the community of their interests and the interests of foreign banks became more solidified. The latter, quite naturally perceived a strong guarantee of safeguarding their common interests. Syndicates of foreign banks frequently aided Russian banks in the issuance of new stock which they subscribed, on condition that the Russian banks would use the capital thus raised for the acquisition of shares in Ukrainian industrial enterprises. This was the manner in which the Russian International Bank acquired shares of the Nikopil-Mariupil Company, the Azov-Don Bank, the shares of the Tahanrih Company etc. "What reason compelled Parisian bankers to take an interest in Russian banks?" This is explained in no uncertain terms by M. Davidov, director of the Petersburg Chastny (private) Bank. Informing the shareholders that the "syndicate" guaranteed a new issue of stock, he said that "Pari-

---

[27] P. Lashchenko, *op. cit.*, p. 365. [28] N. Vanag, *op. cit.*, p. 128.

sian banks have in mind by this operation to facilitate Russian credit institutions becoming intermediaries between industrial enterprises and European markets."[29]

But there is no basis from all this for concluding that in the matter of colonial exploitation the Russian banks were only playing a minor part, or that they were merely in the service of foreign capital.

The way the Russian banks themselves understood their role is best illustrated by the Moscow banking tycoon, Ryabush-insky in his own words spoken at a commercial congress in Moscow. Speaking of the penetration of foreign capital, he said with emphasis: "This does not mean that we should reject foreign capital, but it is necessary that this capital should not feel like a conquerer. It is necessary that we pit our own capital against it, and for this purpose it is necessary to create conditions under which it can accumulate and develop."[30]

The conditions were by no means unfavorable, as far as the support given these banks by the Government is concerned. It is true that the general picture of the Russian money market of the period cannot be termed as blooming. This market depended upon the low saturation point of the market for manufactured goods, determined primarily by the peasants, the basis of the population. For this reason, capital sources outside industry could not take the appropriate part in industrial investments. Peoples' savings, which would accumulate in a banking system and nourish industry were, in a semi-natural economy, very insignificant. In Ukraine, as we have indicated above, almost the entire cash part of the peasants' budget was swallowed up by excessive taxes, excises and leases of land. And wherever there was an excess of income above consumption in a household, it would go mainly toward the acquisition of land. Therefore the greater part of the surplus production created by the rural economy accumulated in the hands of the landlords and was spent by them on non-productive consumption, most often abroad. The low level of the population's purchasing power, the narrow market for goods and the restricted possibilities of non-industrial capital accumulation were responsible for that perpetual cash starvation in the Empire, which was felt all the time and which contributed to the attraction of foreign capital. The condition was made more acute because the Russian Empire,

[29] N. Vanag, *op. cit.*, p. 139.   [30] *Ibid.*, p. 113.

indu;trially backward, desired to go through historical cycles of development at an accelerated pace.

But for all that, in evaluating the banks' role in the industrial economy, we cannot underestimate the resources of internal money accumulations, and must determine the role of banks merely by their own part of stock capital. As Lashchenko correctly states: "Although in the leading banking corporations up to 42% of their stock capital was in the hands of foreign shareholders, yet from this it is still a far cry to the same degree of dependence of Russian banks and of the entire Russian banking system upon foreign capital. Stock capital comprises only between one-third and one-fourth of the credits with which banks operate, and in the concentration of such credits banks depended upon conditions of the Russian money market."[31]

One might argue that on the contrary, in this case we should speak rather of the domination by foreign capital, of internal capital accumulations in the Empire by exercising a leading role in the banks, because such a leading role does not necessarily require possession of a controling 51% bloc of stock because there are always some passive shareholders. This is true. But in this instance it could not be so, because behind the Russian banks, in addition to their stock capital, stood also the power of the state which determined the legal norms of economic processes and thus greatly strengthened the role of Russian capital. This is all the more important, because in the process of bolstering the Russian banking system, the relative importance of foreign capital was gradually diminishing: new issues of shares always had a smaller percentage coming into foreign banks. For instance, in the Azov-Don Bank, French banks had 40,000 shares in 1911 equal to 46% of all stock capital; of the 1912 issue they got 30%, and of the 1913 issue, only 25%.

In spite of the fact that the financial market of the Empire was underdeveloped in relation to the number of population and natural opportunities, nevertheless the process of accumulation of money in the banking system went on at an increasing rate, particularly during the period of the industrial advance in the 1900's. For this reason any conception of the true role of Russian banks cannot by any means be narrowed down to the accentuation of the important role played in them by capital of foreign banks. Huge amounts of internal accumulation went

---

[31] P. Lashchenko, *op. cit.*, p. 365.

through the turnover channels of the Russian banking system, which were many times larger than stock capital, and their management determined the power of their influence on industry, commerce, etc. "In spite of the impressive participation of foreign capital, Russian banks managed to keep the controlling influence in their own hands."[32]

"A group of nine to twelve Petersburg banks, concentrating up to 50% of banking stock capital and up to 65% of all bank deposits, was actually that banking monopoly in Russian financial capitalism. Combining with industrial monopolies, and aided by foreign capital, it held in its hands the financing of the entire industry."[33]

"This process of strengthening the position of the financial oligarchy was accelerated, because in Russia, finance capital cemented its ties with the state apparatus and made large profits on so-called state enterprises, utilizing for that purpose the government's credit, special state loans to industry, etc."[34]

We can get an idea of the amounts handled by the banking system from *Table LXXIV*, savings, deposits, and current accounts of institutions of credit and savings banks (in millions of rubles).

We see from this that huge amounts, for that time, were at the disposal of corporate banks, and we must bear in mind that in reality the data apply only to about nine gigantic banks of Petersburg and Moscow. Outside of these all others constituted a negligible quantity, without any role in financing industry, and whose activities were restricted merely to crediting local commercial transactions.

"The total balance of corporate banks as of Jan. 1, 1910 was 2,611 million rubles, of which ten Petersburg banks accounted for 1,845 million; four Moscow banks for 379 million, and all other seventeen banks for 387 million rubles."[35] The nine gigantic banks were: Russian Bank for Foreign Trade; Petersburg International Bank; Azov-Don Bank; Russian-Asian Bank; United (Soyedinennyi) Bank; Petersburg Private Bank of Commerce; Russian Commercial-Industrial Bank; Petersburg "Uchetno-Ssudnyi" Bank, and Siberian Bank. In some respects we should add: Moscow Commercial Bank, Warsaw Commercial Bank and Riga Bank.

---

[32] P. Lashchenko, *op. cit.*, p. 374.   [33] *Ibid.*, p. 365.
[34] M. Golman, *op. cit.*, p. 311.   [35] P. Lashchenko, *op. cit.*, p. 357.

TABLE LXXIV

Year	State bank	Corporate banks	Mutual credit institutions	City banks	Institutions of small credit (co-ops.)	Savings banks	Total
1900	168	536	178	97	...	662	1,641
1902	257	613	198	102	...	784	1,954
1904	255	776	265	109	...	911	2,316
1906	249	761	203	109	...	1,035	2,357
1908	210	1,060	271	115	113	1,207	2,976
1910	261	1,709	406	146	199	1,397	4,118
1912	266	2,330	545	183	396	1,594	5,314

[36]

36 Ibid.

The transformation of these banks into a financial monopoly came as a result of the centralization of the banking system. This was carried out with the very active support of the Government, and national banks of non-Russian areas were simultaneously destroyed. The United (Soyedinennyi) Bank was formed from the merger of the Moscow International, Orlov the South Russian Banks; the Azov-Don Bank from the Petersburg-Azov which got control of the Minsk Commercial and Kiev Commercial, the Russian-Asian merged with the Northern, etc.

Personal connection played perhaps an even more important part in the formation of a banking monopoly. The Petersburg financial and industrial magnate, Putilov, was chairman of the board of directors of the largest bank, the Russian-Asian; director of the Russian-Chinese Bank; one of the directors of the metallurgical syndicate "Prodamet" based mainly on Ukrainian industry; chief shareholders of many metallurgical enterprises which were members of "Prodamet," also of the Putilov, Sormov, Bryansk, Kolomen and other plants, and of the Neva Shipbuilding Yards. Similarly, the chief operator of the coal industry of Ukraine, Avdakov, was connected with a whole series of industrial enterprises and with influential Russian and foreign banks. The same applies to Utin and Plotnikov, directors of the Petersburg "Uchetno-Ssudnyi" Bank; Kaminka, chief director of the Azov-Don Bank and others.[37]

Both banking houses were in Petersburg, and their directors, chief shareholders of Ukrainian industrial enterprises, were likewise financial magnates of Petersburg.

It is without foundation to maintain, in the light of what was said above, that Ukraine as a result of the influx of European capital into her industries, became a colonial dependency of France or Belgium, who had pushed Russia to the side. Foreign capital bolstered the Russian financial oligarchy, facilitated a deeper penetration into the Ukrainian economy and, leaving the management and exploitation of industrial enterprises in the hands of that oligarchy, restricted itself to a participation in profits. The extent of profits was determined not only by convenient conditions of the advance of the industries of Ukraine, but also by a favorable policy of the Government, directed at increasing the framework of colonial exploitation. Not to men-

[37] P. Lashchenko, *op. cit.*, p. 364.

tion the legal status, in economic matters Ukraine continued, as before, in the role of Russia's colony, for whom foreign capital was another means of increasing the opportunities of exploitation.

"The participation of Russian capital in Ukrainian industry was smaller than of Western European capital. But political influences of Russia upon Ukraine were much greater. The policy of the Russian Empire in Ukraine in the 20th century manifested itself in the forms of an unconcealed economic-political and national-cultural oppression, and curtailment of all and any rights of Ukrainian nationality and culture."[38]

A convincing argument showing the dominant position of Russian banks in Ukrainian industry is provided by a roster of shareholders of Ukrainian industrial corporations. A few are cited as an example. Out of 44,088 outstanding shares of the Tahanrih Consolidated Metallurgy in 1914, 10,000 were in the hands of the Azov-Don Bank, 4,761 in the hands of the Russian-Asian Bank, and 1,700 in the hands of B. Kaminka, director of the Azov-Don Bank. The total is 37.3%. Nine Western European Banks held 12,441 shares of this corporation, 28.2%.

Out of 46,636 shares of the Nikopil-Mariupil Company, 10,000 belonged to the Petersburg International Bank, and 13,653 to its directors, Zolin, Grauman and others. The total is 51%. Out of 25,132 shares of the Auerbach Mercury Mining Company, 11,500 belonged to the Azov-Don Bank, 2,500 to its director Kaminka, and 2,000 to a member of its board of directors Khesin. The total is 64%.[39]

The same can be said of many other industrial corporations in Ukraine. Even toward the end of the 19th century when the flow of foreign capital had not yet reached its peak, securities of industrial enterprises constituted an impressive percentage in the portfolios of banks in the repartition of their own stock capital.

Industrial securities in the portfolios of the then chief banks of Petersburg (in percentages of their stock capital) were as shown in *Table LXXV.*

Foreign capital occupied the positions in these banks shown in *Table LXXVI* (in millions of rubles).

---

[38] O. Ohloblyn, *Peredkapitatlistychna fabryka*, p. 177.
[39] N. Vanag, *op. cit.*, p. 119.

TABLE LXXV

Year	International bank	Uchetno-Ssudyni	Commercial Industrial	Private Commercial
1896	23.4	17.9	31.4	70.4
1897	23.8	17.4	49.0	59.3
1898	25.5	24.3	53.3	62.2

TABLE LXXVI

Bank	Capital Stock	Of this foreign	Of this				Percentage of foreign capital
			German	French	British	Other	
Russian Foreign Trade	60	24.0	24.0	...	...	2.5	40.0
Petersburg International	60	24.0	20.0	1.0	0.5	2.0	40.0
Azov-Don (Petersburg)	60	22.0	8.0	10.0	2.0	2.0	36.7
Russian-Asian (Petersburg)	55	43.5	2.0	36.0	4.0	1.5	79.0
United (Moscow)	40	20.0	1.0	18.0	0.5	0.5	50.0
Petersburg Private Bank of Commerce	40	23.2	0.2	22.8	0.2	..	58.0
Russian Commercial Industrial (Petersburg)	35	15.0	1.0	4.0	10.0	..	42.8
Petersburg Uchetno-Ssudyni	30	4.0	4.0	...	...	..	13.3
Siberian Commercial (Petersburg)	20	8.0	4.0	4.0	...	..	40.0
Total:	400	183.7	64.2	95.8	17.2	6.5	46.0

[40] P. Lashchenko, op. cit., p. 372.

[41] P. V. Ol', Inostrannyi kapital v Rossiyi (Foreign Capital in Russia), Moscow, 1922, pp. 146-150.

Obviously, we cannot underestimate the importance of such a high percentage of foreign capital in Russian banks. It is equally obvious that it must have played a large part in the activities of industrial enterprises which it financed, but all this does not alter the basic fact: because of foreign capital, Russian banks became the controlling centers of Ukrainian industry and its real managers. They became simultaneously reservoirs of the accumulation of money from the whole Empire, and utilized their position to strengthen the economy of Russia proper. It is true that in their activities they safeguarded the interests of foreign capital. The reason for this, however, was not subservience. Their interests were identical.

The Petersburg banks concentrated in their hands a monopoly over disposal of all resources of internal accumulation, over representing the interests of foreign capital and over administering it. They also commanded the huge amounts which the Government collected annually in its budget from the entire population of the Empire and directed to the aid of enterprises of Russian territory proper. We have already indicated that state capitalism institutions were to be seen in Russia long before the Bolsheviks: state railroads; state factories; estates and lands of the treasury; state concessions, etc. All these constituted parts of a large state industry, located almost exclusively on the territory of Russia proper. To finance these, large sums were spent out of the budget, the latter being contributed by the entire population of the Empire. The means of financing these industries were mainly concentrated in the hands of the same banking monopolies, large sums, indeed large. "In the expenditures part of the ordinary state budget which in 1913 reached 3,094 million rubles, a basic part of expenditures, 482 million rubles went into the budget of the Ministry of Finance, with the inclusion of repayable state credits, 906 million rubles; to the Ministry of Roads, 640 million rubles; to the Ministry of the Army and Navy, out of the ordinary budget, went 826 million rubles."[42]

"These expenditures were largely spent by the Government in large part on state subsidies, all sorts of premiums to industrial and railroad capitalists, for the purchase of private enterprises by the treasury, etc."[43]

---

[42] P. Khromov, *op. cit.*, p. 372.   [43] *Ibid.*, p. 375.

Draining the financial resources of the colonies, in this manner, placing them on her own territory concentrating all commerce in her hands and hence also the accumulation of all commercial capital, Russia financially exhausted non-Russian territories, and prevented their organizing any normal financial economy. All initial attempts to create a banking system of their own, as has been indicated by examples given of the experience of the Kharkiv and Kiev Commercial banks, were ruthlessly suppressed in the name of that self-same monopolistic, unchallenged rule over the economic life of these territories.

These occurrences are not exclusively applicable to the prerevolutionary period of the advance of finance capitalism, but to the entire history of Russia's colonial policy. In a work from which we have already quoted, N. Yasnopolsky wrote: "According to Schletzer, even at the beginning of this century (19th) the interest charged on capital loaned was 6% in the Northwestern *gubernias*, 10% in Moscow, and at the same time in Tauria (Ukraine) 25% . . . In Odessa, up to the time of the establishment of a bank in 1815, they charged 3% per month, and after the bank was established the interest rate was reduced to 2% and 1% per month. Even now (the reference is to the 1870's) capital in Odessa is not much cheaper: they pay one, one and a half, and up to two percent per month, and only against absolutely safe collateral, 10%. According to Moscow manufacturers they have credit available at 6% per annum." Yasnopolsky continues and gives the underlying reason of this phenomenon on the basis of reports of the state bank: "Operations of the State Bank and its branches are conducted preponderantly in the North. In 1866, the State Bank, its branches and counters discounted drafts and other time-paper for 96,104 thousand rubles. Out of this amount, Petersburg, Riga and Archangelsk participated in 60,181 thousand rubles, or 62.5% . . . and this lack of credit institutions produced very bad results for the industry of the South."[44]

This is how it was all the time. The conquest of Ukrainian industry (and of other activities) by foreign and Russian capital came about as the result of continually depriving Ukraine of capital by draining cash internally accumulated. It is therefore not surprising that Russian industry which was much more advanced, could lean on Russian capital, while Ukraine, from

[44] N. Yasnopolsky, "Ekonomicheskaya buduchnost . . .," II, 73.

the very beginning of a wider industrial development, went into captivity of alien capital.

In his study of the characteristics of geographic regions of the Empire according to the degree of industrial development, P. Lashchenko puts the Moscow industrial region in first place, "a region of preponderantly Russian national industrial capital and with a large relative percentage of the commercial." He gives second place to the Petersburg and Baltic regions, "regions of a mixed composition of industrial capital, Russian and foreign, mainly German" (the latter was concentrated mostly in non-Russian areas along the Baltic). In third place is the region of Poland, "a region almost completely under the management of German, Polish and Jewish capital." The fourth place is held by the Southern hardcoal and black ore region, i.e. the Left Bank Ukraine, a region "of a controlling position of foreign capital and Russian capital in subsidiary control." Finally, in fifth place comes the Right Bank Ukraine, the region of the sugar industry "with Russian, Ukrainian, Jewish and Polish capital."[45]

In regard to the last-named region, or to be more accurate, in regard to the sugar industry, it would be more appropriate to speak of its complete conquest by Russian capital, in particular after the establishment of the Azov-Don Bank which swallowed up the Kiev Commercial Bank of the sugar refiners. The situation in the sugar refining industry was accurately summarized by the Minister of Finance Kokovtsev, who said: "From the exchange of ideas on the participation of banks in the sugar industry it has become clear that an influence of banks upon the industry cannot be denied, that the influence extends beyond granting of credits, and that the participation of banks in corporate and company enterprises appears to be controlling. Some banks take a very active part in the sugar industry, and this part consists not only of extending credits, but also of taking part in the enterprises themselves and in trading in sugar."[46]

Abuse of the Ukrainian Economy

It is evident that in and of itself the fact of the development of industry in Ukraine, even under foreign control, cannot be regarded as an item on the debit side from the viewpoint of the Ukrainian economy. Merely the fact that because of this development, there was an upsurge of the employment of Ukrain-

---

[45] P. Lashchenko, *op. cit.*, p. 428.   [46] P. Khromov, *op. cit.*, p. 363.

ian workers, was of great importance. But in this evaluation we must not overlook that along with the increase of the Ukrainian national income, there was even a greater increase of that part of the income which was excluded from the Ukrainian economy in favor of Russia and of Western Europe in the form of industrial and commercial profits. These profits were very large.

The pre-revolutionary Russian Empire (thanks to a very low wage scale for labor, a favorable tariff policy of the government and a relatively low "absolute" land rent) was a land of high industrial profits. The average percentage of industrial profit in relation to invested capital was, in the whole Russian Empire, as shown in *Table LXXVII* (in millions of rubles).

TABLE LXXVII

Year	Invested capital	Profit	% of invested capital
1900	2,032	284.9	14.2
1901	2,159	265.0	12.3
1902	2,260	230.4	10.2
1903	2,357	257.0	10.9
1904	2,367	277.2	11.7
1905	2,369	256.1	10.8
1906	2,319	279.0	12.1
1907	2,630	292.6	11.1
1908	2,726	292.4	10.8
1909	2,833	321.8	11.4
1910	2.789	356.4	12.7
1911	3,083	396.3	12.8
1912	3,486	460.2	13.2
1913	3,900	509.8	13.1

[47]

As we can see, the percentage of profit was very high, especially when compared to the yield of capital invested in Western European industry, where "the usual profit was between 4% and 5% and less."[48]

But these averages for the Empire seem quite small when compared with industrial profits in Ukraine. The average annual profit of the large metallurgical associations was, in relation to invested capital in 1912-1914, as shown in *Table LXXVIII*.

It was then two and one-half times higher than the average for the whole Empire. But in order to determine the degree of colonial abuse, the repartition of these profits is of even greater

[47] M. Golman, *op. cit.*, p. 202.   [48] *Ibid.*, p. 298.

TABLE LXXVIII

South-Russian Dnipro Association	57.3%
Russian Tube Association	53.0%
Russian-Belgian Association	28.1%
Kramatorsk Association	28.0%
Sulin Works	21.8%
Konstantiniv Works	23.6%
Mean Average	34.1%

[49]

importance. According to M. Golman, out of that "34.1% profit in relation to invested capital, from 20 to 25% went toward the payment of dividends, and the remaining 9% to 14% went toward capital accumulation, i.e. towards a wider re-investment of capital."[50]

During the period between 1891 and 1914 the total of the increase of industrial capital, of profits received and of dividends paid out, reached throughout the Empire the figures shown in *Table LXXIX*.

TABLE LXXIX

Increase of invested industrial capital	2,370.0 million rubles
Industrial profits received	4,419.8 million rubles
Dividends paid	2,089.7 million rubles

[51]

During the same period the amount that Western European capital had invested in industry, was 1,142.2 million rubles. Hence, industrial capital accumulation achieved internally was 1,188 million rubles, (2,330-1,142). If we make a proportion of profits and dividends to these amounts, then internal imperial industrial capital had 2,349.7 million ruble profits and out of that 1,063.8 million rubles in dividends.

We must stress the relativity of this summary, because, as has been noted above, the percentage of industrial profits was two and one-half times smaller in Russia than in Ukraine, where most of the foreign capital flowed. Therefore the total of profits and dividends of European and Russian capital invested in Ukraine should be higher than their proportion to capital. But even if we assume such a smaller calculation, then "subtracting

[49] V. Ziv, *Inostrannyi kapital v Russkoy chorno-zavodskoy promyshlennosti (Foreign Capital in the Russian Black-Metal Industry)*, Petrograd, 1917, pp. 18-19.
[50] M. Golman, *op. cit.*, p. 305.   [51] *Ibid.*, p. 308.

from the total amount of 2,089.7 million rubles in dividends,
1,063.8 local dividends, there remains the sum of 1,025 million
rubles which must absolutely be considered as taken out and
excluded from the process of local accumulation, and charged
to the profit of foreign shareholders."[52]

For the year 1913 the export of industrial profits was estimated at 721 million rubles. "Foreign capital excluded from our
land (reference is made to the Empire) during only 20 years
(1891-1910) without any equivalent, was almost 2,760 million
rubles in gold. Russia was compelled to pay such high charges to
foreign capital, and towards this went an impressive part of the
national income of the land."[53]

What land are they talking about here? To what extent were
these the losses of Russia? We have already indicated by statistics of the repartition of foreign capital that in Russian industry foreign capital was practically non-existent. It was being
invested in non-Russian territories, in colonies, and to the extent of 75%, in Ukrainian industry. Thus, these huge amounts excluded from the national income apply primarily to Ukraine.
But that is not all. As shown above, an amount of 2,760 million
rubles accrued to "local" capital. But this was not local Ukrainian capital. It was also alien capital which belonged to Russian
banks, although part of it was pumped out of Ukraine. Therefore we can estimate without error that the amount which was
usuriously drawn from Ukrainian industry during the twenty-
five year period of accelerated industrial development reached
approximately 5 billion rubles, an amount much in excess of
the total of capital invested in the entire Ukrainian industry.

This fact cannot be overlooked under any circumstances if
we wish to recognize the real position of industry in Ukraine
and the nature of its development which allegedly contradicts
the colonial status of Ukraine.

Syndicates

Syndicates were tremendously important in the process of
gaining control of Ukrainian industry by Russo-European capital and in it subsequent exploitation. They were established in
the beginning of the 20th century in metallurgy ("Prodamet")
in coal mining ("Produhol"), in sugar refining and in rail-

[52] M. Golman, *op. cit.*, p. 309.
[53] S. Strumilin, *Problemy promyshlennogo kapitala v SSSR* (*Problem of Industrial Capital in the USSR*), Moscow, 1923, p. 11.

road equipment ("Prodwagon"). The syndicates formed an organic unit with the entire system of improving colonial exploitation.

Within a short time, such syndicates as "Prodamet" and "Produhol" became real dictators not only in the area of marketing, but also in large degree in the area of production itself. Their dictatorship was not restricted to the sectors in which they were established, but extended to the entire industrial life, inasmuch as those two sectors of industry (metallurgy and coal) nourish many others.

Syndicates in manufacturing were also being established by Russian industries, and even in the same branches as in Ukraine, as for example, "Krovla" (Roof) in Ural metallurgy. But not one of them succeeded in attaining as dominant a position as the giants of Ukraine. Some even fell at the wayside in their attempt to compete with the giants.

Although neither syndicates, "Prodamet" nor "Produhol" confined itself to the borders of Ukraine in selection of membership ("Prodamet" included fourteen Ukrainian plants, nine Polish, three Baltic and one Central Russian), nevertheless most important were their Ukrainian plants which accounted for nearly three-fourths of the total production of the Empire. This was the cause of the syndicates being identified with Ukrainian industry, and hence the myth of the controlling position of the latter in all industries of the Empire. People who were either unable or unwilling to make a deeper analysis of the situation, drew from this conclusions that it was not Ukrainian industry that was subject to colonial exploitation, but, on the contrary, the whole industry of the Empire was its vassal.

There is no greater error than such concept of the nature of syndicates.

"All those syndicates were established in the form of common trading corporations, under 'commission agreements' for the sale of the products of their members. In reality they were strictly monopolistic organizations which held in the hands of a small group of monopolists the entire industry and dictated all market conditions for the products of industry so important to the national economy."[54]

Who constituted this "small group of monopolists"? In 1902, "Prodamet" was established. "The shares of 'Prodamet' were

[54] P. Khromov, *op. cit.*, p. 368.

granted by law the right to be traded on exchanges and to be
sold freely to outside persons." They were completely concentrated in the hands of owners of plants who were members of
the syndicate, and those owners, as has already been indicated,
were Russian banks and European capital, acting through those
banks. Therefore the manufacturing profits of Ukrainian industry, as well as commercial profits from the marketing of their
production, were in the same hands: Russo-European finance
capital. This fact alone excludes the possibility of any separation of the syndicates from the general system of control of
Ukrainian industry by foreign capital. It also excludes, what has
unjustifiably been attributed to these syndicates, i.e. that they
were the organizers of a national production in the interests of
developing a national economy. But in reality they were not
even accumulators of commercial profits, neither were they crea-
tors of commercial capital. Their only and direct task was the increase of the industrial profits of their member-manufacturers.
The most convincing proof of this that "frequently there were no
dividends declared at all, because the entire profit from operations of the syndicate to its members was not determined by divi-
dend per share, only by an increase of monopolistic prices for
goods sold."[55] The managerial centers of these syndicates were located in Petersburg. They were headed by persons who occupied
leading positions in banks (the chairman of "Prodamet" was P.
Daren, the real executive of "Produhol" was Gruenel, both representatives of French banks). The syndicates themselves were
nothing but an integral part of the financial structure of the
Russo-European bloc for the exploitation of colonies. The mon-
opolization of the market by syndicates was the cause of the
industrial profit of metallurgical enterprises reaching the un-
precedented level of 34.1% in relation to invested capital. This
profit, as has been stated above, which was being excluded from
the national economy in favor of Russian and European finance
capital, was the measure of the colonial exploitation of the
Ukrainian industry.

Undeniably these monopolistic prices injured all consumers,
not only the Ukrainian. Purchasers of Ukrainian metals in Russia were also contributing to these high profits. But the essence
of the matter is that profits made in Russia stayed there in the
national economy, just as did profits from monopolistic prices

---

[55] P. Lashchenko, *op. cit.*, p. 297.

of the Russian textile industry. In Ukraine they were excluded from the national economy. Moreover, for the purpose of competing with Russian metallurgy which was outside the syndicates, prices in Russia were lower than in Ukraine. "At a conference of participants of 'Prodamet' in 1912, prices for assorted and roofing iron were fixed for Ekaterinburg and Nizhni Novgorod (Russia) at 1.15 rubles per 36 pounds, while for Katerynoslav, Kiev, Odessa and Kharkiv they were 1.48 rubles. Thus prices in the main iron producing area were 30% to 35% higher than 'war' prices in the Ural region."[56]

Regarding competition with the Urals, there is no basis for treating it as a fight between Ukrainian and Russian industry. It was nothing more than an internal struggle of various financial groups for supremacy. There was even a struggle within "Prodamet," where two groups were contending, one headed by a majority of French capital (South Russian Dnipro Association), and the other by mixed capital, in large part of Russian banks such as the International, Azov-Don, and Bank for Foreign Trade (the Don-Yurievsky Association). The second group won.

Also opposing "Prodamet" was the group of enterprises of Hughes (controlled by British capital), but in 1905 it knuckled under. Thus, even in this respect the activities of the syndicate cannot by any means be considered a display of Ukrainian national-economic pursuit. The main thing to bear in mind in order to understand the true nature of the syndicates is the fact that the Russian Imperial Government was backing them. They were in the vanguard of the Government's course of policy in non-Russian areas. "Prodamet" was already tightly fused, legally and illegally, with the governmental apparatus which favored its policy."[57]

When, in 1908, under pressure of the State Duma, a conference was called to consider curtailment of the monopolistic trend of the syndicate "a large part of the members of the conference consisted of representatives of those industrialists and of bureaucrats from the Ministry of Industry and of Finance. And the conference did not think it wise to undertake prohibitive measures against the syndicates, being of the opinion that the Government should only fight corruption . . . Assured by the support of official circles, the syndicates continued their policy."[58]

[56] P. Lashchenko, *op. cit.*, p. 312.   [57] *Ibid.*, p. 327.
[58] P. Lashchenko, *op. cit.*, p. 326.

Therefore, the syndicates not only did not promote the interests of the Ukrainian economy, but they acted to its detriment and were an additional, more perfected tool of colonial exploitation. And the damage was not restricted to the mere siphoning off of huge amounts of the national income of Ukraine. Industry itself experienced terrible abuse. "Prodamet" took under control 74% of the total pig iron production of the Empire. At the base of its monopolistic policy "lay the aim to restrict production, as a means of increasing prices and super-profits of the leading enterprises . . . . In reality the policy of 'Prodamet,' directed toward restricting production and increasing prices was supported by the Government itself."[59]

Not a single new plant was established during all this time. Under the protection of the tariff policy which underwent a sharp change the moment Ukrainian enterprises came under the control of Russian banks. "Prodamet" brought the whole Empire by 1911 to a stage of an acute shortage of pig iron. It held production of rails at 20% below the 1904 level. With the aim of a further curtailment of production it shut down two rolling mills, Starachowice and Nikopil-Mariupil. This caused an immediate 40% rise in the price of rails.

Every plant was given a strict production quota by the syndicate. Its violation brought fines of 10,000 rubles plus 1 ruble for every 36 pounds of over-quota production. And conversely a plant would get a premium for producing less than quota. Production for foreign markets was outside of the quota, but in time this was changed, too. When, for example, in 1912 the Druzhkov plant asked "Prodamet" for permission to increase its production for exports to the Middle East, it was denied.

"In the pursuit of these aims 'Prodamet' did not take any needs of the national economy into consideration. It reduced the country to a condition of metal starvation and chronic underproduction of metals. This had a detrimental effect on the development of such important sectors, as the production of agricultural machinery (a sector fairly well developed in Ukraine and whose products were acutely needed in the South of Ukraine—*Author*), construction of railroads, commercial shipping, etc."[60]

---

[59] *Ibid.*, pp. 315, 320.   [60] P. Lashchenko, *op. cit.*, p. 316.

Conventions of manufacturers of agricultural machinery in Ukraine requested lower metal prices on two occasions, in 1910 and in 1913, and their requests were denied both times.

Even when the Minister of Commerce, Timashev, feeling the pinch of a metal shortage, proposed the erection of new plants to take care of the requirements of the War Ministry, he met with an organized opposition and had to withdraw.

There is no point in digressing into the characteristics of the second syndicate, "Produhol" which was established in 1904, because what was said above applies in full measure to all syndicates in Ukrainian industry. This syndicate also controlled 75% of all coal mining in Ukraine. As with "Prodamet," each mine had to adhere to a strict quota of coal sold, and members of the syndicate did not receive dividends, only premiums in the form of a difference between the basic price and the sale price. Between 1904 and 1908 mines were paid this premium in the amount of 2 kopecks per 36 pounds where their cost price was 4.5 to 5 kopecks i.e. 40% to 50% per cost price, over and above normal profit.

"Produhol" also "used all means to curtail the production of coal of enterprises controlled by it. . . . In other words, the 'Produhol' monopoly had as its open aim the stifling of the hard coal mining industry."[61]

In 1906, the Oleksiev Association which had been working with Ukrainian capital for a long time (until the failure of Alchevsky's Kharkiv Commercial Bank) and had preserved its independence, was ordered to curtail its production considerably as a prerequisite to being admitted to the syndicate. And, it was forced to comply. The Zhylov Company was ordered to switch to producing briquettes and to "close the mine . . . . The mine had been producing 480,000 tons of coal annually and employed over 3,000 workers."[62]

Quota violations were punished by a fine of 10 kopecks per 36 pounds, or double their cost price. And conversely, "for rejecting the assigned quota for the home market, the contracting party may, with the assent of the syndicate, receive a separate reward."[63]

This kind of activity of "Produhol" went beyond the bounds of legality, and in 1914 it was hauled into court. "However, fi-

---

[61] P. Lashchenko, *op. cit.*, p. 337.
[62] *Krasnyi Arkhiv, (Red Archives)*, XVIII, p. 139.
[63] P. Lashchenko, *op. cit.*, p. 335.

194   *Ukraine and Russia*

nancial pressure was exerted on the part of French banks and
Russian industrial circles, and the French Government even
made a diplomatic intervention. The case was not prosecuted."[64]

A few more words about the syndicate in the third basic industry of Ukraine, sugar refining. It came into being as early
as 1887 on the basis of a private agreement, uniting 206 out of
the 226 plants then in existence. As has already been noted, the
Ukrainian sugar industry, following the capture of the Kiev
Commercial Bank by the Petersburg-Azov Bank subsequently
changed into the Azov-Don Bank, came under complete control of Russian finance capital, and exports of sugar were monopolized by three Petersburg banks. We have also noted, how the
banks' role in the sugar industry was characterized by the Minister of Commerce and Industry. But even this was not enough:
in 1895 the Russian Government took over the regulation of
production of each refinery for the home market, and thereby
gave the syndicate a compulsory status. Thus, by ruthlessly curtailing the home consumption of sugar (400,000 tons in 1895-96)
and levying a high excise tax on sugar (1.75 rubles per 36 pounds
when the cost price was 3.25 rubles), the Government used all
possible means to favor the exportation of sugar abroad, exempt-
ing exporter banks from the excise tax and paying export premium of 80 kopecks per 36 pounds. "Under such circumstances,
at the expense of increasing prices on the home market, there
arose a possibility of shipping sugar abroad at prices which
were below cost. The price of Ukrainian sugar in London was
almost three times lower than in Kiev," the center of the sugar
refining industry.[65]

It is possible that some of this sugar came back to Petersburg
again in the form of grain raw materials for further processing
into crystal by Petersburg refineries. This is the true nature of
syndicates which existed in the industries of Ukraine. They were
the tools by which an increased colonial exploitation was carried
out, industrial development thwarted and sometimes ruined. In
addition to the exploitation conducted by Russia by means of
centralizing industry on her own territory, by means of excluding
a large part of the national income from Ukraine in the form
of commercial profit, there was yet another means, the system
of financial exploitation of Ukrainian industry. True enough,

[64] *Ibid.*, p. 333.   [65] *P. Khromov, op. cit.*, p. 256.

foreign capital now joined in, but this did not alleviate the exploitation.

The Bolshevik October upheaval of 1917 freed Russia from this partnership in the exploitation of her colonies. Russia confiscated foreign capital and became absolute ruler of the large Ukrainian industry.

"In the course of the history of colonial expansion of Russia during the period of Tsarism, her political, social and economic relations with conquered people brought vividly to the fore these characteristic features of a general economic and historical development which made Russia 'the prison of nations' . . . . The problem of the multi-national system of Russian capitalism, and of its colonial-national policy, is one of the most important for the understanding of the entire social-economic and national-economic development of Russia."[66]

---

[66] P. Lashchenko, *op. cit.*, pp. 421 et seq.

Chapter 5

RELATIONS BETWEEN UKRAINE AND RUSSIA IN OTHER ECONOMIC SECTORS

Transportation

WE HAVE ILLUSTRATED the relations between Ukraine and Russia which existed during the period of the development of capitalism in the provinces of land, industrial capital and finance capital. We have shown that at the base lay the colonial position and colonial exploitation of Ukraine. We could now consider our subject exhausted, at least as to that part which deals with the times before the revolution. As we had indicated at the beginning, it was not our task to provide a characteristic of the development of the national economy of Ukraine. We were to show that the entire development, by its direction, reach and economic consequences was determined by the existence of a colonial dependence of Ukraine upon Russia. Moreover we wished to show that the object of creating there the kind of agrarian conditions and industrial development which were created was the extraction of the entire surplus of the production of Ukraine for the benefit of Russia. Later, of course, Western European capital was drawn into the picture by Russia, to take part in this colonial exploitation.

Economic conditions in the three sectors analyzed above give a complete picture of the real nature of the whole economy, because they are the same for the whole. The conditions which were created here and cemented by legal norms of state economic policy, inevitably had to spread to all economic processes and all aspects of economic life. It made Ukraine, instead of being part of a solid national-state economic body, a restricted national area called upon to serve the advancement of the state-metropolis. Ukraine, like other national areas conquered by Russia, was not a "borderland," but a colony, which made possible Russia's growth into a colonial empire. "Russia's colonial policy of the 17th and 18th centuries consisted of the same form of plundering the borderland colonies, although not on such a vast scale, yet the plundering of Ukrainian localities, particularly during the period of the Muscovite state, was considerable. Therefore it would be erroneous to maintain that colonial sources were not utilized both in the primary, as well as in the subsequent period of capital accumulation."[1]

We venture the opinion that the truth of this thesis becomes irresistible in the light of the facts here cited which characterize the economic relations between Russia and Ukraine. Capital accumulation and economic development in Russia occurred in large measure at the expense of her colonies, primarily of Ukraine as the largest of them. It thwarted the economic growth of Ukraine. Conditions in agriculture, industry and finance irrefutably attest to this.

We will pause for a short time on other sectors of economic relations in order to find that they were also subject to colonial exploitation.

We will start with railroad construction as a most important branch of economic activity. Of itself, it constitutes a large industry, and, without exception, determines the development of all other aspects of the economy.

The attitude of Russia toward the building of railroads in Ukraine can be divided, like industry, into two periods. At first Russia halted the development of railroad construction in Ukraine, just as she had halted the development of industry, wishing to keep Ukraine on the level of supplier of raw material of agricultural production and consumer of Russia's industrial production. Subsequently, when the natural wealth of Ukraine opened wide opportunities for industrial exploitation and contributed to the development of a large industry in Ukraine by Russo-European capital, the attitude toward railroad construction changed. Under the new conditions railroads became an indispensable means toward the realization of industrial exploitation. The pace of the spreading of railroad connections made possible by the influx of foreign capital began to outdistance all other areas of the Empire, and finally placed Ukraine first among all areas in length of rail lines. But even then the direction of rail lines was not determined by the interests of Ukraine, only by the needs of capital exploiting her.

[1] P. Lashchenko, *Istoriya narodnoho khozyaystva SSSR*, II, 12.

The first railroad between Petersburg and Tsarskoye Selo, 27 kilometres in length, was begun in 1837, i.e. not much later than the beginnings of railroads in Western Europe. Almost simultaneously the Warsaw-Vilna line was started, 322 kilometres long, and was completed in 1848. In 1851 work was begun on the Nikolaevsky road between Petersburg and Moscow, 650 kilometres in length. The latter cost the treasury the then staggering amount of 141 million rubles, or 217,000 rubles per kilometre, as against 23,000 rubles for the Warsaw-Vilna line.

In 1857, on the initiative of the Government, and with its aid, the corporation "Glavnoye Obshchestvo Rossiyskikh Zheleznykh dorog" (Central Association of Russian Railroads) was founded. It was to concentrate in its hands all further railroad construction. Its capital was set at 275 million rubles, but only 112 million rubles were subscribed, and within a few years it was indebted to the treasury for 89 million rubles.

The principle of laying rail lines by this corporation was determined in the following order: 1) from Petersburg to Warsaw and the German border, 2) from Moscow to Nizhni-Novgorod, 3) from Moscow via Kursk and Kharkiv to Theodosia in the Crimea, and 4) from Kursk or Orel via Dinaburg to Libau. Thus, one of these lines was to bisect Ukraine, connecting her with Moscow. But along with the construction of these trunk lines, feverish construction of railroads connecting Moscow with producing regions went on. Within twenty years from the beginning of planned railroad construction in 1848, a network of lines was open connecting Moscow with the following regions: the Moscow-Kursk line brought to Moscow the produce of the central *chernozem* region, the Moscow-Kozlovo-Voronizh line brought grain from the Southeast, the Moscow-Nizhni-Novgorod connected it with the whole Volga and Kama region, the Moscow-Petersburg line opened deliveries of grain from the South to Petersburg, and all these lines together opened distant markets to products of the Moscow industrial region. Ukraine was then being taken into consideration when plans were drawn laying out railroads, but only to the extent to which it served the interests of Moscow. "The Imperial Government was primarily concerned with the construction of Russian lines, in order to connect the central manufacturing region with Baltic ports,"[2] through which came most of the imported raw material for the textile industry.

Only after twenty years of railroad construction in Russia was the first line in Ukraine built, between Balta and Odessa. In 1862, when Russia already had 4,030 kilometres of railroads, Ukraine had none. In the entire South there was, at that time, only a 73 kilometre line between the Volga and Don rivers. But even after railroads had already been started in Ukraine, the rate of construction lagged far behind Russia. (See *Table LXXX*).

TABLE LXXX
Length of Railroads (in kilometres)

Year	Ukraine	Russia	% Ukraine
1869	366	7,277	5.0
1871	434	12,278	3.5
1876	587	17,652	3.3
1879	1,057	20,034	5.3

[3]

Such a miserable percentage applied to Ukraine not only with respect to railroads, but to roads in general: "In 1864, out of a total of hard-surface roads of 7,664 kilometres, Ukraine had only 942 kilometres, and even out of this the Kiev-Beresta highway goes almost along the northern border of South Russia (Ukraine), the Kharkiv-Moscow and Kiev-Petersburg highways hardly penetrate Ukraine from the North, and the Simferopil-Sevastopil are insignificant in length."[4]

Needless to say, this deeply affected the Ukrainian economy with its large amount of commercial grain, cattle, sugar and by then also coal. The cost of transporting one *chetvert* (360 pounds) of wheat a distance of 100 kilometres cost up to 2 rubles, or almost 30% of the value of the wheat itself. We also must bear in mind the specific conditions existing in Ukraine as to animal-drawn transportation. First of all, autumnal rains and spring thaws preclude all transportation in the black soil regions. Further, the winter (in Russia this is the main season of transportation, when a horse can pull three times as much on a sled) in Ukraine is short and uncertain. The main thing is, however, that in Ukraine most of the hauling was done by oxen and not

² M. Slabchenko, *Materialy* . . ., p. 312.   ³ *Ibid.*, p. 314.
⁴ N. Yasnopolsky, "Ekonomicheskaya buduchnost . . . .," II, 77.

by horses, and during the winter no hauling by oxen was possible because they were used to grazing on the roads (200 feet wide). During the summer heat they would not budge, either. Thus, the transportation period was restricted to April-June and August-October, a period of the greatest activity in the farm fields. In addition the pace of transportation by oxen was extremely slow, 10 to 15 kilometres per day, and, with the great distances from seaports, the *chumaks* (oxen teamsters) could manage to make one annual round trip, to the coast with grain, and back with fish or salt.

Under such circumstances transportation of goods required a lot of manpower and other means. It is estimated that in the Poltava region alone there were about 210,000 teamsters in the 1860's. Two-thirds of all cargoes taken in the ports of the Black and Oziv Sea were delivered by *chumaks*. Although this provided the peasants with some additional income, the time was not free from labor in the fields, and thus was costly. It was otherwise in the North. In addition, the financial load of transportation costs fell upon the price of grain, the basic product of the peasants. The cost of hauling produce to Ukrainian markets alone amounted to 100 million rubles every year.[5]

The above cited is sufficient evidence for us to understand how acutely Ukraine felt the need of an early development of railroad communications, and why the landlords of Ukraine made such persistent demands upon Moscow in this regard.

But "the matter was slowed down by Moscow patriots who, through their mouthpiece *Moskovski Vedomosti* (an organ of official circles) said that it is not so necessary to connect Ukrainian points with Ukrainian export centers, as to connect Russia with Ukraine, Moscow with Kiev and Odessa, so that ties with Moscow 'the collector of Russian lands' should not be weakened."[6]

The divergent interests of Ukraine and Russia were probably wider in the matter of railroad building than in any other field. This applied to the amount of construction of lines, as well as their direction. "The interests of the Ukrainian economy demanded that railroads should first be built from Ukrainian centers to Ukrainian Black Sea ports, and also to the Western borders of the Empire, i.e. the Austrian and Prussian (through Poland). The Imperial Government, under pressure of the Rus-

[5] *Ibid.*, p. 78.   [6] M. Slabchenko, *op. cit.*, p. 289.

sian bourgeoisie, decided upon other directions of the first
Ukrainian railroads (in the first place Moscow-Kharkiv-Theodo-
sia). This direction, as a basic one, was inconvenient to the
Ukrainian economy. And if we consider that it put the brakes
on other projects of railroad construction in Ukraine, it is clear
that it was detrimental to Ukraine. The problem of directions
of railroads caused an animated discussion. Even an official
Russian publication (Central Statistical Committee of the Ministry of Internal Affairs) stated in 1864 in a paper *O napravlen-
iyi zheleznikh dorog v Yugo-Zapadnoy Rossiyi* (On the direction of railroads in Southwestern Russia) that "after the termin-
ation of the Crimean War all efforts of the state were concentrated on the construction of railroads in the North, whereas the
South, the most productive part of Russia, remained neglected.
Southern Russia is feeling more and more convinced that her
interests are, in the eyes of the Government, in second place,
and that the income of the entire state is being directed toward
the benefit and convenience of its northern part. If such con-
viction takes root it can bring about a complete disunity of the
interests of the North and of the South."[7]

By means of this policy of railroad construction the Russian
Government of the time (up to the 1880's) desired to accom-
plish two ends: first of all to secure the economic dependence
of Ukraine upon the metropolis, and in the second place to promote more activity in the Baltic ports which were of much
more interest to the Petersburg and Moscow industrial areas
than Black Sea ports. This caused an artificial routing of Ukrainian grain over great distances, and as a result there was a high
differential land rent on the realization of the products of the
Ukrainian agricultural economy, in the form of a difference of
transportation costs. In the balance of goods accounting, the
profitability of a unit of land in Russia increased thereby.

"Ukraine suffered from this very much, being obliged to
ship grain too far. The relationship between exports through
Baltic and Black Sea ports was, in the form of a percentage of
the Empire's total exports, as shown in *Table LXXXI*. Thus, commensurate with the increase of the railroad network the participation of the Baltic increases at the expense of the participation
of the Black Sea, adjacent to whose shores were directly located
the exporting regions of Ukraine, Kuban and the Don Cossack

[7] O. Ohloblyn, *Peredkapitalistychna fabryka*, p. 172.

TABLE LXXXI

Year		Baltic	Black Sea
1870	....	22%	59%
1871	....	29%	53%
1872	....	19%	61%
1873	....	37%	32%
1874	....	33%	34%
1875	....	33%	43%
1876	....	40%	37%

region. Only after railroad construction (in the South) was increased considerably did a process in the reverse of the one indicated above begin taking place."[8]

The amount of the surplus profit which fell to the seller of Russian grain under these circumstances can be pretty accurately imagined from the comparison in *Table LXXXII*, of prices of wheat and rye in Odessa and Petersburg in 1874 (per unit of one *chetvert*—360 pounds).

TABLE LXXXII

	Petersburg	Odessa
Wheat	12 to 16 rubles	8 to 14 rubles
Rye	7.8 to 8 rubles	5.7 to 7 rubles

[9]

It would seem that the needs of the Ukrainian economy for railroad connections between its producing regions and the Black Sea, and the general need of railroads in Ukraine were quite obvious. But, as we have already noted, until the end of the 1870's, Ukraine was in reality outside of the plans of railroad construction. At the same time in Russia, up to 1877 private capital amounting to 878 million rubles and 1,833 million in state railroad loans had already been spent on railroads. Moreover, even later, when Western European capital intervened in the matter of railroads in Ukraine, the proposition of a large-scale connection with ports of the Black Sea encountered a determined opposition of Russian commercial and industrial circles, "which were stubborn in trying to prove by all possible means that it would be a useless loss of money, n.b. not their own, but foreign British, French and German to build railroads to the Black Sea. They maintained that freight from Black Sea

[8] M. Slabchenko, *op. cit.*, p. 278   [9] *Ibid.*, p. 274.

ports to Marseilles or London is too high compared with the closer Baltic network of ports, and the amount of goods too small. Furthermore, they said, many loads of grain come to the ports of the Black Sea by water of the Dnipro, Don and Buh, or by oxen from nearer regions. Only a small part can be hauled by rail. Therefore, railroads in Ukraine will never become an important means of transportating grain and they will be unable to compete with the cheap *chumak.*"[10]

Basic changes in the matter of railroad construction took place in Ukraine in the 1880's under the pressure of new conditions in the Ukrainian coal mining and metallurgical industries, in whose conquest Russian and Western European finance capital were very much interested.

The already then impressive network of railroads in Russia, and its further increase, represented a great demand for coal and metals. Satisfying those needs as heretofore, by imports, became difficult because of the lack of foreign exchange. In addition, hand in hand with the conquest of Ukrainian industry by Russo-European capital, the official policy of the state, as has been noted above, changed also. In the order of 1857 entitled *Polozheniye ob osnovnikh usloviyakh dla ustroystva zheleznikh dorog v Rossiyi* (*Order concerning basic conditions of railroad construction in Russia*), section 18 permitted duty-free importation of all material used in railroad construction (rails, cars, engines, steel, etc). But already during the construction of the Kursk-Kharkiv line the Government required that "rails, cars, etc. needed for the construction of the line must be purchased in Russia in such quantities as Russian factories are able to supply."[11] Only the amount which could not be supplied by domestic factories could be imported without duty. Subsequently, the restrictions became more stringent.

A duty was also imposed on coal, and it was being increased all the time. The proprietors of the Ukrainian coal and metal industry, Russian and French banks, desirous of monopolizing the market, did everything within their power to isolate the market from foreign lands. This helped increase the importance of Ukrainian industry in the economy of the railroads, and simultaneously in the entire economy of the Empire. Under these circumstances, railroad construction in Ukraine became an acute

---

[10] M. Yavorsky, *Ukraina v epoku kapitalism,* II, 78.
[11] M. Sobolev, *Tamozhennaya politika Rossiyi,* p. 335.

necessity, flowing from the needs of finance capital. The Minister of Finance, Kokovtsev gave a clear picture of the situation in his letter to the French banker, Verneuil. Although the letter refers to a subsequent period (1908 in connection with the construction of the North-Donets railroad), nevertheless it characterizes completely the motives of foreign capital in the development of railroads in Ukraine, it reads: "This matter interests the Russian Government, which admits the whole importance of railroad construction in Russia, but it interests equally French capitalists who invested their capital in coal and metallurgical enterprises of the Donets basin. I am even convinced that these enterprises will not be able to exist, build up and grow otherwise than with the aid of the North-Donets railroad. Without this railroad coal enterprises will not be able to transport all their production, and metallurgical plants will not have orders of which they are acutely in need."[12]

The Katerynska railroad was started in 1879 which connected the iron ore region of Kryvyi Rih with the Donets coal basin. From that time on, railroad construction went at a fast pace, declining during the period of crises in the late 1890's and picking up again after 1907. Railroad construction was particularly intensive in the Donbas itself. In 1891, there were only 118 kilometres of railroads there; in 1893, they grew to 1,691 kilometres; in 1896, to 2,272 kilometres, and in 1898 to 2,865 kilometres. At the outbreak of the revolution in 1917 Ukraine possessed the railroads shown in *Table LXXXIII*. Of this, 14,770 kilometres

TABLE LXXXIII

Name	Length in kilometres
Donets	3,204.8
Southern	3,270.0
Katerynska-Moscow-Kiev-Voronizh	4,932.6
Southwestern	3,470.8
Odessa	1,125.0
Total	16,003.2 kilometres

were within the borders of Ukraine, out of the total of 70,300 in the whole Empire or 21%.[13]

From a land almost without railroads, Ukraine soon became, in regard to railroads, the best equipped territory of the Empire.

[12] N. Vanag, "Finansoviy kapital v Rossiyi nakunne mirovoy voyny," p. 111.
[13] P. Fomin, *loc. cit.*, and *Bolshaya Sovietskaya Entsiklopedia*, Vol. 55, USSR, p. 374.

For each 1,000 square kilometres of area Ukraine had 23.7 kilometres of railroads, as against 22.3 kilometres in the central black soil area; 17.9 kilometres in the central industrial, and 17.5 kilometres in the Western area. In the Urals there were at that time only 2.2 kilometres of railroads per 1,000 square kilometres, in Siberia, 1 kilometre, and in the Far East only 5 kilometres.[14]

Financial sources out of which railroad construction was undertaken were the state budget and state loans, floated in the main abroad, and private capital, mostly foreign as far as Ukraine is concerned.

Initially, as has been stated above, the Imperial Government started building railroads out of the state budget, but subsequently the so-called "concession system" was applied. Its objective was wide-spread attraction of foreign capital. It existed until 1879, that is prior to widespread construction in Ukraine. The Government looked with great favor on associations which took concessions for railroad construction, and gave them very convenient terms. First of all the Government guaranteed interest and profit on bonds, as well as payment of bonds. These guarantees were issued not to the associations, but to each bondholder. The same principle was later applied to shares. In addition, the Government knowingly permitted inflated cost estimates, thus facilitating the issue of more bonds. The stock capital was supposed to constitute between one-third and one-fifth of the cost estimate, but in reality it was only one-ninth, one-twelfth, and later even one-nineteenth. The fact of the matter is that frequently the subscription of capital was entirely fictitious. The sale of government-guaranteed bonds was completely free of control and the founders would subscribe to certain blocks of bonds at low prices, sell part of them at a higher price and enter the difference as the payment of their own subscription price.[15]

It was a process of artificial enrichment of Russian entrepreneurs at the expense of the state budget, and this gave them the initiative to build more railroads. Even the railroads which were built directly out of the budget were, when finished, turned over to these corporations. By 1881, all railroads, with the

---

[14] P. Khromov, *Ekonomicheskoye razvitiye Rossiyi . . . .*, p. 337.
[15] K. Zagorskiy, *Ekonomika transporta (Economy of Transportation)*, Moscow, 1930, p. 270.

exception of one narrow-gauge line, were in private hands.[16]
Beginning in 1880, after the abandonment of the concession
system, the state took over railroad construction, and soon began to purchase private railroads, among them also those which
had previously been state-owned.

On these operations of transferring railroads to private corporations and then buying them back, and on the guarantees
of bonds and shares, the Government suffered considerable
losses.

Capital invested in railroad construction is shown in *Table
LXXXIV* (in millions of gold rubles). This total of 7.7 billion

TABLE LXXXIV

End of year	Length of railroad (kilometres)	Capital in shares	Capital in bonds	Total	Additional investment	Grand total
1885	25,676	577	1,682	2,259	314	2,573
1890	29,890	510	2,092	2,602	439	3,041
1895	35,050	193	3,056	3,249	408	3,662
1900	54,374	120	3,886	4,006	819	4,825
1905	61,493	134	4,221	4,355	1,599	5,954
1910	67,253	137	4,378	4,515	2,361	6,876
1913	70,525	130	4,575	4,705	2,978	7,683

[17]

rubles consisted of 4.7 billion rubles of state and private corporation loans and 3 billion rubles out of the state budget.[18]

Out of the 4.7 billion rubles borrowed, 2.7 billion can be
apportioned to state loans and 2 billion to loans of private corporations. But even in the latter 2 billion there is a certain share
of the treasury, and prior to the purchase of private railroads
by the state, the state had contributed up to 90% of the capital
of these private enterprises. *Table LXXXV* indicates, at ten-year
intervals, the accumulation of private capital in railroad construction, and the part of the treasury in it (in millions of rubles).

Thus, even out of 1,990 million rubles which were, on the
eve of World War I, in the hands of private capital, one-fourth

[16] *Bolshaya Sovietskaya Entsiklopediya*, Vol. 24, p. 760.
[17] *Ibid.*, Vol. 24, p. 762. See also, I. Glivits, *Zhelezodelatelnaya promyshlennost' Rossiyi*, p. 114.   [18] *Ibid.*

TABLE LXXXV

	1873	1883	1893	1903	1913
Shares	636	675	406	131	130
Bonds	1,155	1,500	1,744	1,551	1,860
Total	1,791	2,175	2,150	1,682	1,990
Treasury in above					
Shares	84.5	12.7	....	....	....
Bonds	754.1	991.4	851	269.5	265.7
Treasury guarantee					
and other	305.1	869.7	876	106.7	217.6
Total	1,143.7	1,873.8	1,727	376.2	483.3
In percentages of total					
amount of capital..	63.8	90.2	80.4	22.3	24.3
					[19]

belonged to the treasury. We may therefore figure that out of 7,683 million rubles capital in the railroads, 6,173 million rubles, or 80.5%, belonged to the treasury, and only 1,507 million rubles, or 19.5%, to private capital. It is therefore permissible to consider the railroads in the Russian Empire as nationalized. This is of prime significance for the determination of the role played by the railroads as an arm of the state economic policy and in regard to colonial exploitation. In this regard we can come to full agreement with the conclusions of Soviet Russian economists. Albeit the conclusion was not addressed to themselves, nevertheless it is to the greatest extent applicable to Russia: "Colonial railroads were, in the hands of capitalist countries, siphons for drawing from the colonies raw material, a means of colonial exploitation of the colonies in all forms, and finally, a means of their political enslavement. The policy of state acquisition of railroads of the colonies was in this respect in accord with this objective, and profitable to foreign finance capital which, on the one hand, bleeds the colonies, drawing off local capital and preventing its entry into industry, and, on the other hand, strengthens its strategic positions in the national economy."[20]

This is correct because by this means the state takes into its hands such a very important economic factor, as railroad tariffs. Utilizing this factor, the state has an opportunity to exert a basic influence upon the entire economy of the land. "Tariff management, instituting these, or other tariff payment has as its object the influence upon the course and development of economic life of the land in those directions which, in the opinion of the

[19] *Bolshaya Sovietskaya Entsiklopediya, loc. cit.*   [20] *Ibid.*, Vol. 24, p. 758.

Government, represent at the given time, what is desirable from
the general-state viewpoint," and "to solve such problems, as
to which areas are to engage in agriculture, which in animal
husbandry, which in extracting or manufacturing industries, and
which are not to do so, what roads and directions appear to be
the most attractive for commercial relations, etc." By means of
raising and lowering railroad tariffs, the Government has the best
opportunity to realize its economic policy in the direction "of
the best (from the standpoint of the Government's interest—
Author) repartition of capital and productive forces of the land
among the various forms of industry and commerce, among the
various producing regions and commercial-industrial centers."[21]

Such was the significance ascribed to railroad tariffs in the
economic policy of the state, by one of the greatest Russian ex-
perts in this matter, Professor K. Zagorskiy. And we must state
that the Russian Government made full use of this economic
fulcrum in its colonial policy. A State Tariff Commission was
established in 1889, and it was given the power to draw up
tariffs both for state, as well as for private railroads. It worked
out a very complicated system of tariffs, depending upon the
nature of the freight and the distance in the form of so-called
differential tariffs, i.e. progressive lowering of the freight rate
per *pood-kilometre* (36 pounds per two-thirds mile) on long
hauls.

Ukraine was placed in a much worse position than Russia
in all respects, be it in the matter of tariffs according to the
nomenclature of goods, or tariffs according to distance of haul-
age. Moreover, different freight tariffs applied to identical loads
on Russian and Ukrainian railroads. Thus, the freight tariff on
grain in Ukraine was one-thirty-second kopecks per *pood-kilometre*, while in Russia it was one-fortieth to one-fiftieth kopecks.[22] "The losses of grain producers at the place of production, because of high tariffs and disorder on railroads amounted
to no less than 15 kopecks per *pood*, or between 6 and 7.5 rubles
per *desiatyna* of land, depending upon the harvest."[23]

It is fit to recall here that the gross profit form 1 *desiatyna*
of land in the steppe area of Ukraine amounted to 4.5 to 5 rubles.
The excessive tariff load on Ukraine can be judged from such

[21] K. Zagorskiy, *op. cit.*, p. 179.   [22] M. Slabchenko, *op. cit.*, p. 323.
[23] N. Ratzig, *Finansovaya politika Rossiyi s 1887 g.* (*Russia's Financial
Policy Since 1887*), St. Petersburg, 1903, p. 39.

facts. For example, in 1900 the freight on 36 pounds of grain from Chicago to New York cost 11.2 kopecks for a distance of 1,378 kilometres, and for the same distance between Kherson and Moscow it was 22.56 kopecks, which was the equivalent of 35% to 40% of the value of the grain at the place of its origin.

The same applies to other products. We have noted already that the tariff on coal from Shakhtna in the southerly direction of the Oziv Sea was higher then in the northerly, or Moscow direction. Coal mining industrialists attempted to prove that "in connection with high tariffs we have such misunderstandings that a *pood* of coal costs 23 to 25 kopecks, in Kharkiv (the cost price at the mine being 4.5 to 5 kopecks) while wood, a more expensive fuel, costs in the same city of Kharkiv 15 to 17 kopecks per *pood*."[24]

Russian industrialists stood firmly behind this tariff policy of the Government. It was so favorable to them that in 1896, when tariffs on grain were being revised, they demanded "protection of Central Russia from the competition of 'borderlands,' basing their demands upon the historical merits of the center in the matter of the establishment of the Russian state."[25]

On this occasion the tariff struggle against the central manufacturing region was renewed. That region had for a long time considered itself the exclusive supplier of manufactured goods to Ukraine. At the commerce and industry meeting in Odessa, Weistein, the mill-owner, said: "For a distance such as that between Moscow and Odessa, the freight on textile in inland transportation (within Ukraine) costs 1 ruble, 15.9 kopecks per *pood*, and in through transportation (into Ukraine), 41.05 kopecks, i.e. on goods coming out of Moscow the tariff is lowered by 65% . . . . A representative of the stock-exchange committee, Petakoros, showed that the railroad tariff policy caused a receding of freights from such regions bordering directly on Odessa, as Bessarabia, to Koenigsberg and Danzig. The system of differential tariffs had a considerable influence upon the loss of grain loadings by the port of Odessa particularly because the only railroad leading to the port goes in a very crooked line."[26]

We need not pause to consider the particular tariff items as to each form of goods. It is sufficient to cite in general that "the total income of Ukrainian railroads in 1913 was 318,206

[24] M. Slabchenko, *op. cit.*, p. 325.   [25] *Ibid.*, p. 321.
[26] M. Slabchenko, *op. cit.*, p. 319.

thousand rubles, which is the equivalent of 16,400 rubles per kilometre (*verst*). If we compare the net profit of Ukrainian railroads (property of the Russian Government) with the net profit of railroads in all other lands, it appears that the profit of the Ukrainian railroads was the highest in the world."[27]

When we recall that the Government guaranteed railroad shares and bonds as to fixed income, then the annual payments of the Government to the operators of Russian railroads were "nothing else but a system of money grants and premiums, paid out not directly from the treasury, but through the intermediary of railroad ticket offices," grants really going to Russian industry and commerce.[28]

But this is not the end of the matter. As we shall see later the load of interest payments and capital retirement of state loans incurred for the construction of railroads, fell in greatest measure upon Ukraine, though the railroads were built all over Russia.

Not only the tariffs, openly protective of Russia hurt the economy of Ukraine, but it suffered no less from the direction of railroad connections. Just a look at a map of Ukraine convinces one that the main objective of railroad construction in Ukraine was not the safeguarding of the economic interests of the area. The trunk lines go only in one direction, North-South. The North is connected with all the main producing areas of Ukraine, agricultural, sugar, metallurgical and coal mining, while within Ukraine there are no trunk lines between these areas. From West to East Ukraine has in reality only one direct rail line, Kovel-Sarny-Kiev-Poltava-Donbas. All the others are indirect and, considering the high tariff, contribute greatly to the increase of costs of transportation in Ukraine. The whole South of Ukraine below Katerynoslav has no west-east lines at all. Such localities, as e.g. the triangle between Kherson, Nikopol and Melitopol, which by area is almost as large as all of Belgium and produces huge quantities of commercial grain, have no feeder line at all. Many villages are located between 30 and 50 kilometres from the nearest railroad station, in a land where, during the trackless spring and fall seasons, even a distance of 10 kilometres is insurmountable. With a lack of hard surfaced roads, transporting goods by horse even a short dis-

---

[27] S. Ostapenko, "Kapitalizm na Ukraini," p. 201.
[28] K. Zagorskiy, *op. cit.*, p. 184.

tance frequently doubled the cost of the load. It must be noted that the products of the Ukrainian economy are goods of great bulk and weight and are priced low per unit of weight. Costs of transportation reflect heavily on price.

Neither must we forget that Ukraine had very poor connections with seaports, in no way commensurate with the real interests of the Ukrainian economy. Ukraine's largest port, Odessa has only two trunk lines, and one of them, Odessa-Petersburg (Leningrad) goes along the former frontier, and is of importance only to the sugar refining industry. The other, Odessa-Bakhmach, does not connect the sea with either the metallurgical, or the coal region. Other ports, such as Mykolaiv and Kherson, have only one trunk line. It is also without direct connection to industrial regions, and the latter Kherson-Merefa (Kharkiv) which was only completed after World War I, is used principally for hauling grain and other agricultural products to Moscow. The coal producing region is only connected with the port of Mariupil, and the metallurgical region with an undeveloped port of Berdyansk. Both ports are on the unimportant Sea of Oziv. One other line leads from the Donbas to Taghanrog, also on the Sea of Oziv, but it is beyond Ukraine.

With the North, however, all industrial regions are connected by many direct trunk lines. To the two previous lines between the Donbas and Moscow, another one has recently been added, via Starobilsk Luhanske (Voroshilovgrad).

As a result of such specific layout of railroad directions, freight loads, in the absence of direct and short connections with Ukrainian ports, went to the great trunk lines connecting Ukraine with the North. Therefore "The Kursk-Kharkiv-Oziv railroad hauled the same grain both north and south . . . The Kiev-Berestya railroad south and towards the western border."[29]

It is not surprising therefore, that the "most overloaded lines were those which connected the Donbas and Kryvyi Rih with the center (Moscow), Leningrad and the Volga region. Over them were hauled the main loads of coal, iron ore, metals, lumber, grain, mineral building material, both within Ukraine, as well as beyond Ukraine's borders."[30]

The development of railroads in Ukraine was thus subservient to the general goal: tying the Ukrainian economy with

[29] D. Chuprov, *Zheleznodorozhnoye khozyaystvo* (*Railroad Management*), Moscow, 1897, II, pp. 69-70.
[30] *Bolsh. Sovietsh. Entsikl.,* Vol. 55, p. 728.

the metropolis and making it dependent upon it. Western European capital, which played such an important part in the development of these railroads, was likewise interested in this layout. That capital, in partnership with Russian finance capital, thus automatically assured itself a monopolistic repartition of the products of Ukrainian industry on the markets of Russia.

Hence, the nature of the Ukrainian railroad economy was incompatible with the total interests of Ukraine. This reflected her colonial position and not the requirements of internal commercial-industrial exchange of goods, nor foreign ties dictated by natural conditions. This explains the disproportion between external and internal railroad operations in Ukraine, as compared with Russian regions like the central-agricultural, or the Volga, not to mention the central industrial regions. *Table LXXXVI* indicates the percentage relationship between external (through) and internal (home) railroad connections.

TABLE LXXXVI

Region	External connection	Internal connection
Central agricultural	42.1%	57.19%
Volga region	47.0%	53.0%
Southern Ukraine	75.4%	24.6%
Southwestern Ukraine	72.8%	27.2%

31

Beside the harm from the tariff policy and the railroad lines, the routing of the external trade of Ukraine to its natural seaports was in great measure stymied by the condition of the ports and freighter fleet. The Russian Government, interested in increasing operations on the Baltic, and directing traffic to Baltic ports by means of its tariff policy, deliberately neglected the development of harbors and shipping in the Black and Oziv Sea. The Ukrainian coast of the two seas has eight ports, of which the three Crimean (Evpatoria, Sevastopol and Yalta) are of no commercial importance. To the remaining five, we must add Mykolaiv and Kherson, situated on the estuaries of the rivers Boh and Dnipro. These seven ports are numerous and well enough located to take care of all the needs of Ukrainian commerce, but in reality were far from fulfilling their destiny.

31 P. Lashchenko, *op. cit.*, p. 365.

The finest and largest of all Ukrainian harbors, is Odessa, followed in size and importance by Mariupil, the harbor serving the Donbas and Kryvyi Rih. But even these two principal ports were very poorly equipped. "Berths, for example, were very small. Foreign ships sometimes had to wait for a month and a half for their turn to unload. Docks were awkwardly located. In Odessa the location of the coal harbor was such that ships could not be berthed lengthwise."[32]

General inadequacy, and in some localities a complete lack of river shipping, also had its detrimental influence upon Ukrainian overseas commerce. Specific layout of railroads and expensive and difficult rail deliveries of goods to seaports created a real need for cheap and easy river transportation, which was not forthcoming. Ukraine possesses rivers that are conveniently located for commercial purposes. Three great rivers flow through Ukraine from north to south, the Dnister, Southern Boh and Dnipro. The big bend of the latter around Katerynoslav-Zaporozhe encompasses the metallurgical region and comes very close to the Donbas. Donbas in turn, is bisected by the river Donets, the largest tributary of the Don. It, in turn connects the coal region with the Sea of Oziv. All those rivers have tributaries from West and East, covering all Ukraine with a fairly dense network.

The Dnister, 1371 kilometres long, has nine important tributaries, which are hardly used for shipping at all. The river itself is used for shipping along only about 800 kilometres although it is navigable much farther North than this. Matters are much worse with the Boh, 750 kilometres long, where steamers go only between Voznesensk and Mykolaiv, a distance of 100 kilometres. The principal river, Dnipro, 2,150 kilometres long, of which 1,400 is in Ukraine, is utilized for navigation along almost its entire length, with the exception of 80 kilometres of rapids (at present flooded and locked, following the construction of the Dnipro Electric Power Station). Its tributaries, Prypiat and Desna, are also navigable. But hardly any of the other nine large tributaries, as well as the tributaries of the Prypiat and Desna, are navigable, because of a complete neglect of the regulation of their flows. Similarly on the river Donets, in the part which flows through Ukraine, there is no navigation.

[32] M. Slabchenko, *op. cit.*, p. 291.

The large water areas with an annual water deficit which are so badly needed by the Ukrainian economy are not properly utilized because this would aid the economic consolidation of the Ukrainian national territory contrary to Russian interests. "River navigation in the South does not aid the economic development of the land. For each inhabitant there is only 25 pounds of river freight for a charge of 73 kopecks, while in Russia, in the North it is 300 pounds for 3.5 rubles. If, for the betterment of South Russian communications, both by water and by land, thus far as much had been done as in the North, the results would be greater for all of Russia than heretofore, because the immense natural wealth makes the land of the South more suitable for wider development than the North."[33]

All these circumstances, point to a situation where the Ukrainian seas were far from carrying out the task commensurate with natural conditions.

The privileged position of the Baltic ports, upheld by the Government, and the niggardly equipment of the Black Sea in tonnage of home registry, influenced existing conditions.

In their competition with Baltic ports, lower shipping rates were as necessary as favorable railroad connections and protective railroad tariffs. The freight on 36 pounds of grain from Odessa to London was in the late 1890's 24 kopecks, while from Baltic ports it was only 13 kopecks. "It is not surprising, therefore that the latter have such pre-eminence over Southern ports."[34]

Freight cost was in large measure also heavily influenced by the lack of balance between ocean imports and exports. Steamships had to go empty to Ukraine. In 1912, in the main ports of the Black and Oziv Sea 3,718.4 thousand tons were loaded for overseas shipment, while only 416 thousand tons were unloaded.[35]

During the same period 75% of the ships arriving at the ports of the Baltic Sea came fully loaded.

We have a different picture in coastwise shipping, i.e. basically an intra-Ukrainian sea trade. Against 1,766.4 thousand tons of loadings, we have 2,139.2 thousand tons of unloadings. These figures would have been much higher if the ports had not been working under handicaps described above, because, in spite of

[33] M. Yasnopolsky, *op. cit.*, II, 78.   [34] M. Yasnopolsky, *op. cit.*, I, 285.
[35] I. Feshchenko-Chopivsky, *Ekonomichna heohrafiya Ukrainy*, p. 81.

all difficulties, the advantages of shipping via the Black Sea were indisputable. The freight cost of 36 pounds of oil products from Batum via Odessa to Kharkiv was 38.2 kopecks, and to Kiev 35.6 kopecks in spite of the high railroad tariff in Ukraine. At the same time, transporting the same quantity and product by rail via Tsaritsin (Stalingrad), even at the low railroad tariff on Russian railroads cost respectively 42.2 kopecks and 46.9 kopecks.

This comparison is all the more applicable to transportation exclusively by water. Thirty-six pounds of freight from Odessa to Vladivostok in the Far East cost 51 kopecks and never more than 1 ruble, 12 kopecks. Transportation over the same distance via Siberian railroad cost 12 rubles.

But in spite of everything, in spite of the obvious advantages of utilizing southern sea routes, and in spite of the undeniable need to connect the commerce of Ukraine with her geographical position, the policy of the Russian Government remained unchanged. Grain deliveries to ports of the Black Sea, at a time when exports of grain were on the increase frequently declined on a large scale. Grain deliveries to Black Sea ports were (in thousands of tons) as shown in *Table LXXXVII.*

TABLE LXXXVII

1895	2,825.6	1898	2,264.0
1896	2,598.4	1899	1,876.8
1897	1,929.6	1900	1,704.0

[36]

At the same time we can observe such a phenomenon in dissonance with natural conditions, as an increase of overland exports. There was such a paradoxical situation: exports declined when the French Government reduced duties to a minimum, and increased when, in consequence of large imports from abroad, the French tariff was increased by 28%. "The fact that foreign countries' demand declined, released the brakes upon domestic trade."[37]

Brakes upon domestic trade experienced by Ukraine were more effective than a boom on foreign markets. Things came to such a stage that the Southwestern Railroad attempted to escape the rule of the Ministries of Transportation and of Fi-

[36] M. Slabchenko, *op. cit.*, p. 294.   [37] *Ibid.*, p. 296.

nance and "to conclude a separate agreement with German railroads to combat Russian protectionism by lowering the tariff on imported goods and exported sugar."[38]

This clearly shows why so little attention was being paid to the problem of rebuilding a home commercial fleet on the southern seas, which had been nearly destroyed in the Crimean War.

Ten ports of the Ukrainian coast, including Sevastopol had, at the outbreak of World War I, a total of 310 ships with a net of 200,000 tons, and 657 coastwise ships weighing 25,300 tons. The average weight of one seagoing vessel was 680 tons, and of a coastwise vessel 38 tons. Both the numbers, as well as the tonnage of ships, provide clear evidence of the absolute disproportion between the means of water transportation and commercial tonnage of Ukraine. At that we must bear in mind that 58% of all ocean-going and 62% of all coastal shipping was handled by Odessa. The remainder has to be apportioned among the other nine ports, of which e.g., Skadovsk, a good harbor close to a wealthy region, had only one vessel of 7 tons.

Under such circumstances the role of a home commercial fleet in water transportation was very insignificant. Whereas the participation of domestic ships in transporting goods of the European part of the Empire was equal to 11.8%, in the Black and Oziv Seas in 1912 it was only 5.8%. British ships handled 47.5%, Greek 16.1%, Austrian-Hungarian 10%, and others lesser amounts.[39]

The situation in river transportation was no better. On the entire Dnipro river with all its tributaries there were only 187 freight-passenger steamers, total tonnage, 13,500 tons, and 177 barges. On the Dnister there were 14 steamers and 7 barges, and so on. As of 1900 the entire import and export trade of the Empire by water is represented by the figures (in percentages) in *Table LXXXVIII*.

TABLE LXXXVIII

	Imports	Exports
Baltic Sea	70.4	43.6
Black and Oziv	22.3	50.5
White	.5	3.0
Caspian	6.8	2.9 [40]

[38] *Ibid.*   [39] P. Fomin, "Ekonomichna kharakterystyka Ukrainy," p. 47.
[40] P. Khromov, *op. cit.*, p. 251.

Ignoring the interests of Ukraine in laying out railroads, neglecting river transportation, inadequate highways, these were what kept the domestic trade from assuming its proper proportions. This also explains the disproportionate importance of fairs in Ukraine. The ten largest fairs handled almost half of the domestic trade in goods in Ukraine. It is also characteristic that out of the ten fairs, eight were located in close proximity to the Russian border: four in Kharkiv, two in Kiev and two in Poltava. At these fairs the bulk of goods produced by Russian industry was sold. This system of trade, peculiar to ancient times, is a vivid indication of the weakness of domestic communications. It is understandable why, in the middle of the 19th century "all goods sold at fairs were valued per one inhabitant of Kharkiv region at 15 rubles, Poltava at 12 rubles, Katerynoslav at 6 rubles, whereas in Petersburg province at 35 kopecks, Moscow at 27 kopecks, Tula at 23 kopecks and Ryazan 20 kopecks."[41]

Market

In the chapter which studied the characteristic of relations between Ukraine and Russia in industry, we have already analyzed the extent of trade in three basic branches of industry, coal, metallurgy and sugar. These three branches were the leading ones of Ukrainian industry, and conditions existing there characterized the entire system of economic relations with Russia. Nevertheless, for a more complete picture of the colonial nature of the Ukrainian economy, we shall pause to consider the position of the Ukrainian market. This is more important since we have not clarified the situation in the grain trade which was of tremendous importance to the Ukrainian economy.

Here again, the center of our attention will not be the particular branch of commerce alone, but the relationship between Ukraine and Russia in this sector.

We shall consider first the problem of the general exchange of goods in Ukraine as they were subject to official statistics of the Government, the trade of those enterprises which were licensed to do business. For this purpose we are making use of data on commerce and industry in the regions of European Russia, as published by the Ministry of Commerce and Industry in 1908. We are unfortunately compelled to adhere to regional

[41] M. Yasnopolsky, *op. cit.*, II, 81.

boundaries used in the official report. They do not correspond
to the boundaries of Ukraine. One of the regions cited, the region of grain commerce, includes a small part of the South
of the Don Land. But for our purpose such slight variation in
the figures of one region is not too important and can have no
serious effect upon the general conclusions.

The Ministry of Commerce and Industry divided Ukraine
into three regions: 1) grain commercial (Number VIII)
which included the Oziv Seaboard, the Crimea, the Dnipro-Boh
strip and Bessarabia; 2) black-industry (iron and coal), (Number IX) including the Donbas, Katerynoslav and Kryvyi Rih
regions; and 3) the Southwestern, (Number X) which took in the
regions of Kharkiv, Poltava, Kiev, Chernihiv, Volhynia and
Podilla. The gross business figures of commerce and industry
of these three regions, are (in thousands of rubles) as seen in
Table LXXXIX.

TABLE LXXXIX

Region	Gross Commerce	Gross Industry	Total
VIII	580,620	177,542	758,162
IX	152,614	254,419	407,033
X	517,983	401,152	919,135
Total	1,251,217	833,113	2,084,330

According to groups of goods, the gross commerce figures
were (in thousands of rubles) as shown in *Table XC.*

According to groups of goods, the gross figures of industry
were (in thousand rubles) as shown in *Table XCI.*

Before we begin an analysis of the above figures we must pin-
point two basically important sets of figures, those of the food
industry and iron and coal industry which, together, constitute
89% of the entire gross figure for industry.

TABLE XC

Region	Agricultural products	Animal products	Lumber	Minerals and metal	Textiles	Beverages	Not specified	Total
VIII	197,413	28,548	18,601	57,625	97,668	52,976	127,889	580,720
IX	25,479	6,514	12,934	14,405	36,394	25,095	31,793	152,614
X	78,375	33,982	20,228	45,632	124,235	83,439	132,092	517,983
Total	301,269	69,044	51,763	117,662	258,297	161,510	291,774	1,251,319 [42]

TABLE XCI

Region	Food	Non-edible animal products	Lumber	Mining	Textiles	Chemicals	Not specified	Total
VIII	86,147	10,594	8,300	51,192	3,184	10,208	7,917	177,542
IX	23,163	349	2,854	215,415	123	3,744	8,771	254,419
X	329,405	5,357	8,025	39,999	4,702	6,592	7,072	401,152
Total	438,715	16,300	19,179	306,606	8,009	20,544	23,760	833,113 [43]

[42] Minister Torgovli i Promyshlennosti (Minister of Commerce and Industry), *Torgovla i promyshlennost Yevropeyskoy Rossiyi po rayonam*, 1908, VIII-4, IX-5, X-5.

[43] *Ibid.*, VIII-5, IX-6, X-6.

The gross figure of the food industry is broken down into the groups shown in *Table XCII* (in thousands of rubles).

TABLE XCII

Groups	VIII	*Regions* IX	X	Total	*In percentage relation to the total*
Milling	33,256	17,270	47,679	98,205	22.4
Sugar refining ..	16,899	.....	237,121	254,020	58.1
Wines and spirits	6,493	....	18,688	25,181	5.7
Tobacco	12,989	....	11,729	24,718	5.6
Vegetable oil..	3,705	....	2,944	6,649	1.5
Confectionary..	2,803	....	2,514	5,317	1.2
Grits	1,991	....	....	1,991	0.4
Baking	2,802	....	1,754	4,556	1.0
Meat	958	....	732	1,690	.4
Fish	1,373	....	....	1,373	.3
Brewing	2,424	....	....	2,424	.5
Others	2,445	5,893	4.253	12,591°	2.9
Total	88,138	23,163	327,414	438,715	100.0

44

°The group "others" in the official report also includes some items from among specified groups which are in small amounts.

44 *Ibid.*, VIII-13, IX-16, X-15.

Table XCIII is a similar breakdown of figures of the iron and coal industry (in thousands of rubles).

TABLE XCIII

Groups	VIII	Regions IX	X	Total	In percentage relation to total
Metallurgy and metal-working	32,731	119,665	16,832	169,228	55.2
Coal and clay extraction ..	1,897	69,680	1,148	72,725	24.2
Iron ore	529	11,965	11	12,568	4.0
Agricultural tools and machinery	3,556	2,319	8,945	14,820	4.9
Bricks and pottery	2,495	4,128	5,234	11,857	3.8
Tin and metalware ..	2,690	64	1,914	4,668	1.5
Salt mining ...	1,923	1,877	....	3,800	1.2
Mercury mining	....	1,417	....	1,417	.4
Manganese mining	....	759	....	759	.2
Repair-shops ..	1,705	298	1,868	3,871	1.3
Cement, chalk, alabaster ...	1,616	1,368	1,514	4,498	1.4
Glass and faience	....	1,438	1,501	2,939	.9
Zinc	284	....	....	284	.1
Carriage-making	589	167	676	1,432	.4
Electro-mechanical..	354	....	....	354	.1
Others	760	270	356	1,386	.4
Total	51,129	215,415	39,999	306,606	100.0

[45]

It is not worthwhile to spend time on the textile industry, in spite of its basic importance, because of its very insignificant figure (8 million rubles), and also for the reason that this group includes mostly goods of secondary use such as twine, bags, etc. Thus, we actually find in two main branches of industrial production, only two groups in each which have a preponderance over all others, constituting 80% of the total. In the first it is milling and sugar-refining, and in the second, metallurgy and coal. The gross figures of all other groups are so insignificant that their per capita repartition will give no more than a few

[45] *Ibid.*, VIII-17, IX-7, X-11.

kopecks per person. Thus, in analyzing the Ukrainian economy from the standpoint of the market, we find again the same situation that we have already observed in the realm of industry: the manufacturing process is indisputably one-sided, which is a characteristic of colonial countries.

Even more telling in this respect is a comparison of the gross industrial and commercial figures. The sales of textiles reached 258,297 thousand rubles, and this is doubtless an incomplete figure, since many textile articles are included in the "not specified" group. Ukraine's own production of textiles reached only 8 million rubles, of secondary use. A similar picture is revealed in the comparison of production of wines and spirits (25 million rubles) with sales in this group (161 milion rubles). From the comparison of just these two groups we can estimate the huge amounts of foreign production consumed by Ukraine, i.e. what great part of the national income went out of the Ukrainian economy in the form of commercial profits.

One might reply to such argument that there were other industries in Ukraine at the time producing more than was required for home consumption (sugar, metals, etc.), and that these industries produced goods which went into foreign economies creating commercial profits in favor of the Ukrainian economy. This would be an apt observation, provided the industrial and commercial capital engaged in these activities had been Ukrainian capital, and that the profits from them accrued to Ukraine. But, as has been amply illustrated above, none of the capital was Ukrainian, and thus the loss of surplus production was not compensated for by these return processes.

In support of this, we cite below some data on the distribution of goods in the Ukrainian market according to production classification groups. It is to be borne in mind that, in addition to commercial distribution as accounted for by the Ministry of Commerce and Industry for licensed enterprises, there was also a distribution through local bazaars, where the vendors were not subject to licenses. This includes such enterprises as peasants offering their wares, and local mongers. According to Ostapenko, this distribution, mostly in agricultural products, added up to the value of 751 million rubles in 1913.

According to the same scholar, the Ukrainian market handled on the eve of World War I, the annual quantities of its own products (in thousands of tons) as shown in *Table XCIV.*

TABLE XCIV

Coal	24,000,000	Grain	9,600,000
Coke	4,800,000	Sugar beets	8,960,000
Iron ore	6,720,000	Sugar	1,280,000
Manganese ore	256,000	Grits	1,600,000
Salt	800,000	Spirits	168,000
Pig iron	640,000	Potatoes	3,840,000
Iron and steel	2,400,000	Vegetables	352,000
Machinery and tools	224,000	Corn (maize)	480,000
Textiles	56,000	Horses	265,000 head
Leather	160,000	Steers and cows	915,000 head
Leather goods	144,000	Calves and heifers	1,025,000 head
Paper	40,000	Hogs	950,000 head
Books	16,000	Sheep	3,500,000 head
Chemicals	48,000	Eggs	1,600,000 thous. pieces
Tobacco	56,000	Poultry	35,300 thous. pieces
Oils (edible)	43,200	Milk	1,180,000 tons [46]

In addition to the above home production figures, Ukraine imported, during the year 1913 the quantities of goods (in thousand tons) shown in *Table XCV*.

TABLE XCV

Lumber	1,248,000	Tea	4,800
Machinery and		Gasoline and kerosene	480,000
metal goods	320,000	Fertilizer	140,800
Textiles	80,000	Cement	137,600
Notions	6,400	Wool	16,000
Herrings	112,000	Leather goods	48,000
Other fish	80,000	Fruits	8,000 [47]
Rice	16,000		

At the same time, goods exported from Ukraine are shown in *Table XCVI* (in thousand tons).

TABLE XCVI

Coal	9,600,000	Clover seed	16,000
Grain	7,200,000	Beans	59,200
Sugar	960,000	Peas	160,000
Ore	1,600,000	Corn	112,000
Pig iron	480,000	Potatoes	96,000
Iron and steel	1,440,000	Leather	16,000 tons
Salt	384,000	Alcoholic beverages	37 million litres
Grits	432,000	Agricultural machinery	44,800 tons
Grits (fine)	25,600	Horses	100,000 head
Middlings	232,000	Horned cattle	385,000 head
Bran	96,000	Hogs	135,000 head
Sunflower seed		Poultry	16,200,000 pieces
and hemp seed	91,200	Eggs	70,400 tons [48]

[46] M. Ostapenko, *op. cit.*, p. 204.   [47] *Ibid.*, p. 203.   [48] *Ibid.*, p. 113.

The total export figure of all goods shipped from Ukraine in 1913 was 1,022,780 thousand rubles, and import, 647,960 thousand rubles.[49]

Thus, Ukraine's exports were in excess of imports by the amount of 374,820 thousand rubles.

This relationship between exports and imports was not a matter of chance, nor did it apply only to the year 1913. M. Volobuyev indicates that Ukraine's active foreign trade balance in 1900 amounted to 367 million rubles; in 1901, to 740 million rubles; in 1902, to 468 million rubles; in 1904, to 287 million rubles, and in 1905, to 301 million rubles.[50]

The annual excess of exports over imports is estimated by M. Shrah for the years 1909 to 1911 at 319 million rubles. Out of this 262 million applies to foreign trade and 57 million to trade with Russia.[51]

Ostapenko estimates the excess figure for 1912 at 260.4 million rubles. There were obvious variations from year to year, but exports always exceeded imports. In this instance we are not so much interested in the amount of that excess as in the fact of its existence, because it is indicative of the economic relations between Ukraine and Russia. The Empire as a whole also had an active foreign trade balance, and we have to inquire by what means this was achieved. Professor P. Fomin cites (*Table XCVII*) the abbreviated trade balance sheet of Ukraine's foreign trade for the year 1912, compiled by Professor Halytsky (in millions of rubles):

TABLE XCVII

	Exports	Imports	Excess Exports	Imports
Food products	663.2	37.1	626.1	....
Animal products	24.7	.1	24.6	....
Raw material and semi-manufactured goods	91.5	64.8	26.7	....
Manufactured goods	9.5	158.8	....	149.3
Total for Ukraine	788.9	260.8	677.4	149.3
Active balance			528.1	

[52]

[49] *Ibid.*, p. 114.   [50] M. Volobuyev, "Do problemy Ukrainskoyi ekonomiky."
[51] M. Shrah, "Zovnishnya torhivla USSR ta yiyi blyshchi perspektyvy" ("Foreign Trade of the Ukrainian SSR and its Immediate Prospects"), *Chervony Shlakh* (*Red Path*), Kharkiv, No. 6, 1924, p. 117.
[52] P. Fomin, *op. cit.*, p. 119.

At the same time, the Empire as a whole exported goods abroad of the total value of 1,276.9 million rubles, and imported goods valued at 841.9 million rubles which gives an active trade balance of 435 million rubles. This balance, as we can see, is 93 million rubles lower than the balance of Ukraine. This means that the Empire, without Ukraine, imported goods from abroad for almost 100 million rubles more than it exported. If we consider that the Empire also included such non-Russian territories as the Kuban, Azerbaijan, etc., then we must come to the conclusion that Russia proper imported much more than she exported. This was done at the expense of the colonies. We have already indicated that in commerce with Ukraine, Russia received 100 million rubles worth more than she gave to Ukraine.

Out of the total Ukrainian export figure, the amounts shipped to Russia were as shown in *Table XCVIII.*

TABLE XCVIII

Grain and cereals ..	720,000 tons	Coal over	8,000,000 tons
Iron and pig iron...	1,024,000 tons	Cattle over	200,000 head
Sugar	720,000 tons	Hogs	90,000 head
Seed	144,000 tons	Meat	16,000 tons
Ores and salts	760,000 tons	Clay, lime, etc.	80,000 tons

[53]

Such was the nature of Ukrainian exports to Russia, chiefly agricultural products, raw materials and semi-manufactured goods, exports peculiar to colonies. This situation is even more marked in Ukrainian exports going outside the borders of the Empire. During the period 1909 to 1911 agricultural products constituted 85% of the entire value of exports from the Empire. Thus, in spite of the relatively high level of industrial development, in exports to foreign countries Ukraine appeared in the role of a typical colony supplying industrial countries with food products. To Russia, however, Ukraine shipped industrial raw materials and semi-manufactured goods, playing the role of a raw material market for Russia's industry. "Economic relations between Ukraine and Russia were based on industries to the extent of 75%, and not on agriculture."[54]

The extent to which Ukraine participated in the exportation of agricultural products of the whole Empire can be determined

[53] I. Feshchenko-Chopivsky, *op. cit.,* p. 81.   [54] M. Shrah, *op. cit.,* p. 117.

from the fact that out of a total of 7,107,200 tons of grain exported by the Empire in 1900, Ukraine furnished 5,952,000 tons,
or 84%. The average participation of Ukraine during the period
1900 to 1913 was about 75%. At the same time Ukraine harvested
24.2% of the four principal grain crops which made up the export figure. (The total Empire figure being 70,704,000 tons; and
Ukraine, 17,136,000 tons.)[55]

"This region of huge cultivation and extensive grain farming
(Ukraine) was transformed into a region of capitalist-commer-
cial agriculture, engaged partially in shipments to home provinces, but mostly for export. The region was becoming a typical
colony which delivered its grain products to the metropolis and
to foreign markets, and imported manufactured goods from the
metropolis."[56]

We have deliberately emphasized the fact that Ukraine had
an active trade balance with Russia. This was not meant to im-
ply that this is, of itself, detrimental to the economy of a country. Much depends upon the conditions under which this phenomenon makes its appearance, and upon the proprietary rights
to the trade balance surplus. Under ordinary circumstances a
country appropriately organizes its commerce and can advisedly create reserves for a definite economic objective, such as
strengthening its currency, etc. This in general is one of the
means of accumulating national capital. Therefore, in our emphasis upon this position of the external trade of Ukraine, it
was not our intention to evaluate it as an economic ill in itself.
But under the existing relationships between Ukraine and Russia, this excess of exports over imports was yet another form
of colonial exploitation.

The surplus derived from Ukraine's external trade did not
join the reserves of Ukrainian capital accumulation. It went
into the hands of those who controlled Ukrainian exports. Russian commercial and finance capital was that controlling factor.
We have had occasion to remark that exports of sugar were exclusively concentrated in the hands of two Petersburg banks, the
"Petersburg International" and the "Russian Bank for Foreign
Trade . . . . Ninety per cent of sugar exports went through their
hands."[57]

[55] B. Dzinkevvch, *Produktsiya khliba v Ukraini (Grain Production in
    Ukraine)*, Kharkiv, 1923, No. 1, p. 23, and P. Khromov, *op. cit.*, p. 253.
[56] P. Lashchenko, *op. cit.*, p. 487.
[57] M. Golman, "Russkiy Imperializm," p. 354.

The second most important export item, grain, was also handled by Russian exporters, primarily by the state bank.

The surplus did not return to Ukraine in the form of capital accumulation, but was consumed in Russia. Russia proper, as we have stated, exported less than she imported, and the difference was covered by the surplus of Ukraine. Russia not only shipped more goods to Ukraine than she took from Ukraine, but also received more from abroad than she gave at the expense of Ukraine.

Russia accounted for her financial loan operations with foreign countries, floated for the development of her economy, in the same manner.

"Ukraine, which had been up to the time of the war illegally part of the former Russian Empire, in spite of being one of the wealthiest parts making up the property of the autocrats, in spite of being one of the basic contributors to the achievement of Russia's active foreign trade balance, not only did not participate in the organization of foreign trade, not only did not appear on foreign markets as an economic unit, but in general had very little advantage from the Russian active trade operations with foreign lands. The profits were used to pay off Russia's foreign debts, or to the Imperial Treasury, or to the pockets of private dealers, who reaped tremendous profits by taking advantage of the producers, the peasants and workers of Ukraine who were the suppliers of cheap raw material."[58]

We must also bear in mind that thanks to the monopoly enjoyed by the exporters, profits were in large measure determined by their price policy, aimed at lowering prices paid to Ukrainian producers in spite of constantly rising taxes, excises, and, most important, a stormy increase of the land rent in the shape of the price of land and rentals. Export prices for basic products of the agriculture of Ukraine declined in the manner shown in *Table XCIX* [the figures are in kopecks per 36 pounds (1 *pood*)].

TABLE XCIX

Years	Wheat	Rye	Barley
1871-75	90.1	65.7	60.6
1876-80	85.1	63.1	56.1
1881-85	76.7	63.4	52.0
1886-90	64.6	42.5	37.6
1891-1900	55.6	46.6	35.9 [59]

[58] M. Shrah, *op. cit.*, p. 108.   [59] P. Khromov, *op. cit.*, p. 254.

For a better understanding of the repercussions upon the general profitability of Ukrainian agriculture, we must bear in mind that the decline in grain prices between 30% and 40% was accompanied by an increase in productivity of only 19%. This means that the Ukrainian peasants, burdened by taxes, rents and prices, were continually forced to sell more and more of their produce, and thus consume less. Most Ukrainian peasants were short of food. This went on in a land which was called "the breadbasket of Europe" and about which the poet A. Tolstoy wrote: "Know you the land where all things breathe abundance?"

Such is the fate of all lands, richly endowed by God, that are made into colonies. India, the pearl of the British crown, was frequently visited by famine which ravaged millions of the population. The fellahin of wealthy Egypt lived in utter squalor. So also, most of the peasants and workers of Ukraine, who were forced to give up a large part of their labor's fruits to Russia, lived in misery and the entire Ukrainian population was deprived of the opportunity of developing its national economy.

It becomes quite apparent, then, why those diseases that vividly indicate the existence of a low material level of life were widespread in Ukraine. Typhoid is often called "hungry typhus," not without reason. This cannot be charged to the negligence of the Ukrainians. On the contrary, all visitors from foreign lands have always remarked that in this respect the Ukrainians are far ahead of the Russians. The quaintness and cleanliness of the Ukrainian peasant's home has become his national pride which he has carried with him wherever fate would compel him to go.

Under these circumstances the prevalence of some diseases traceable to malnutrition is yet another illustration of the social and economic position of Ukraine.

From 1910 to 1914, the incidence of disease prevailed per 10,000 of the population,[60] as shown in *Table C.*

TABLE C

	Typhoid	Typhus	Recurrent typhus	Dysentery	Diphtheria
Ukraine	41.2	10.9	4.8	29.6	45.9
European Russia	23.4	5.4	2.5	22.6	20.4

[60] *Bolsh. Sovietsk. Entsikl.*, Vol. 55, Ukr. SSR.

It could not be otherwise: acute need of employment created by agrarian conditions and a restricted market for labor in industry compelled the workers to accept low wages and hard conditions of work. "The condition of the workers was awful, just like that of slaves on plantations . . . In the underground stone quarries of Odessa, workers did not come out into the air for weeks at a time, they slept on bundles of straw on which they poured water, so they would steam and keep their bodies warm. Without question first place in criminal negligence and unfitness of dwellings for human habitation goes to the enterprises of Hughes. The laborers have to shift for themselves. They make dirt huts, about 60 square feet for two people, without any windows, damp, musty, something like animal dens, where it is not only morally revolting to enter, but frightening."[61]

We have made this brief digression from the main subject of market conditions in order to emphasize the significant influence of the policy of colonial exploitation upon the standard of living of the labor classes, and in order to stress the falsehood of statements made about the alleged flowering of Ukraine. Such flowering is impossible under conditions of perpetual and excessive diversion of a large part of the national income in favor of the metropolis. In respect to market conditions Ukraine was also the object of colonial exploitation. Russia concentrated in her hands the manufacture of goods of universal consumption, derived large profits from the distribution of these goods in Ukraine, and assuring herself of the control of Ukraine's ties with foreign markets, siphoned Ukraine's favorable trade balance to service her own foreign debts.

The Budget

We have noted above that colonial exploitation consists in the exclusion from a nation's economic body in favor of the metropolis of a part of the national income—"the surplus production" in the shape of land rent, industrial and commercial profits, as well as of budget surpluses. Therefore, in order to provide a complete picture of the nature of the economy of Ukraine prior to the revolution of 1917, we must consider, if only briefly, the budget relationship of Ukraine and Russia.

[61] S. Ostapenko, *op. cit.*, p. 219.

It must be borne in mind, for a better understanding of state finances of the Russian Empire, that the Russian Government, unlike governments of other large European countries, always took a large and active part in the economic life of the land as proprietor of many enterprises. Even during the period of serfdom and before industrial capitalism, the state owned huge tracts of land inhabited by millions of state serfs. During the reform of 1861 the state kept a large number of land estates, which continued under a form of state feudal ownership. The state engaged not only in agriculture and lumbering. Even during the reign of Peter I state industries were established, particularly in iron and coal in the Urals. Subsequently the industrial development of the Empire frequently took the shape of state enterprises such as state railroads, state distilleries and distribution of alcoholic beverages, state banks engaged in the operations of grain exports, state land banks engaged in trading on the exchanges and in underwriting mortgages and state ownership of stock in corporations.

All these economic undertakings were obviously of a different financial nature than the ordinary state budget, and for that reason the budget itself had many peculiarities. The apportionment of state income and expenditures based on collection of all sorts of taxes from the population was supplemented by the so-called "extraordinary budget" which provided a close link between the budget and credit financing, banking and finance capital. Part of the budget covered the area of finance capital, and vice versa. The latter contributed to the maintenance of state enterprises with the result that the budget included items of credit operations.

Between 1887 and 1901 a total of 1,600 million rubles was excluded from the state budget in the form of an excess of ordinary income over ordinary expenditures, and this amount was used for so-called "extraordinary expenditures," for enterprises of a fiscal-economic nature.[62]

By 1903 these "extraordinary expenditures" reached 1 ruble, 47 kopecks per capita of the Empire's population and continued to increase from year to year. Expenditures for education were only 28 kopecks per capita. This nature of the state economy of the Russian Empire was the cause of a peculiarity of Russia's credit operations with foreign countries. Russia did not seek for-

[62] N. Ratzig, *op. cit.*, p. 49.

eign loans to supplement budget deficits caused by unusual occurrences such as war, but to finance state commercial and industrial enterprises. This must be stressed since the Russian State
Government, in servicing these obligations, exercised its sover-
eign prerogatives and was a direct participant in colonial exploitation. The economic policy was thus adapted to the regulation of industrial and commercial relations, to customs, and thus
the budget itself was draining surplus profits. The indebtedness
of the Russian Imperial Government at the end of the 19th century exceeded 5 billion gold rubles, or the equivalent of a three-
year budget of that period.

Subsequently the national debt increased at a slower pace,
but the increase still was considerable. See *Table CI* (in millions
of gold rubles).

TABLE CI

Year	Outstanding debt	Annual payments on debts	Percent relation of payment to state budget
1901	6,392	277	15.4
1906	8,626	357	15.7
1908	8,852	398	16.5
1909	9,055	395	16.1
1911	8,958	399	15.7
1913	8,824	424	13.5

[63]

These state loans were floated partly within the Empire but
in large measure abroad.

As we have already stated, in addition to state loans, shares
of private and state corporate enterprises were also floated in
the financial markets of foreign lands.

The total amount of Russian securities, according to group
origins and location markets, can be properly evaluated according to data for the period 1908 to 1912, a period of the peak of
operations of this sort. See *Table CII* (in millions of rubles).[64]

The bulk of the securities is located, as we can see, in mortgages which almost wholly constitute land bank obligations.
They were a *sui generis* nature, basically like current accounts
and only within the last few years preceding World War I did
foreign exchanges begin to quote them. They came into existence as a result of the sale of land to the peasants by landlords,

[63] M. Golman, *op. cit.*, p. 12.   [64] N. Vanag, *op. cit.*, p. 261.

TABLE CII

	1908 Total	1908 Russian	1908 Foreign	1909 Total	1909 Russian	1909 Foreign
State Bonds	272	203	69	209	7	202
Mortgages	278	278	....	272	272	...
Securities of credit institutions	11	10	1	23	18	5
Railroad bonds	156	18	138	169	70	99
Industrial stocks	183	137	46	123	83	40
Total	900	646	254	796	450	346

	1910 Total	1910 Russian	1910 Foreign	1911 Total	1911 Russian	1911 Foreign
State Bonds	74	42	32	28	17	11
Mortgages	463	463	...	635	635	...
Securities of credit institutions	95	62	33	114	93	21
Railroad bonds	120	41	79	78	15	63
Industrial stocks	169	107	62	381	226	155
Total	921	715	206	1,236	986	250

	1912 Total	1912 Russian	1912 Foreign	Total Total	Total Russian	Total Foreign
State Bonds	57	2	55	640	256	375
Mortgages	645	545	100	2,293	2,193	100
Securities of credit institutions	171	167	4	414	350	64
Railroad bonds	205	26	179	728	170	558
Industrial stocks	272	158	114	1,128	711	417
Total	1,350	898	452	5,203	3,680	1,514

	% of total securities	% of foreign floated securities
State Bonds	12.3	58.6
Mortgages	44.1	4.4
Securities of credit institutions	7.9	15.5
Railroad bonds	14.0	76.8
Industrial stocks	21.7	36.7
Total	100.0	29.2

the peasants making their purchases with the aid of credit extended by the Land Bank. These securities were used to pay off the main part of the purchase price due to the landlords for land sold through the Bank. The latter (landlords) paid off their mortgages by these securities. The landlords owed huge amounts of mortgage monies to banks at that time, mainly to the Dvoryansky Pozemelny Bank. Thus the real meaning of the banking operations could be reduced to the following: by settlement of accounts between two banks, the Dvoryansky (Nobility) and Selyansky (Peasants') with the aid of bonds, the mortgage indebtedness of the landlords was transferred to the peasants.

These operations reached their peak in Ukraine, particularly following the Stolypin reform.

If we exclude from the total amount of securities issued such mortgage bonds then the percentage of securities floated abroad reaches 48.6% of the total. Part of this indebtedness falling upon the state cannot merely be determined by the appropriate amount in the cited table, for, as we have noted, the railroads were almost all the property of the state. Hence the location of their bonds on foreign markets was also an indebtedness of the state. In addition, with some securities the state had assumed a guarantee of payment of both dividends and capital. We have had occasion to quote the total amounts payable by the state on credit operations with foreign lands. This provides an answer to the disproportionately high amount of debt service payments as compared with the indebtedness of other nations. The amount of interest was of some significance in this respect, as Russia generally had to pay more interest than other nations. Among the seven largest countries in the world, the Russian issue of securities during the ten-year period of 1903 to 1912 amounted to 10.4%, while annual service payments amounted to 25% in the year 1910.[65]

It is therefore not surprising that the servicing of loans constituted such a large part of the budget (between 13.5% and 16.5% as indicated by a preceding table). Some economists (especially Golman) estimate loan servicing at 25.2% of the budget. From the tables cited it is easy to imagine what a heavy load foreign loan servicing put upon the currency balance of Russia's foreign trade. Thus exports became the main source of covering investments in Russian industry which were undertaken with the aid of borrowed capital.

Although the balance sheet of payments of the Russian Empire compiled by N. Ole is conditional and statistically imperfect, yet it provides a fairly accurate characteristic of currency account settlements with foreign lands. For this reason we are utilizing it in *Table CIII*, all the more so, as our task is an analysis of the nature of economic phenomena, and not so much their quantitative expression:

Balance of Payments of Russia (in millions of rubles):

[65] *Vyestnik Finansov Promyshlennosti i Torgovli (Financial, Industrial, and Commercial News)*, St. Petersburg, 1912, No. 37, p. 547.

TABLE CII

	1881-1897	1898-1913		1881-1897	1898-1913
Payments for imports	8,140	13,313	Income from exports	10,775	17,432
Foreign payments of interest and dividends	2,900	5,000	Foreign capital investments:		
Bond retirement:			a) in industry	200	1,500
a) of banks	100	....	b) in railroads	550	....
b) of railroads	....	400	c) in credit institutions	....	350
Spent by Russians abroad......	1,000	2,000	d) in municipalities	....	375
Other expenditures	287	415	Government loans	1,050	2,000
Increase of foreign currency reserves	273	772	Other income	125	240
Totals:	12,700	21,900	Totals:	12,700	21,897

[66] P. Lashchenko, *op. cit.*, pp. 385, 386.

We can see from the above the extent to which exports contributed to the balance of foreign payments. A place of highest importance was held by grain exports, 75% of which was contributed by Ukraine, and of equal importance was sugar, almost all of which came from Ukraine. "The Tsarist Government used all available means to bolster exports of grain at the expense of malnutrition of the workers. 'We are not going to eat as much as we need, but we shall export' was the cynical remark made by the Minister of Finance Vishnegradsky."[67]

Most of the grain came from Ukraine. "The Tsarist Government aimed at increasing exports by all means, because the Government's balance of payments could as a rule be only covered by having an active trade balance. Industrial development required the importation of metals, machines, etc.; it was necessary to make annual payments of large amounts of interest on bonds of the Tsarist Government, as well as on loans of private railroad companies and interest on other credit amounts. All these payments contributed heavily to the passive side of the payments balance and were covered in the main by bolstering exports, primarily of grain and raw materials, inasmuch as Russia did not possess any other worthwhile sources of income (from freights etc.)."[68]

It is now clear to what degree the results of Ukraine's commerce influenced the Imperial budget. Russia not only withdrew from Ukraine more value than she delivered, but also balanced her foreign payments at the expense of exports of Ukrainian grain, sugar, cattle and ores. These foreign payments of Russia were for loans negotiated for military purposes and for the development of Russia's own industry. "Hence, one can now state openly that a large part of what constituted the difference between the exports and imports of Ukraine was being taken away, as capitalist robbery, to pay for debts."[69]

It was not only through the medium of the "extraordinary budget," but also through the ordinary budget that Ukraine was a source of Russia's enrichment. In contributions to the state, such as taxes and others, Ukraine paid more than the Empire spent on Ukraine. *Table CIV* is the income side of the Imperial budget for 1885 to 1913 (in millions of rubles).

[67] P. Khromov, *op. cit.*, p. 253. [68] *Ibid.*, p. 252.
[69] S. Ostapenko, *op. cit.*, p. 207.

TABLE CIV

	Taxes and collections				State monopolies, enterprises, estates	Payments for land purchased by peasants, 1861	Total gross budget of Empire
	Direct	*Indirect*	*Other*	*Total*			
1885	130.1	360.1	49.3	539.5	80.5	47.3	765.0
1890	90.7	474.6	59.8	625.1	144.8	90.5	952.0
1895	105.7	586.1	71.8	763.6	310.4	101.2	1,255.8
1900	131.7	657.2	87.3	876.2	650.4	96.0	1,704.1
1905	126.7	408.3	99.7	634.7	1,239.1	55.3	2,024.4
1909	198.6	529.7	151.4	879.7	1,523.1	.7	2,526.3
1911	223.9	629.7	193.4	1047.0	1,778.2	.8	2,952.0
1912	243.2	650.4	199.2	1,092.8	1,882.4	.8	3,105.9
1913	249.8	671.0	218.2	1,139.0	1,966.2	.9	3,240.6 [70]

[70] M. Golman, *op. cit.*, p. 376.

The column of income from monopolies, enterprises and estates is very interesting. It provided 10.5% of the budget in 1885 and increased to 60.7% of the budget within 28 years. The chief item of this income figure is from the sale of alcoholic beverages (nearly one billion rubles). It is not surprising that the Russian budget of that period was called "the drunken budget." In general, this column provides a good illustration of the extent of the spread of state capitalism in Russia by that time. Hence the present total nationalization of the entire economy had its beginnings before 1917. Equally noteworthy are also incomes derived from indirect taxes. They more than double direct taxes and those coupled with income from the sale of spirits, again provide a close parallel between the budget of that period and those of the present day, under which indirect taxes, or so-called receipts taxes, constitute almost 80% of the entire budget.

We can see that even then a characteristic of the state economy was that a decisive role in the budget was played by commercial and industrial profits from state enterprises. These were based on the appropriation by the state of certain enterprises and a monopoly in certain economic processes, in place of financial obligations to the state of the population and business. And to the extent that the same state authority was at the same time subject to the law, to that extent the regulation of economic processes was in a large measure determined by law enforcement which always stood on guard for the interests of the dominant Russian economic system.

The significance of this moment cannot be underestimated, inasmuch as it determined Ukraine's losing battle with Russia in the realm of economics. We have emphasized on several occasions the part played by statutory regulation and official government policy in agriculture, industry, transportation, and commerce. This found its repercussions in the structure of the budget. Let us take, for example, just the indirect taxes. Excise collections are their backbone. In 1900, the total of 658 million rubles indirect taxes consisted of: excise tax on spirits, 317 million; on tobacco, 41 million; on sugar, 63 million; on kerosene, 25 million; on matches, 7 million, and collection of duties, 204 million. As we can see, excise taxes were imposed on goods chiefly of non-Russian origin: spirits, tobacco and sugar from Ukraine, kerosene from the Caucasus, matches from Finland and Belorussia. Yasnopolsky is correct when he says: "the present excise taxes on grain, spirits and salt (there was an excise tax on salt at that time—*Author*) imposes a double burden on the agricultural part of Russia, both on the producers, and the consumers. And that excess of income over expenses which is created in the agricultural part of Russia, is diverted Northward in impressive amounts for the state treasury."[71]

Excise taxes thwarted the development of the Ukrainian distilling industry, and the tax paid on sugar was lost to the Ukrainian manufacturers when it went into the hands of the two Petersburg sugar exporting banks. All this indicates that relations between Ukraine and Russia in the realm of the budget were, similarly of a colonial nature. The budget was another tool of colonial exploitation.

Yasnopolsky, in his basic text on the geographic repartition of state income and expenditures, states that during the 13-year period "since 1868, the nine Ukrainian *gubernias* gave the Russian state an income of 2,899.2 million rubles and received from the state, 1,749 million rubles."[72]

The Ukrainian national economy lost, by means of the budget, 1,150.2 million rubles. This is nothing but colonial exploitation.

In the same text, Yasnopolsky also cites statistics compiled by M. Porsh. According to these: "The Russian state had from Ukraine (during the period of 15 years at the end of the 19th and beginning of the 20th centuries) an income of 3,289.6 million rubles, and expenditures of 2,605.2 million rubles."[73]

The following table of budgetary income and expenditures for the year 1912 is found in the work of Professor Feshchenko-Chopivsky:[74]

Table CV
(In Millions of Rubles)

	Income	Expenditures
Empire total	3,107	3,171
Ukraine	683	377

Here again is a siphoning of 306 million rubles from Ukraine. We might allow that all these statistics are not absolutely ac-

[71] N. Yasnopolsky, *op. cit.*, II, 116.
[72] N. Yasnopolsky, *O geograficheskom raspredeleniyi gosudarstvennikh dokhodov i raskhodov* (Geographic Distribution of State Income and Expenditures), Kiev, 1893, p. 69.
[73] M. Yavorsky, *op. cit.*, II, 123.
[74] I. Feshchenko-Chopivsky, *op. cit.*, p. 161.

curate and that the amount actually taken out of Ukraine varies one way or the other. There is room for error in view of the absence of a proper subdivision and localization of certain categories of expenditures in the official sources, although Yasnopolsky's calculations have been made with the utmost regard for scrupulous veracity. For the purpose of our research any possible inaccuracies may properly be disregarded, inasmuch as our task is not to determine the *extent* of colonial exploitation, but rather to find its *presence*. To prove in other words that economic relations between Ukraine and Russia were based on principles of colonial dependence. Hence, it is of no great import how much the state budget succeeded in pumping out of the Ukrainian economy in favor of Russia, be it 300 million rubles annually, or less. The gist of the matter is that such pumping existed, that Ukraine always paid more than she received, and that this was the consequence of her colonial position. "The Tsarist regime of the second half of the 19th and the beginning of the 20th centuries imposed upon Ukraine a greater financial burden than during the old times of the Hetmanate."[75]

A similar structure of the Imperial budget on the expenditures side vividly illustrates the diversion of funds of the colonies in favor of the metropolis. *Table CVI* is a summary statement of budget expenditures in percentage groupings.

TABLE CVI

	1910	1911
Military establishments	30.6%	31.7%
Debts	26.6%	25.2%
State administration	26.0%	25.7%
Education	7.4%	8.3%
Agriculture	3.5%	3.8%
Industry	5.9%	5.3%
Total	100%	100%

[76]

We have already amply illustrated the part of Ukraine in the repartition of debts. The debts of the Empire were being paid off by Ukrainian grain, the proceeds of those loans having been used by Russia. Concerning expenditures for the military establishment, their preponderance in the budget mirrors the imperialist nature of Russia and her continuous military expan-

[75] M. Yavorsky, *op. cit.*, II, 124.　　[76] M. Golman, *op. cit.*, p. 357.

sion, something which had nothing in common with the interests of Ukraine. Even a proportionate participation of Ukraine in providing funds for state needs is not justified to the extent that the maintenance of part of the state apparatus was not the result of the needs of the population but merely an assurance of political domination of subjected nations. Only the last three categories of expenditures, together totaling 17% to 18% of the Imperial budget can be considered as giving Ukraine a proportionate share. In all others, Ukraine gave more than she received, thus making it clear that in the state budget branch of the economy, part of Ukraine's national income was diverted in favor of metropolitan Russia.

To repeat our former statements on the nature of colonialism in the sphere of economic relations: its essence is that the surplus production of one national economy is appropriated by another national economy by military and political superiority. This appropriation goes on by siphoning of land rents, industrial and commercial profits and tax budget burdens out of proportion to expenditures. In order to insure continued exploitation, the economy of the colony is developed in a certain direction which precludes the creation of a harmonious and unified economic body on the national territory of the colony and for this purpose legal norms are promulgated, regulating economic processes in the direction desired by the metropolis.

We have analyzed all primary branches of the Ukrainian economy during the period between the abolition of serfdom and the revolution of 1917, i.e. during the period which is justly called the period of industrial-capitalist development of the Russian Empire. We have illustrated the nature of the main and decisive economic processes in their historical development during that time, and we have invariably come face to face with the fact of the existence of characteristics peculiar to colonies.

This undeniably justifies to state that *during this period Ukraine was a colony of Russia, and that the industrial and economic growth of Russia was to a great extent based upon a colonial exploitation of Ukraine.*

Unless this is properly recognized, there can be no correct evaluation made either of the real nature of the economic development of Russia, or of those peculiar economic processes which took place in Ukraine.

This problem has, unfortunately, not been sufficiently clarified to this day. Very many people perceive in the economic centralism of Russia, peculiar to colonial empires, a sign of economic unity. This leads them to regard the non-Russian colonial national territories as provinces of Russia and as component parts of a single economic organism.

For obvious reasons, this matter has thus far not been given sufficient attention either in the literature of economics, or history. It is not in the interest of Russia, with her deeply rooted Imperialism, to have this matter clarified.

As justly stated by Lashchenko: "The development of capitalism 'in depth' and 'in breadth', i.e. the spreading of capitalism to new terrains . . . appeared with great force and continued to spread in Russia following the reform (of 1861—*Author*). This most important problem has thus far not been solved either by the economists or the historians. No separate work on the development of Russian capitalism on national territories, nor on such new economic conditions which appeared against this background, has as yet been written." During this period "the development of capitalism 'in breadth' meant primarily the colonial subjugation of national territories . . . . The Russian state began to transform into a centralized, multi-nation state in the 16th and 17th centuries with many nations economically and politically subject forming its composition . . . . In the economic respect, the national terrains of Russia were to the metropolis for the most part colonies or semi-colonies, suppliers of all sorts of raw material."[77]

This in no way contradicts another undeniable fact: the desire of Russia to assimilate Ukraine completely by destroying her unique national character. Oppressing all manifestations of the Ukrainian national spirit, Russia never showed any intention of obliterating the boundary in social and economic relations by placing the economy of Ukraine in a position of equality with the economy of Russia. A Ukraine russified would continue as a colony of Russia and a source of Russia's enrichment. Economic centralization was being carried out against the background of imperialism.

Such contradictory nature of two lines of Russia's Ukrainian policy obviously acted to strengthen the resilience of the Ukrainian people. Russianization unified Ukraine spiritually and

---

[77] P. Lashchenko, *op. cit.*, pp. 418-421.

economic exploitation physically in opposition to the Russian steamroller.

The idea of Ukrainian separation was, under these circumstances, the result of logical thinking in terms of reality.

M. Volobuyev is therefore perfectly right in his conclusions made after an analysis of the so-called unity of the Russian Empire's economy: "Those who speak of the unity of the pre-revolutionary economy of Russia or Ukraine, have only in mind the first tendency (towards centralism—*Author*) and forget about the second, the centrifugal, or rather the desire to join in the world system directly, not through the intermediary of the Russian economy. The process of concentration on a capitalist basis goes on counter to the forms of autarchic tendencies, therefore we should not deceive ourselves by the fact of concentrating tendencies in the Russian pre-revolutionary economy. Behind such tendencies we must perceive separatist forces of the Ukrainian economy. Hence, the question of whether there was a single Russian pre-revolutionary economy should be answered as follows: it was a single economy on an antagonistic, imperialist basis, but from the viewpoint of centrifugal forces of the colonies oppressed by her, it was a complex of national economies . . . . The Ukrainian economy was not an ordinary province of Czarist Russia, but a land which was placed in a colonial position."[78]

This ends the analysis of social and economic processes in Ukraine prior to the 1917 revolution. We end by stating that it is a proven fact that Ukraine was transformed into a colony, exploited by Russia for the development of her own economy. A natural question arises, how did this position of Ukraine influence the thinking of her population and what were its repercussions upon the social trends in Ukraine? This question cannot be answered by the scope, nor significance of the social-economic processes herein analyzed. This is quite understandable. When we speak of the history of one or another enslaved nation, the decisive matter is not its subjected position, but rather the realization of the position by the people themselves, and a crystallization of the peoples' will around the idea of national and political liberation. The factor of liberation is in no way determined by the extent of oppression, but by the strength of the nation's will which comes into existence when the nation realizes its op-

[78] M. Volobuyev, *loc cit.*

pressed condition. In the light of the above it would be essential to provide an analysis of psychological processes in the Ukrainian community and of the social movements. But to do this, it would be necessary to write a history of social and political developments in Ukraine, and this goes far beyond the scope of this undertaking.

It is also necessary to postpone an analysis of this problelm for the further reason that thus far we have concerned ourselves with economic conditions to the time of the revolution of 1917. Almost forty years have gone by since, forty years of weighty events, in all spheres, including economics. Without any change of their inner nature, the processes continued under an entirely different set of circumstances. The social structure underwent a basic change, likewise the nature of social trends. To speak of a society's desires as of a factor which determines the historical pathways of a nation, the expression of such desires in a single historical moment will not suffice, the general trend must be known.

Our task has been to show that social and economic relations between Ukraine and Russia prior to the revolution were based upon principles of national oppression. This is the kind of soil in which the idea of nationalism takes root. Therefore, wishing to discuss contemporary Ukraine, we must find out whether any changes have taken place in this respect, and if so in what direction. It is necessary to illuminate the nature of subsequent social and economic processes. This is the task of our undertaking in the second volume of this work.

There we hope to characterize the awareness of the community, its desires and social movements in the entire historical process to this day. This might give us an insight into the future of such continued processes.

Without pausing at the present moment to consider the development of a national awareness in the Ukrainian people, or the content and course of social movements in Ukraine before the revolution of 1917, we wish to quote an historical fact which provides a summary of all those social processes and constitutes their clearly visible peak.

We speak of the revolution of 1917 in Ukraine.

From the very first days of the revolution, the problem of reshaping the social structure was inextricably connected with the national problem.

The social-political revolution immediately became a national Ukrainian revolution.

A new social order was being introduced into the framework of a separate national-state organism.

There was nothing surprising about this. It came as the logical conclusion to many centuries of the Ukrainian nation's existence, as a fact of historical necessity.

That it had to be thus was clear to all who were aware of the real situation in Ukraine. The best testimony to the existence of this situation is in the words of the most prominent statesman in the Russian Government of the 20th century, Prime Minister P. Stolypin, who said as early as 1906: " . . . the national and political aims are so closely intertwined in the Ukrainian movement that it is absolutely impossible to separate them."[79]

Neither will they be separated in the future.

[79] S. Shchogolev, *Sovremennoye Ukrainstvo, yego proiskhozhdeniye i zadachi (Contemporary Ukrainianism, its Origin and Aims)*, Kiev, 1915, p. 37.

Bibliography

Books and Annual Publications .. ..

Aristov, N. *Promishlennost drevnoy Rusi* (*Industry of Ancient Rus'*). St. Petersburg, 1866.

Bogolepov, P. *Gosudarstvenniye i miestniye nalogi* (*State and Local Taxes*). Kharkiv, 1902.

Bolshaya Sovietskaya Entsiklopediya (*Great Soviet Encyclopedia*). Volume 55, 1947.

Brant, B. *Inostranniye kapitaly* (*Foreign Capital*). St. Petersburg, 1899.

Bukovetsky, A. (ed.) *Materyaly po denezhnoy reforme, 1895-1897 g.* (*Materials on the Currency Reform of 1895-1897*). Moscow, 1903.

Chuprov, D. *Zheleznodorozhnoye khozyaystvo* (*Railroad Management*). Moscow, 1897.

Dzinkevych, B. *Produktsiya khliba v Ukraini* (*Grain Production in Ukraine*). Kharkiv, 1923.

Feshchenko-Chopivsky, I. *Ekonomichna heohrafiya Ukrainy* (*Economic Geography of Ukraine*). Kiev, 1923.

Filimonov, M. *Materiali po voprosu ob evolutsiyi zemlevladeniya* (*Materials on the Problem of Evolution of Land Ownership*). Second edition, Perm, 1895.

Glivits, I. *Zhelezodelatelnaya promyshlennost' Rossiyi* (*The Iron-Working Industry of Russia*). Moscow, 1911.

Imshenetsky, N. *Opys Poltavskoiy huberniyi* (*Description of Poltava Governorship*). Poltava, 1907.

Kasperovich, G. *Zhelezodelatelnaya promishlennost v Rossiyi za 1903-1913 g.g.* (*The Iron-Working Industry in Russia during the Years, 1903-1913*). Moscow, 1914.

Keypen, N. *Krizis 80-tikh godov* (*The Crisis of the Eighties*). Moscow, 1903.

Khromov, P. A. *Ekonomicheskoye razvitiye Rossiyi v XIX-XX v. v.* (*Economic Development of Russia in the Nineteenth and Twentieth Centuries*). Moscow, 1950.

Knipovich, A. *K Voprosu o diferentsiyatsiyi krestyanskogo khozyaystva* (*On the Problem of the Differentiation of the Peasants' Economy*). Katerynoslavkoye Gubernia Zemstvo, 1903.

Koshkarev, M. *Denezhnoye obrashcheniye v Rossiyi* (*Money Circulation in Russia*). Moscow, 1898.

Kosinsky, V. *K Agrarnomu voprosu* (*The Agrarian Problem*). Moscow, 1911.

Krasny Arkhiv (*Red Archives*). Volume XVIII.

Lashchenko, P. *Istoriya narodnoho khozyaystva SSSR* (*History of the National Economy of the USSR*). Leningrad, 1952.

Lazarevsky, A. *Opisaniye Staroy Malorossiyi* (*Description of Old Little-Russia [Ukraine]*). Kiev, 1888.

Maslov, P. *Agrarniy vopros v Rossiyi* (*The Agrarian Problem in Russia*). St. Petersburg, 1908.

——————————*Razvitiye zemledeleniya v Rossiyi* (*Development of Land Distribution in Russia*). Moscow, 1912.

Materyali Redaktsionnoy Kommissiyi (*Materials of the Editing Commission*). St. Petersburg, 1876.

Minister Torgovli i promyshlennosti (Minister of Commerce and Industry). *Torgovla i promyshlennost Yevropeyskloy Rossiyi po rayonam* (*Commerce and Industry of European Russia by Districts*). St. Petersburg, 1908 & 1912.

Myakotin, V. *Ocherki sotsialnoy istoriyi Ukrainy v 17-18 v. v.* (*Outline of the Social History of Ukraine in the Seventeenth and Eighteenth Centuries*). Prague, 1924.

Ogonovsky, M. *Individualnoye zemlevladeniye* (*Individual Land Ownership*). Moscow, 1912.

Ohloblyn, O. *Peredkapitalistychna fabryka* (*Pre-Capitalist Factories*). Kiev, 1925.

_____ *Ocherki Istoriyi Ukrainskoyi fabryki. Manufaktura v Hetmanshchyni (Outline of History of Ukrainian Factories. Manufacturing in the Hetman Period).* Kiev, 1925.

Ol', P. V. *Inostranniyi kapital v Rossiyi (Foreign Capital in Russia).* Moscow, 1922.

Olezhko, N. *Agrarna polityka Bolshevykiv (Agrarian Policy of the Bolsheviks).* Munich, 1947.

Pokrovsky, M. *Marksizm i osobennosti istoricheskogo razvitya Rossiyi (Marxism and Peculiarities of Russia's Historical Development).* Moscow, 1923.

Ratzig, N. *Finansovaya politika Rossiyi s 1887 goda (Russia's Financial Policy since 1887).* St. Petersburg, 1903.

Sbornik Svedeniy i materyalov Ministerstva Finansov za 1867 god yun' (Collection of Reports and Materials of the Ministry of Finance for the Year, 1867, June). St. Petersburg, 1867.

Shary, D. (ed), *Statisticheskiy Yezhegodnik na 1914 god (Statistical Yearbook for 1914).* St. Petersburg, 1914.

Shchogolev, S. *Sovremennoye Ukrainstvo, yego proiskhozhdeniye i zadachi (Contemporary Ukrainianism, its Origins and Aims).* Kiev, 1915.

Skalkovsky, K. *Russky torgoviy flot (Russian Merchant Marine).* St. Petersburg, 1909.

Slabchenko, M. *Materialy do ekonomichno-sotsialnoyi istoriyi Ukrainy 19-oho Stor. (Materials on the Economic-Social History of Nineteenth Century Ukraine).* Kharkiv, 1925.

_____ *Orhanizatsiya khozyaystva Ukrainy (Organization of the Economy of Ukraine).* Kharkiv, 1925.

Sobolev, M. *Tamozhennaya politika Rossiyi (Russia's Customs Policy).* Tomsk, 1911.

Statistika po dvizheniyu zemlevladeniya v Rossiyi (Statistics on Development of Land-ownership in Russia). 1911 edition.

Statisticheskiye tablitsi Rossiyskoy imperiyi za 1856 g. (Statistical Tables of the Russian Empire for the Year, 1856). St. Petersburg, 1856.

Strumilin, S. *Problemy promyshlennogo Kapitala v SSSR* (*Problem of Industrial Capital in the USSR*). Moscow, 1923.

Troynitsky, N. *O chisle krepostnikh v Rossiyi* (*On the Number of Serfs in Russia*). Poltava, 1907.

Trudi Kharkovskogo obschestva selskogo khozyaystva (*Proceedings of Kharkiv Agricultural Society*). Kharkiv, 1889.

Vasylenko, S. *Kustarni promysly* (*Home Industries*). Kiev, 1913.

Vobly, K. *Ekonomichna heohrafiya Ukrainy* (*Economic Geography of Ukraine*). Kiev. 1927.

Voznesensky, V. *Deystvuyushche zakony o krestyanakh* (*Binding Laws Pertaining to Peasants*). Moscow, 1910.

V. V. *Ocherki krestyanskogo khozyaystva* (*Outline of the Peasant Economy*). Moscow, 1903.

Vyestnik Finansov Promyshlennosti I Torgovli (*Financial, Industrial and Commercial News*). St. Petersburg, 1912.

Vyestnik Evropy (*European News*). St. Petersburg, 1870.

Witte, S. I. *O napryazheniyi platezhnikh sil naseleniya* (*The Strain on the Paying Ability of the Population*). Stuttgart, 1903.

———————Zapiske po krestanskomu delu (*Notes on Peasant Affairs*). Stuttgart, 1903.

Wolf, M. V. *Geograficheskoye rozmyeshcheniye Russkoy promishlennosti* (*Geographic Distribution of Russian Industry*). Moscow, 1925.

Yasnopolsky, N. *O geograficheskom raspredeleniyi gosudarstvennikh dokhodov i raskhodov* (*Geographic Distribution of State Income and Expenditures*). Kiev, 1893.

Yavorsky, M. *Ukraina v epokhu kapitalismu* (*Ukraine in the Era of Capitalism*). Odessa, 1924.

Yefremov, S. *Istoria Ukraineskoho pysmenstva* (*History of Ukrainian Literature*). Kiev, 1924.

Yezhegodnik ministerstva finansov (*Annual Report of the Ministry of Finance*). St. Petersburg, 1869.

Zagorskiy, K. *Ekonomika transporta* (*Economy of Transportation*). Moscow, 1930.

Ziv, V. *Inostrannyi kapital v Russkoy, chorno-zavodskoy promyshlennosti* (*Foreign Capital in the Russian Black-Metal Industry*). Petrograd, 1917.

ARTICLES .. ..

Danilov, F. "Obshchaya polityka pravitelstva i gosudarstvenniystroy" ("General Policy of the Government and State Structure") *Obshchestvennoye dvizheniye v Rossiyi* (*The Social Movement in Russia*). St. Petersburg, 1910.

Fomin, P. "Ekonomichna kharakterystyka Ukrainy" ("Economic Characteristics of Ukraine"). *Nauchnaya Mysl* (*Educational Ideas*). Kharkiv, 1923.

Golman, M. "Russkiy Imperyalizm" ("Russian Imperialism"). *Priboy* (*The Surf*). Leningrad, 1926.

Lazarevsky, A. "Malorossiyskiye pospolitiye krestyane" ("Little-Russian [Ukrainian] Common Peasants") *Zapiski Chernigovskogo statisticheskogo komiteta* (*Proceedings of the Chernihiv Statistical Commission*). Chernihiv, 1866.

"Natsionalne pytannya na skhodi Evropy" ("The Nationality Problem in Eastern Europe"). *Materyaly i Dokumenty* (*Materials and Documents*). Prague, 1925.

Ohloblyn, O. "Problema Ukrains'koyi ekonomiky v naukoviy i hromadskiy dumtsi" ("The Problem of the Ukrainian Economy in Scientific and Community Thought"). *Chervony Shlakh* (*Red Path*). Kharkiv, 1928.

Ostapenko, S. "Kapitalizm na Ukraini" ("Capitalism in Ukraine"). *Chervony Shlakh* (*Red Path*). Kharkiv, 1924.

Peshekhonov, A. "Zemlevladeniye" ("Land Ownership"). *Narodne Khozyaystvo Ukrainy* (*National Economy of Ukraine*). Kharkiv, 1922.

Porsh, M. "Iz statystyky Ukrainy" ("From Ukrainian Statistics"). *Ukraina*, Volume III, Kiev, 1907.

_____ "Statystyka zemlevolodinnya i mobilizatsiya zemelnoyi vlasnosty v Ukrainy" ("Statistics of Land Ownership and Mobilization of Land Property in Ukraine"). *Ukraina,* XI, XII, Kiev, 1907.

Shrah, M. "Zovnishnya torhivla USSR ta yiyi blyshchi perspektyvy" ("Foreign Trade of the Ukrainian SSR and its Immediate Prospects"). *Chervony Shlakh (Red Path).* Kharkiv, 1924.

"Sils'ke hospodarstvo Ukrainy" ("Ukrainian Agriculture"). *Narkomzem Ukrainy (Peoples' Commissar of Agriculture).* Kharkiv, 1923.

Vanag. N. "Finansoviy kapital v Rossiyi nakanune mirovoy voyny" ("Finance Capital in Russia on the Eve of the World War"). *Proletariy (The Proleterian).* Moscow, 1930.

_____ "Finansoviy kapital v tyazheloy industriyi" ("Finance Capital in Heavy Industry"). *Protelariy (The Proletarian).* Moscow, 1930.

Volobuyev, M. "Do problemy Ukrainskoyi ekonomiky" ("On the Problem of the Ukrainian Economy"). *Bolshevyk Ukrainy (The Ukrainian Bolshevik).* Kharkiv, 1928.

Yasnopolsky, N. "Ekonomicheskaya buduchnost yuga Rossiyi i sovremennaya yego otstalost" ("The Economic Future of South Russia and its Present Backwardness"). *Otechestvenniye Zapiski' (Home Notes).* St. Petersburg, 1871.

Translator's Postscript

READERS WILL NOTICE from the method of transcription of certain words, especially of geographic designations and names of persons, that there is a discrepancy between this method and generally accepted transliteration standards for Soviet (Russian) names. This discrepancy stems from the fact that the overwhelming majority of geographic designations and names of persons refer to Ukraine, thus differing from their Russian counterparts.

A few examples will illustrate the problem: throughout this book *Kryvy Rih* has been used instead of *Krivoy Rog*, *Tahanrih* instead of *Taganrog*, *Mykolaiv* instead of *Nikolayev;* also *Hryhory* and not *Grigorii*, *Mykhailo* and not *Mikhail*. The reason for this is that the names are Ukrainian, and hence the author, as well the translator, believe that they should be emphasized as such in order not to confuse them with somewhat similar Russian names and terms, or with names deliberately changed by Russians as part of the so-called process of Russification. An illustration from a different area will bring out the point with even more clarity: during their occupation of Poland at the time of World War II, the Nazis changed the name of the Polish city of Lodz to *Litzmannstadt;* the city, however, never lost its right to its original name, and after the German withdrawal it became Lodz again as a matter of course. So it is with Kryvy Rih, Mykolaiv and others; no amount of change by fiat of Moscow could change their original Ukrainian names.

In this connection, it might be added, according to all Soviet official declarations, that the Ukrainian Soviet Socialist Republic is a soverign nation (although the veracity of this statement within its Western meaning is disputed), and as such it has its own geographical terminology, obligatory within its political boundaries, which is officially recognized by the other Soviet Republics. Once such names and terms are used in official Ukrainian governmental designations, they also deserve application outside Ukraine.

Finally, we wish to refer again to the factor of Russification or Russianization. For a considerable length of time, the Russian conquerors of Ukraine (particularly since the time of Peter I, following Mazepa's and Charles' XII defeat at Poltava in 1709), have attempted to transform Ukraine to their own image, and following this policy, they began to impose Russian place names in substitution of the original Ukrainian names. Inasmuch as the Ukrainians have offered political resistance to these plans of conquest and colonization, it is only fair that a concession to the fighting Ukrainians should be made in the realm of terminology.

Index

THE MARQUETTE SLAVIC STUDIES

Published by the Marquette University Press
Milwaukee 3, Wisconsin

I. *The Doctrine of Anarchism of Michael A. Bakunin* (1955) by Eugene Pyziur.

II. *Hitler's Occupation of Ukraine (1941-1944)* (1956) by Ihor Kamenetsky.

III. *History of Slavic Studies in the United States* (1957) by Clarence A. Manning.

IV. *Ukraine and Russia* (1958) by Konstantin Kononenko.

Available in paper or case bindings. Prices on application.